This book examines the relationship between the theologies of atonement and penal strategies. The question of the impact of religious sensibilities, or the structure of affect surrounding the crucifixion, on penal practice, and the correlative effects of the development of criminal law on the understandings of atonement, is Timothy Gorringe's theme. Christian theology was the most potent form of ideology in Western society until the nineteenth century, and atonement theology (in particular, the so-called 'satisfaction theory' of the atonement) interacted and reacted with penal thinking and practice. Satisfaction was, and remains, powerful because expiation or atonement for wrongdoing seems to be one of the most powerful human impulses, operating on both individual and collective levels. Drawing on the work of Norbert Elias and David Garland, the author argues that atonement theology created a structure of affect which favoured retributive policies. Gorringe ranges freely between Old Testament texts, St Anselm, and eighteenth- and nineteenth-century British social history, to show that the integral connection between sin and crime, the moral and the legal, was fundamental to the way satisfaction theology changed in response to alterations in the accounts of criminal law. But the question arises if the preaching of the cross not only desensitised us to judicial violence but even lent it sanction.

The last two chapters review theory and practice in the twentieth century, and Gorringe makes concrete proposals for both theology and criminal and societal violence. He contends that the balance needs to shift from satisfaction to biblical conceptions of redemption and reconciliation.

CAMBRIDGE STUDIES IN
IDEOLOGY AND RELIGION 9

GOD'S JUST VENGEANCE

CAMBRIDGE STUDIES IN IDEOLOGY AND RELIGION

General Editors: DUNCAN FORRESTER *and* ALISTAIR KEE

Religion increasingly is seen as a renewed force, and is recognised as an important factor in the modern world in all aspects of life – cultural, economic, and political. It is no longer a matter of surprise to find religious factors at work in areas and situations of political tension. However, our information about these situations has tended to come from two main sources. The news-gathering agencies are well placed to convey information, but are hampered by the fact that their representatives are not equipped to provide analysis of the religious forces involved. Alternatively, the movements generate their own accounts, which understandably seem less than objective to outside observers. There is no lack of information or factual material, but a real need for sound academic analysis. Cambridge Studies in Ideology and Religion will meet this need. It will give an objective, balanced, and programmatic coverage to issues which – while of wide potential interest – have been largely neglected by analytical investigation, apart from the appearance of sporadic individual studies. Intended to enable debate to proceed at a higher level, the series should lead to a new phase in our understanding of the relationship between ideology and religion.

A list of titles in the series is given at the end of the book.

GOD'S JUST VENGEANCE

Crime, violence and the rhetoric of salvation

TIMOTHY GORRINGE

Reader in Contextual Theology, University of St Andrews

CAMBRIDGE
UNIVERSITY PRESS

Published by the Press Syndicate of the University of Cambridge
The Pitt Building, Trumpington Street, Cambridge CB2 1RP
40 West 20th Street, New York, NY 10011–4211, USA
10 Stamford Road, Oakleigh, Melbourne 3166, Australia

© Cambridge University Press 1996

First published 1996

Printed in Great Britain by Athenaeum Press Ltd, Gateshead, Tyne and Wear

A catalogue record for this book is available from the British Library

Library of Congress cataloguing in publication data
Gorringe, Timothy.
God's just vengeance: crime, violence and the rhetoric
of salvation / Timothy Gorringe.
p.   cm.
Includes bibliographical references and index.
ISBN 0 521 55301 6 (hardback) – ISBN 0 521 55762 3 (paperback)
1. Satisfaction for sin – History of doctrines.
2. Revenge – History of doctrines.
3. God – Wrath – History of doctrines.
4. Crime – Religious aspects – Christianity – History of doctrines.
5. Violence – Religious aspects – Christianity – History of doctrines.
6. Punishment – Religious aspects – Christianity – History of doctrines.
7. Crime – Great Britain – History.
8. Punishment – Great Britain – History.
9. Correction – Great Britain – History.
10. Reconciliation – Religious aspects – Christianity.   1. Title.
BT263.G67   1996
261.8′336–dc20   95–17196   CIP

ISBN 0 521 55301 6 hardback
ISBN 0 521 55762 3 paperback

No one seemed to realize that the gilt cross with the enamel medallions at the ends, which the priest held out for the people to kiss, was nothing else but the emblem of the gallows on which Christ had been executed for denouncing the very things now being performed here in His name.

Tolstoy, *Resurrection*

Contents

General editors' preface

In the early 1970s it was widely assumed that religion had lost its previous place in Western culture and that this pattern would spread throughout the world. Since then religion has become a renewed force, recognised as an important factor in the modern world in all aspects of life, cultural, economic and political. This is true not only of the Third World, but in Europe East and West, and in North America. It is no longer a surprise to find a religious factor at work in areas of political tension.

Religion and ideology form a mixture which can be of interest to the observer, but in practice dangerous and explosive. Our information about such matters comes for the most part from three types of sources. The first is the media, which understandably tend to concentrate on newsworthy events, without taking the time to deal with the underlying issues of which they are but symptoms. The second source comprises studies by social scientists, who often adopt a functionalist and reductionist view of the faith and beliefs which motivate those directly involved in such situations. Finally, there are the statements and writings of those committed to the religious or ideological movements themselves. We seldom lack information, but there is a need – often an urgent need – for sound objective analysis which can make use of the best contemporary approaches to both politics and religion. Cambridge Studies in Ideology and Religion is designed to meet this need.

The subject matter is global and this will be reflected in the choice of both topics and authors. The initial volumes will be concerned primarily with movements involving the Christian religion, but as the series becomes established movements involving other world religions will be subjected to the same objective critical analysis. In all cases it is our intention that an accurate and sensitive account of religion should be informed by an objective and sophisticated application of perspectives from the social sciences.

The purpose of this book is to explore, by means of judiciously selected historical and theological examples, the relationship between atonement theology (in particular, the so-called 'satisfaction theory' of the atonement) and ideas about punishment. Timothy Gorringe shows that the role retributive ideas have played in atonement theology is largely a function of the close relationship between law and religion, which are equally concerned with the question of what it is that sustains a human community. From his account, which ranges freely between Old Testament texts, St Anselm, and eighteenth- and nineteenth-century British social history, it emerges that the integral connection between sin and crime, the legal and the moral, was fundamental to the way satisfaction theology changed in response to changing accounts of criminal law. Motivated by the strong sense of social justice which has characterised much of his work, the author tries to show how a Christian theology of the atonement ought to bear on penal thinking; and his contention that the balance needs to shift from satisfaction to biblical conceptions of redemption and reconciliation has clear contemporary implications.

DUNCAN FORRESTER AND ALISTAIR KEE
New College, University of Edinburgh

Acknowledgements

I should like to thank my colleagues Mark Freedland, Malcolm Vale and David Faulkner for much advice on reading in unfamiliar areas, and likewise Joanna Innes of Somerville College. Readers familiar with the subject will at once recognise my debt to the work of David Garland and Antony Duff, which is gladly acknowledged. It is also a pleasure to acknowledge the remote origins of the present study in Henry Chadwick's inspirational lectures in the Chapter House of Christ Church, Oxford, now a quarter of a century distant, which first introduced me to theology, and in particular to the work of R. C. Moberly.

Abbreviations

CC   *Corpus Christianorum, series latina* (Turnhout, 1953–)

LW   *Luther's Works* (Missouri, Concordia, 1958–75)

PL   J. P. Migne, *Patrologia Latina* (221 vols., Paris, 1844–64)

TDNT   *Theological Dictionary of the New Testament*, ed. G. Kittel, tr. G. W. Bromiley (9 vols., Grand Rapids, Mich., Eerdmans, 1964–74)

WA   Luther, *Weimarer Ausgabe* (Weimar, 1883ff.)

CHAPTER I

Religion and retribution

Christianity is Parcel of the Laws of England: Therefore to
reproach the Christian Religion is to speak in Subversion of
the Law.

Matthew Hale, Lord Chief Justice

By the satisfaction of justice, I mean the retribution of so
much pain for so much guilt; which is the dispensation we
expect at the hand of God, and which we are accustomed to
consider as the order of things that perfect justice dictates
and requires.

William Paley

John Fletcher, of Madeley, is one of the most attractive figures of
the eighteenth-century English church. Born and brought up in
Switzerland, and attending university at Geneva, he learned
English only after coming to Britain in his early twenties, and his
early sermons, at any rate, were delivered with so thick an accent
that English congregations found him difficult to understand. He
had intended to be a soldier, but a series of accidents prevented
him, and on coming to England he came under Wesley's
influence, took up residence in Madeley, and after ordination by
the Bishop of Bangor began to assist the incumbent. About
Madeley it was observed that it was 'remarkable for little else
than the ignorance and profaneness of its inhabitants, among
whom respect to men was as rarely observed as piety towards
God'. When the vicar died in 1760 Fletcher was offered the living
and accepted, even though he was simultaneously offered one of
much greater value. He remained at Madeley for the rest of his
life, twenty-five years. He was an indefatigable visitor, and when
people maintained that they could not wake up on Sunday

mornings in order to get to church he took to going round the
entire parish with a handbell, beginning at four o'clock in the
morning. The year after his induction he formed a religious
society within the parish, which met in private houses, the rules of
which were as rigorous as those of any monastic community,
though it was typical of Fletcher that it included the provision not
to be unkind to those who chose not to join the society. Amongst
the rules we also find the injunction to 'do good to the Bodies of
all Men; by giving food to the Hungry, cloathing to the naked,
visiting the sick, and helping those in trouble'. Fletcher himself
took this so seriously that, according to an early biographer, 'it
frequently unfurnished his house, and sometimes left him destitute
of the most common necessaries ... That he might feed the
hungry, he led a life of abstinence and self denial; that he might
cover the naked, he clothed himself in the most homely attire;
and that he might cherish such as were perishing in a state of
extreme distress he submitted to hardships of a very trying
nature.'[1] These included struggling for almost his entire ministry
against the tuberculosis which eventually killed him. If there was
ever an Anglican St Francis, Fletcher is the man. When John
Wesley preached at his funeral, in 1785, he declared that he never
expected to meet so holy a man this side of eternity. This helps us
to understand why, when the brother of his servant girl was
sentenced to death in March 1773, he at once asked Fletcher to
intervene.

The name of the youth in question was John Wilkes. His father
had died when he was still a child, and his mother bound him
apprentice to a collier who himself died in a pit accident, though
not before introducing the boy to the pleasures of cock fighting
and gaming. At the age of fifteen he was arrested and whipped
for stealing fowls. He then broke into a house, and finally robbed
a man of a watch and some money on the public highway. Under
the Black Act both housebreaking in daytime and robbery on the
highway were capital offences. Still not nineteen, he was arrested
and sentenced. When he appealed for Fletcher's help to have the
sentence commuted, the vicar refused. 'I neither can nor will

---

[1]   Joseph Benson, *Life of J. W. de la Flechere* (London, 1805).

meddle in that affair', he wrote, 'nor have I any probability of success if I did.'

Apply then *yourself*, night and day, to the *king of heaven* for grace and mercy. If you cry to him, from the bottom of your heart, as a condemned dying man, who deserves hell as well as the gallows; if you sincerely confess your crimes, and beg the Son of God, the Lord Jesus Christ, to intercede for you, it is not too late to get your soul reprieved: he will speak for you to God Almighty: he will pardon *all* your sins: he will wash you in his most precious blood: he will stand by you in your extremity: he will deliver you out of the hands of the *hellish* executioner; and though you have lived the life of the wicked, he will help you to die the death of the penitent ... Consider him [Jesus] as hanging upon the cross by the nails that fastened him there. See him bearing your curse, your shame, your punishment. Behold him opening his arms of mercy to take you in, letting out his vital blood to wash away your sins.

After the boy's execution Fletcher later published this letter, and the story of his repentance and conversion, together with a litany for use by prisoners condemned to death.[2]

Wesley's Journal, and early Methodist history, is full of this kind of scene. Both John and Charles Wesley began visiting in Oxford Gaol as early as 1730. We read in the Journal entry for 25 April 1739 how John Wesley preached to the prisoners in Bristol: 'I was insensibly led without any previous design to declare strongly and explicitly that "God willeth all men to be saved." Immediately one, and another, and another sunk to the earth: they dropped on every side as thunderstruck.' Charles Wesley's Journal for July of the previous year records his ministry in Newgate. On the night before the execution of nine prisoners, 'We wrestled in mighty prayer ... Joy was visible in all their faces.

---

[2]   *The Penitent Thief or A Narrative of Two Women, fearing God, who visited in prison a Highwayman, Executed at Stafford, April 3rd 1773* (London, 1773). In the hymns he proposed for condemned prisoners we find the following verses:

> I own my punishment is just
> I suffer for my evil here,
> But in *thy* suffering, Lord, I trust
> *Thine*, only *Thine*, my soul can clear.
>
> This is the faith I humbly seek,
> The faith in thine all cleansing blood:
> That blood which does for sinners speak
> O let it speak for me to God.

We sang "Behold the Saviour of Mankind: Nailed to the shameful tree. How vast the love that him inclined, To bleed and die for thee." It was one of the most triumphant hours I have known.' The next morning he accompanied them to the gallows: 'They were all cheerful, full of comfort, peace and triumph, assuredly persuaded that Christ had died for them and waited to receive them into paradise ... I never saw such calm triumph, such incredible indifference to dying.' He returned home, he wrote, 'Full of peace and confidence in our friends' happiness. That hour under the gallows was the most blessed hour of my life.'[3]

When, at the end of May 1831, two men were hanged, one for sheep stealing and one for stealing in a dwelling house, even though no violence had been used, the *Spectator* commented: 'In England "law grinds the poor" – and why? The remainder of the line supplies the ready answer – "rich men make the law"! There is the secret of our bloody code – of the perverse ingenuity by which its abominations have so long been defended – of the dogged obstinacy with which all attempts to wash them away has been withstood! "Whoso stealeth a sheep, let him die the death" says the statute: could so monstrous a law have been enacted had our legislators been chosen by the people of England? But our lawmakers hitherto have been our landlords.'[4] Fletcher, the Wesleys, and their followers were genuinely concerned for the poor – that is not in doubt. John Wesley may have been an old-fashioned high Tory, but he was concerned to do something about poverty and frequently made unpopular (and fairly simplistic) suggestions to the Government in the newspapers. What was it, then, which prevented them from seeing what the editors of the *Spectator* so clearly perceived? How was it that they could see people like Wilkes, whose hopeless background they perfectly understood, go to the gallows for offences which were trivial and which involved no violence against the person, without exerting themselves to have the sentence commuted? Fletcher's one

[3] Cf. P. Linebaugh, *The London Hanged: Crime and Civil Society in the Eighteenth Century* (Harmondsworth, Penguin, 1991), pp. 214–15.

[4] *Spectator*, 4: 152 (28 May 1831). Cited by L. Radzinowicz in *A History of English Criminal Law and its Administration from 1750*, vol. 1 (London, Stevens, 1948), p. 600. The allusion is to Goldsmith, *The Deserted Village*: 'Each wanton judge new penal statutes draw, / Laws grind the poor, and rich men rule / the law.'

concern, as we see it in the pamphlet, was that the boy repented of his sin, and this is what appears in the Journals of both Wesleys.[5] The *Spectator* editorial was, of course, sixty years on, but many of Fletcher and Wesley's contemporaries had already raised the question of penal reform. Eden's *Principles of Penal Law*, which advocated extremely sparing use of the death penalty, and which attacked the inhumanity and irrationality of large parts of the criminal law, had appeared in 1771. How is it that the question whether the law might be wrong, or even wicked, does not arise for these good Christian people? How could they come away from scenes of judicial murder feeling that this was 'the most blessed day of their lives'?

Mutatis mutandis the same question can be raised with respect to earlier theologians. In Anselm's day, at the end of the eleventh century, the life of a stag was worth more than that of a serf, but, although he was sensitive to the needs of 'Christ's poor', Anselm nowhere adverts to the fact. This was not a blindness shared by all. Two generations later, in 1159, John of Salisbury makes a spirited attack on the forest laws, precisely in the name of the Christ who died for all, but by and large this was not the concern of the great theologians.

A number of reasons for this failure can be adduced. One is that 'social blindfolds' prevented even saintly figures like Anselm from really seeing what was going on. Anselm, Archbishop of Canterbury when *Cur Deus Homo?* appeared, might find himself in conflict with the king on the grounds of sexual morality, or on the question of who appoints bishops, but not on the grounds of criminal justice. Bishops and archbishops could hardly read Scripture except from the position of those who exercise power. However genuinely reluctant to take office (and there is no doubt at all where Anselm's heart lay), once in post it was they who underwrote the legitimacy of rulers.

One can also point to the idealist character of almost all

[5] P. J. R. King argues that good character, youth, poverty and the absence of violence were taken into account in deciding on reprieve, but this was clearly not the case for Wilkes, nor did these considerations bear on Fletcher, who had, he argued, helped save one young man from the gallows who had since turned out 'very bad'. 'Decision-Makers and Decision-Making in the English Criminal Law, 1750–1800', *Historical Journal*, 27 (1984), 25–58.

Western theology. Idealism functions to direct attention away from the messiness and injustice of ordinary life to 'eternal' realities and truths. It puts a phantasmal object in place of the real human being. So the Christ of doctrine was far removed from the Galilean preacher, with his teaching about forgiveness, who mingled with the poor, and ideas about making up the number of fallen angels took the place of concrete attention to the miseries and oppression of the poor.

Again, Louis Dumont draws our attention to the fact that today we are individuals in the world, *inworldly* individuals, in his terms, whereas the early Christians, and figures like Anselm, were *outworldly*, characterised by renunciation of the world. In his view the change from one to the other begins in the mid eighth century and culminates with Calvin.[6] We still find it, however, in the pietist theology of the eighteenth and nineteenth centuries. Further reasons for this blindness, at least after the Reformation, include the character of Enthusiasm, and theological debates about law, authority, and the nature of God.

Amongst all these factors I wish to suggest that the satisfaction theory of the atonement has a role which must not be underestimated. This theory formed the very heart not only of Enthusiast but of Establishment theology. On the cross, according to the *Book of Common Prayer*, Christ made a 'full, perfect, and sufficient sacrifice, oblation and satisfaction, for the sins of the whole world'. The doctrine of satisfaction here implied drew on legal notions. Together with debates about natural and divine law, and the theology of justification, it formed part of a formidable body of legal-theological rhetoric which exercised a potent ideological function. It is this function which I hope to explore in this book. I wish to do three things. First, to look at the way satisfaction theory changed in response to changing accounts of criminal law. Second, to ask about the validity of the presuppositions behind it, and in particular to try and understand what is meant by expiation. I shall try and show the ways in which expiation and retribution have been

---

6　　L. Dumont, 'The Christian Beginnings of Modern Individualism', in *The Category of the Person*, ed. M. Carrithers, S. Collins and S. Lukes (Cambridge, Cambridge University Press, 1985), pp. 93ff.

read together in the Christian tradition. Third, in the light of this, to ask how a Christian theology of the atonement *ought* to bear on penal thinking. I shall argue that whilst a powerful tradition in Christian atonement theology reinforced retributive attitudes, an alternative tradition, as I hope to show more squarely rooted in the founding texts, always existed to critique these. In understanding the roots of retributivism I hope at the same time to contribute to its deconstruction. Though the bulk of my argument will be narrative I must begin, not with history, but by taking a little further the suggestion that the doctrine of satisfaction formed part of the 'ideology' of Western Christendom.

THEOLOGY, IDEOLOGY AND CULTURAL THEORY

All theology is ideology. This is true in the tautologous sense in which Marx first uses the word 'ideology' in *The German Ideology* to mean all forms of discourse in any given society, from poetry to metaphysics.[7] By extension we can use the word to characterise the articulation of the position of any specific group or person, or the point of view of a particular text, so that we can speak of Anabaptist or Methodist ideology, or the ideology of Blake's *Jerusalem*. It is also frequently appropriate, however, in the strong and usually pejorative sense in which Marx used the word, to speak of the role which forms of discourse may play in justifying particular social interests.[8] In this sense it has to be said that Christian theology constituted the most potent form of ideology in Western society for at least a thousand years, up to the eighteenth and nineteenth centuries, and its ideological importance is by no means dead. In this strong sense satisfaction theory played an important ideological role. It was both influenced by, and influenced, penal thinking. It represented a construal of the crucifixion, by no means inevitable, which reinforced retributive thinking, according to which sin or crime have to be punished, and cannot properly be dealt with in any other way.

[7] K. Marx and F. Engels, *Collected Works*, vol. v (Moscow, 1976), p. 30.
[8] K. Marx, *Political Writings, II* (Harmondsworth, Penguin, 1973), p. 37.

In a series of observations which are not elaborated at length
Marx characterised the relation of ideology to specific modes of
production in terms of the relation of base to superstructure.
'What else does the history of ideas prove', asks the Communist
Manifesto, 'than that intellectual production changes its character
in proportion as material production is changed? The ruling
ideas of each age have been the ideas of its ruling class.'[9] Sub-
sequent discussion has wished to insist on a dialectical interaction
between ideas and forms of society, which is in any case the most
obvious reading of the *Theses on Feuerbach*. David Nicholls has
recently offered us a compelling account of such a dialectical
interplay in exploring the relationship between ideas of God and
different polities. Images for God may be borrowed from
political discourse, he argues, but they then develop a life of
their own and in turn come to affect political ideas. Thus,
'Theological rhetoric, child of political experience, may also be
mother of political change.'[10] At the heart of Nicholls' case are
analogies for God, such as king, lord or judge, and models and
allegorical inferences which take these analogies further. Such
analogies constitute what cultural theory speaks of as 'mentalities'
or ways of thinking, and these are the focus of Nicholls' account.
When we turn to satisfaction theory, however, we need to
broaden our understanding of ideology to include cultural
representations and practices. Under 'ideology' are included not
only mentalities but also 'sensibilities', or ways of feeling, which
constitute 'structures of affect'. Thus we have mentalities, a
framework of belief, in the work of the great theologians, but
even more importantly we find in the imaging of the cross in
Western art, carried to the remotest corners of Europe in
cathedrals and parish churches, in hymnology, and in decisively
important construals of the Christian liturgy, a structure of affect,
embracing rich and poor, of great power. That this pattern of
sensibilities was focussed week in week out by *ritual* was vitally
important, for 'rituals do not just "express" emotions – they
arouse them and organize their content; they provide a kind of

---

[9]   K. Marx, *Political Writings, I, The Revolutions of 1848* (Harmondsworth, Penguin, 1973),
       p. 85.
[10]   D. Nicholls, *Deity and Domination* (London, Routledge, 1989), p. 14.

didactic theatre through which the onlooker is taught what to feel, how to react, which sentiments are called for.'[11]

The account of cultural theory to which I am referring is laid out in Norbert Elias' *The Civilizing Process*, and developed with regard to the sociology of punishment by David Garland. Impetus for this development came from the Dutch historian Pieter Spierenberg, who challenged Foucault's account of the rise of the penitentiary. Where Foucault discounted humanitarian impulses, Spierenberg argued that the change in punishment from public torture to imprisonment was bound up with changes in sensibility evident from 1600 onwards.[12] Like all contemporary theories of ideology such cultural theories recognise a dialectic between theory and practice. In its cognitive aspect, Garland argues, culture embraces 'all those conceptions and values, categories and distinctions, frameworks of ideas and systems of belief which human beings use to construe their world and render it orderly and meaningful'.[13] As such it is inextricably bound up with material forms of action and ways of life, so that the 'interwoven webs of significance', which make up the fabric of a culture develop in a dialectical relationship with social patterns of action. Amongst other things punishments and penal institutions 'help shape the overarching culture and contribute to the generation and re-generation of its terms' – including, of course, the formulation of atonement theology.[14] At the same time we need to recognise 'the incorrigible complexity and overdetermination of the cultural realm as it relates to practice'. While it may be easy to show in broad terms the influence of a particular cultural form upon penal practice, he notes, 'the actual route by which one comes to influence the other, and the exact nature of that influence, are often much less easy to specify'.[15] For this reason there is no master key to understanding the relation of ideology and praxis or, in this case, theology and

---

[11] David Garland, *Punishment and Modern Society* (henceforth cited as *PMS*) (Oxford, Clarendon Press, 1990), p. 67.

[12] P. Spierenberg, *The Spectacle of Suffering: Executions and the Evolution of Repression* (Cambridge, Cambridge University Press, 1984); N. Elias, *The Civilizing Process* (Oxford, Blackwell, 1994).

[13] Garland, *PMS*, p. 195.

[14] ibid., p. 249.

[15] ibid., p. 209.

penal practice. The sociology of punishment has drawn on Marx, Durkheim and Weber, and Foucault has extended the discussion to take in the question of discipline and conformity in society as a whole. In my view all of these frameworks of analysis provide essential insights into understanding how and why society punishes, and to recognise this is to respect the complexity of cultural data rather than to seek to tame critical discourse through a petit bourgeois synthesis.[16]

Garland argues that socially constructed sensibilities and mentalities have major implications for the way in which we punish offenders. 'These cultural patterns structure the ways in which we think about criminals, providing the intellectual frameworks ... through which we see these individuals, understand their motivations, and dispose of them as cases.'[17] If we wish to see how theology and penal practice have interacted, this form of cultural analysis at once suggests itself. Theology and piety form subsets of mentalities and sensibilities and also influence the ways we think about criminals. In both mentalities and sensibilities an image of judicial murder, the cross, bestrode Western culture from the eleventh to the eighteenth centuries. How did this bear on understandings of penality? Michael Ignatieff's study of the rise of the prison, unlike Foucault's, gives many examples of the way in which religious sensibilities influenced new penal thinking, and they could even be claimed to have played a decisive role.[18] The question of the impact of religious sensibilities, or the structure of affect surrounding the cross, on penal practice, and the correlative effects of the development of criminal law on understandings of the atonement is then the theme of this study which can be taken as an extended footnote to specialist accounts by sociologists of punishment.

---

[16] So Adrian Howe on David Garland's *Punishment and Modern Society* in *Punish and Critique* (London, Routledge, 1994), p. 70. Garland cites Peter Gay: ' "overdetermination" is in fact nothing more than the sensible recognition that a variety of causes – a variety, not infinity – enters into the making of all historical events, and that each ingredient in historical experience can be counted on to have a variety – not infinity – of functions'.

[17] Garland, *PMS*, p. 195.

[18] M. Ignatieff, *A Just Measure of Pain: The Penitentiary in the Industrial Revolution 1750–1850* (henceforth cited as *JMP*) (Harmondsworth, Penguin, 1989), cf. pp. 49, 56, 84, 152–3, and see chapter 7 below.

Satisfaction theory, finding expression both in art and liturgy, as well as intellectual discourse, has functioned in the way that Malinowski described myth. Myth, he said, is 'a narrative resurrection of a primeval reality, told in satisfaction of deep religious wants, moral cravings, social submissions, assertions, even practical requirements ... it expresses, enhances and codifies belief; it safeguards and enforces morality; it vouches for the efficiency of ritual and contains practical rules for the guidance of men.'[19] So construed, myth is the bearer of cultural meaning and just so has satisfaction theory functioned. It has decisively informed that culture which constitutes the framework for social action.

One reason satisfaction theory was, and remains, so powerful is that in so many areas it is true to human experience. The need to make expiation or atonement for wrongdoing seems to be one of the most powerful human impulses, operating both on the individual and the collective level. If the problems of guilt and violence and the need to deal with them are not definitive of human culture, then they certainly are of civilisation, i.e. the attempt of human beings to live together in settled communities. Part of the power of Christianity as a missionary religion is that its central symbol, the cross, targets both guilt and violence, and offers a remedy to both through the 'bearing' of guilt and the refusal to meet violence with counter-violence. That it is a *symbol* which is central, and not a doctrine or a philosophy, is important, for the cross focusses feelings of guilt, shame and repentance which go far beyond words to the very roots of human culture and the individual psyche. That it squarely faces the universal human problem of guilt and violence is its claim to be redemptive. Satisfaction theory in particular addressed the need for order both in society and in the human soul; it addressed the sense of justice and the need to express moral outrage; it gave voice to the experience that suffering might sometimes be redemptive; above all it was a means of dealing with guilt. All of these things were brought together by the satisfaction theory, adumbrated at each celebration of the eucharist, painted in representations of the passion, given voice in the hymns of pietism. The power of this

19 B. Malinowski, 'Myth in Primitive Psychology', in *Myth, Science and Religion and Other Essays* (Westport, Conn., Negro Universities Press, 1971), p. 101.

combination of factors was enormous. No artist or ideologue could have dreamed up anything remotely as effective.

I do not suggest, of course, that satisfaction theory arose simply to meet a societal need. The relation of mentalities to social and economic structures is, as Garland insists, highly complex and resistant to a simple unravelling. On the other hand it seems clear that there are connections, and in this case it is true that the need to punish, to torture, to hang, to imprison was never quite self-evident. Even in the days when punishment was a popular spectacle there were those who condemned its use, as we shall see, and the attitude of the crowds which turned up to watch executions was ambivalent. Moral and metaphysical justifications for these acts were therefore always sought. In England 'The Church by Law Established provided the intellectual and theological justification for hanging ... Had the church denounced it, it would have withered and died.'[20] The theology of satisfaction, I contend, provided one of the subtlest and most profound of such justifications, not only for hanging but for retributive punishment in general.

I shall attempt to explore the relation of satisfaction theory to penal practice through a narrative which runs from the eleventh to the nineteenth century, but before doing so I need to clarify what is meant by retributivism, and outline its theological roots, in the remainder of this chapter and in the two chapters which follow. Having considered the relation of religion and law, sin and crime, I shall ask, in a preliminary way, what structure of affect arose from the dominance of a particular construal of the crucifixion. Those of us who are conditioned to think of Christianity as a civilising and progressive influence need to be aware of its shadowside, to which Nietzsche and, more recently, Girard have drawn attention. Why is it that, in the United States today, surveys of public opinion show that Christians tend to favour capital punishment slightly more than the overall population?[21] Could it be that the preaching of the cross not only desensitized us to judicial violence but even lent it sanction?

---

[20] H. Potter, *Hanging in Judgement* (London, SCM, 1993), p. vii.
[21] H. Prejean, *Dead Man Walking: An Eyewitness Account of the Death Penalty in the United States* (New York, Random House, 1993), p. 124.

RELIGION AND LAW

In the law books of the Old Testament, cultic and what we now call civil and criminal law are all inextricably interrelated, as we shall see in detail in the next chapter. The framework of all these laws is an apodictic narrative: 'God said'. Law as a whole is understood as revelation, even though it is certain that the different laws emerged over many centuries in a variety of cultures. In this way Israel expressed an ultimate sanction for its law codes, and this connection between law and religion is taken for granted in the ancient texts of many cultures. 'In early law ... a supernatural presidency is supposed to consecrate and keep together all the cardinal institutions of those times, the State, the Race, and the Family.'[22] Even for Plato, religion provides the ultimate metaphysical justification for human laws.[23] For the Stoics, who were pantheists, the whole cosmos expressed divine rationality, and thus discernment of the world's immanent rationality was discernment of how human beings should live. Natural law was the codification of this discernment. Roman law was profoundly affected by Stoicism, which, through the writings of Cicero and Seneca, came to influence Christianity.

The provision of ultimate justification for morality, or for law, is only one way of conceiving the relationship between religion and law, however. Religion and law are related at the deepest level, I shall argue, as being equally concerned with the question of what it is which enables and sustains human community. All theories of law are concerned with setting out the conditions under which the life of a given community is thought to be sustainable, a task implied in the etymology of the Greek word for law, *nomos*. It derives from *nemo*, 'to distribute', 'deal out', in the sense of assigning land or pasture. When qualified it comes to express ethical judgements: to grant equally, exercise fairness, be impartial.[24] 'Human nature cannot by any means subsist without the association of individuals', wrote Hume, 'and that association

---

[22] H. S. Maine, *Ancient Law* (London, John Murray, 1906), p. 5.
[23] Plato, *Laws* x.
[24] See H. H. Esser in *Dictionary of New Testament Theology* (Exeter, Paternoster Press, 1975), vol. II, p. 438.

never could have place were no regard paid to the laws of equity and justice.'[25] Human community, in other words, is only ultimately sustainable when morally founded. Tyrannies collapse because they run against the grain of human community.

Both Judaism and Christianity claim that God has revealed the true meaning of human life, and that an essential part of that meaning is 'life together'. Both law and religion, therefore, in different ways, embody normative views of the human, moral perceptions which underwrite a vision of human community.[26] The connection between law and morality has been taken for granted by all Christian reflection on law, and finds its most typical expression in Aquinas' hierarchy of divine, natural and positive law, where natural law reflects the divine law, and positive law which is worthy of the name reflects natural law. In the background is the confluence of Stoicism and the Mosaic law, understood as God's divinely revealed will for human community. When Aristotle's emphasis on the appeal to reason by law is added, as by Aquinas, then we can say that law is a rational enterprise which addresses and respects the citizen as a rational and responsible agent, and makes moral claims in moral terms about what it is which enables life together.[27] 'Law is nothing other than an ordinance of reason for the common good made by the authority who has care of the community.'[28]

Aquinas' hierarchy of laws was echoed by Blackstone in his *Commentaries*, written at precisely the time of our opening story, though stated in a characteristically eighteenth-century form. Blackstone began by defining law as a rule of action prescribed by a superior to an inferior, a view which looks back through Hobbes to Ockham and theological nominalism. He glossed this, however, to make it compatible with natural law. 'Man considered as a creature must *necessarily* be *subject* to the *laws* of

25 Hume, *Treatise of Human Nature* III.ii.
26 The tension between law and gospel, as understood by Augustine and later Western theorists, is not a rejection of law so much as a demand that we need to go beyond it. Law represents as it were a surface dimension which we need to internalise and radicalise if we are to be truly moral.
27 R. A. Duff, *Trials and Punishments* (Cambridge, Cambridge University Press, 1986), p. 89.
28 *Summa Theologiae* 1a 2ae 90.4. I use the New Blackfriars edition (60 vols., London, Eyre & Spottiswoode, 1964–81).

his creator, for he is entirely a *dependent* being ... as man depends absolutely upon his maker for every thing, it is necessary that he should in all points conform to his makers's will. This will of his maker is called the *Law* of Nature.'[29] Bentham objected to this: 'there are no such things as any "precepts", nothing by which man is *"commanded"* to do any of those acts pretended to be enjoined by the pretended law of Nature. If any man knows of any let him produce them.'[30] As opposed to what he took to be the vagaries of English case law he wanted a rational system of laws founded on the principles of utility, an idea he took from Beccaria. Bentham initiated a debate, which continues to the present day, between 'positivist' philosophers of law and those who maintain that law rests overtly on moral principle. Bentham's most famous successor, John Austin, echoed Blackstone in defining laws 'strictly so called' as the commands of political superiors to inferiors, and insisted on the separation of law and morality. 'The existence of law is one thing; its merit or demerit another.'[31] The best-known contemporary proponent of this position, H. L. A. Hart, defines legal positivism as 'the simple contention that it is in no sense a necessary truth that laws reproduce or satisfy certain demands of morality'.[32]

Definitions like this can be misleading, as neither Hart nor other positivists have wished to deny intimate connections between law and morality. Hart in effect reinstates natural law as comprising those 'rules of conduct which any social organization must contain if it is to be viable'.[33] These include systems of 'forbearances', respect for persons and property based on an understanding of the 'approximate equality' of persons, and the fact that human beings are motivated by 'limited altruism'. These are considerably more minimal than the 'basic goods' presupposed in John Finnis' reworking of natural law, but they move in

[29] W. Blackstone, *Commentaries on the Laws of England* (1769), vol. I, p. 38.
[30] J. Bentham, *A Comment on the Commentaries*, ed. C. W. Everett (Oxford, Clarendon Press, 1928), p. 38.
[31] J. Austin, *The Province of Jurisprudence Determined* (London, Weidenfeld & Nicolson, 1954), p. 184.
[32] H. L. A. Hart, *The Concept of Law* (Oxford, Clarendon Press, 1961), p. 181.
[33] ibid., p. 188.

the same direction.[34] Both ask what constitutes human flourishing
and make non-cynical judgements about human motivation.
Such judgements mark legal positivism off from the Sophists
whom Plato contested, who also believed that law was simply a
matter of convention, but used this argument to justify the
tyranny of the strong. De-coupling law and morality, then, is
purely in the interests of analytical clarity. Hart believes that
rather than argue, as Augustine and Aquinas did, that bad law is
no law, the formula 'This is law but too iniquitous to obey or
apply' makes for clearer thinking.[35] In Hart's view the sense that
there is that beyond the legal system which judges it (i.e. a moral
code) is better protected by this approach than by the approach
which believes that nothing iniquitous can anywhere have the
status of law. In jurisprudence we need to distinguish between
social control enforced by purely moral sanctions, by brute force,
and by law. Those who insist on the identity between law and
morality make the understanding of the specific realm of law
difficult.

Part of the problem with the positivist account of law is that it
is counterintuitive. As Hart himself notes, 'The law of every
modern state shows at a thousand points the influence of both the
accepted social morality and wider moral ideals.'[36] It is this sense
which Ronald Dworkin has appealed to, over many years, in
insisting that principles are appealed to in sentencing, rather than
a simple clarification and application of the law.[37] Antony Duff
points up the connection between law and morality by asking why
it was that someone had to be 'fit to be hanged'. It was universally
agreed that it was immoral to hang the insane. 'A creature
unprepar'd, unmeet for death', comments the Duke of the
drunken Barnadine, in *Measure for Measure*; 'to transport him, in
the mind he is were damnable.'[38] The reason for this, Duff

[34]   J. Finnis, *Natural Law and Natural Rights* (Oxford, Clarendon Press, 1980). Finnis
       proposes life, knowledge, play, aesthetic experience, sociability, practical reason-
       ableness and religion as basic human goods.
[35]   Hart, *The Concept of Law*, pp. 205ff. Cf. Augustine, *De Libero Arbitrio* 5; Aquinas, *Summa
       Theologiae* 1a 2ae Qu. 95 arts. 2, 4.
[36]   Hart, *The Concept of Law*, p. 199.
[37]   See *Law's Empire* (Cambridge, Mass., 1986).
[38]   Act 4, sc. 3.

argues, is that 'punishment aims ... to *address* the offender as a rational and responsible agent: if she cannot understand what is being done to her, or why it is being done, or how it is related as a punishment to her past offence, her punishment becomes a travesty'.[39] Legal obligation, then, is a species of moral obligation:

the obligations which the laws of my community impose on me are aspects of my moral obligation to care for the good of that community. To claim, prescriptively, that someone has a legal obligation is to claim that a law is morally binding on her; to accept a legal obligation is to accept it as morally binding.[40]

The theologian's intervention in the continuing dispute between legal positivists and their opponents takes roughly the form Duff indicates. The engagement of religion, or at any rate the Christian religion, with law is in its account of what it means to be human, and therefore of what constitutes human or sub-human forms of community. Of course, such positions call for a hermeneutic of suspicion. Marxists have argued that law is essentially a means of class domination, and there is much to be said for that view.[41] Blackstone and Paley clearly understood Christianity as providing ideological support for laws which functioned to oppress the poor, and in this they could appeal to a venerable Christian tradition. I shall seek to argue, however, that the founding texts point in another direction, and that this alternative voice is also represented throughout the development of atonement theology and criminal justice. To accept that religion is concerned with law because it offers an account of the common good is not to commit oneself to a dominant ideology. This can be illustrated by examining a subset of the religion–law relationship, the relation of sin and crime.

SIN AND CRIME

Despite the importance of positivism in British jurisprudence, the identification of morality and law was often accepted very

---

[39] Duff, *Trials*, p. 27.
[40] ibid., p. 93.
[41] Classically in E. B. Pashukanis, *Law and Marxism: A General Theory*, ed. C. Arthur (London, Ink Wells, 1978).

roundly. 'In order that an act should be punishable', said Lord Denning, 'it must be morally blameworthy. It must be a sin.'[42] 'The distinction between crimes and sins can be found only in considerations of social utility', announced Rashdall. 'A crime is simply a sin which it is expedient to repress by penal enactment.'[43] Three centuries earlier Hobbes, a proto-positivist, had already proposed an important de-coupling of crime and sin: 'A Crime', writes Hobbes, 'is a sinne, consisting in the committing (by Deed, or Word) of that which the law forbids, or the Omission of what it hath commended. So that every crime is a sinne; but not every sinne a crime.'[44] Sin, according to this definition, is whatever is against the law. The eighteenth-century penal reformer William Eden made the more obvious distinction in the opposite direction:

Crime is distinguishable from sin: for every crime must be a positive breach, or wilful disregard, of some existing public law. But many offences against earthly authority are no otherwise sinful in the eye of Heaven, than as infractions of that implied contract of obedience to the legislature, to which every member of Society is subjected: and there are many species of sin, which, in a legal sense, cannot be criminal, because in their nature not obvious to human accusation.[45]

As Eden points out, crime, which is breach of legal obligation, and sin, which is breach of moral obligation, are often not identical. Selling off nationalised industries to the highest bidder, or using the services of prostitutes, are not crimes, though they are sins. For the eighteenth-century peasant poaching was no sin, though it might cost you your neck. Nevertheless Lord Denning is right to the extent that 'a certain kind of immorality should be a necessary, though not a sufficient, condition of criminality'.[46] One of the difficulties of an extreme positivist position is that bad laws, like the eighteenth-century poaching laws, for example, or the Poll Tax, cannot ultimately command assent and cannot be enforced. They go against the grain of that moral consensus

[42] T. Denning, *The Changing Law* (London, Stevens, 1953), p. 112.
[43] H. Rashdall, *The Theory of Good and Evil* (Oxford, Oxford University Press, 1907), vol. 1, p. 296.
[44] *Leviathan*, Part 2, chap. 27.
[45] W. Eden, *Principles of Penal Law*, 2nd edn (London 1771), p. 84.
[46] Cited in Duff, *Trials*, p. 93.

which is the heart of natural law theory, and indeed which underlies the principle of trial by jury. The possibility of trial by jury rests on the view that 'justice should be administered to the members of a community in accordance with the standards of morality and common sense prevailing in a community'.[47] It presupposes, in other words, that form of moral consensus which Hart calls 'natural law'. If, then, an adequate law expresses a genuine moral obligation, there ought to be no crimes which are not at the same time sins. But this raises the question of our understanding of 'sin'.

In Scripture we find accounts of some of the earliest law codes of the human race. They emerged to serve either tiny nomadic communities, or small city states. It is a testimony to how well the work was done, and how little the human condition has changed over the millennia, that these law codes continue to speak to us to the extent that they do, and the experience of the past inevitably informs current debate on crime and punishment. On the other hand, neither theories of criminal justice nor theologies of the atonement can remain the same in the face of changed human conditions.

Moral codes differ because they adjust themselves to historical and environmental conditions. If we divide economic history into three stages – hunting, agriculture, industry – we may expect that the moral code of one stage will be changed in the next. In the hunting stage ... Pugnacity, brutality, greed, and sexual readiness were advantages in the struggle for existence. Probably every vice was once a virtue – i.e. a quality making for the survival of the individual, the family or the group. [48]

This is overstated, but there is truth in it. The Uruguayan theologian Juan Luis Segundo takes an evolutionary view of sin and guilt. He points out that the word 'humanity' designates not something ready made and morally responsible from the word 'go', as post-Augustinian theology constantly imagined it, but a painfully slow process in which one animal species is being

47   P. Vinogradoff, *The Jurisprudence of the Greek City* (London, Oxford University Press, 1922), p. 11.
48   W. and A. Durant, *The Lessons of History* (New York, Simon & Schuster, 1968), pp. 37–8.

hominised, a process which continues to this moment. In particular, moral conscience is still unfolding from the tangle of
instincts and determinisms. In the course of evolution moral
standards have changed.

Two consequences follow from such an evolutionary view. One
is that, although sin is condemned, it is also recognised as
something which forms part of our evolutionary base. In a certain
sense 'sin' is necessary. It is not that there is a simple contest
between love and egotism, grace and sin, liberty and law.
'Evolution is not a contest between two contradictory forces that
would cancel each other out, unless one should partially or totally
eliminate the other. Though they point in opposite directions,
these two vectors – or tendencies, or forces – are indispensable
and complementary, *each in its own way*.'[49] 'Original sin' on this
understanding constitutes part of the 'negative vector' of evolution, speaking not of an original act from which guilt or punishment, or both, follow but of patterns and structures in which we
find ourselves caught up whether we like it or not, and which we
are not free to choose. In the same way the individual moral life is
not most appropriately viewed as a heroic contest, notwith-
standing the New Testament metaphors which suggest this.
Actions, situations, events do not come to us labelled 'good' or
'bad', but ethical value adheres to the whole project within which
they are inscribed as means and tools. It is the task of a whole
lifetime to try to imprint the reflexes of gratuitousness on our way
of life. 'Sin', then, does not constitute a revealed absolute by
which we can assess what is, or is not, a crime. Rather, when we
submit the biblical uses of the word to scrutiny, we find that sin is
always something which in one way or another damages human
life. Idolatry, for example, is a sin because it commits people to
false and destructive values which lead to the oppression of the
poor and systematic injustice.

Many theologians have insisted on a distinction between sin
and crime on the grounds that crime refers only to breaches of
human law, whereas sin springs from indifference to, or rebellion
against, God. The difficulty with such distinctions is that, as Jesus

[49] J. L. Segundo, *Evolution and Guilt*, tr. J. Drury (London, Gill and Macmillan, 1980),
    p. 129.

and the Scriptural authors repeatedly insist, honouring God is bound up with honouring our neighbour, and vice versa. We can distinguish sin and crime on the ground that there are unjust laws; it is less easy to do so on the ground that some acts have a reference to God which others lack.

It is also pertinent to ask whether we need the concept of sin at all. The question is put to us not only by Freud, who ascribes the notions of sin and guilt to the super ego, but by the fact that there are great cultures, such as the Hindu and Buddhist, which seem to have managed without it. They focus more on suffering and transcience, and for them redemption is escape from the wheel of reincarnation. Good deeds help one to achieve this, and bad deeds keep one bound to reincarnation, but both good and bad deeds arise, to a considerable extent, from one's karma. In the same way for classical Greek culture it was ignorance which was the fundamental human problem, rather than an evil will, the *mens rea* so crucial to Western legal discussion.[50] As far as Aristotle is concerned, when a person has understood what he or she should do, then he or she can do it.[51] Again, it has been suggested that many people do not feel guilt at all and that absence of guilt may be not so much pathological as normal. So perhaps we can do without sin? The response to these questions is to insist that, whilst there are many societies which do not work with sin as a category, there have not yet been societies for which 'anything goes'. All societies up to the present have been *constituted* by drawing boundaries which ought not to be transgressed, by defining behaviour which is, or is not, acceptable. This drawing of boundaries is the function of law which, if it is to command assent, appeals, as we have argued, to shared values. Whilst there are societies without the concept of 'sin', therefore, there are no societies without the concept of 'crime', i.e. behaviour which destroys and is therefore unacceptable to the community. In this context both 'sin' and 'crime' describe patterns of behaviour which damage human society, and therefore the possibility of

---

[50] According to Democritus 'the cause of sin is ignorance (*amathiee*) of the better way' (Fr. 83, Diels II, 78, 13). Cf. the Oedipous tragedy.

[51] See *Eth. Eud.* VIII.I, 1246a; *Pol.* III.II, 1231b. For Aristotle *hamartia*, translated in the NT as 'sin', means error, often committed in good faith.

being human, to varying extents. It is this interrelation of sin and crime, the legal and the moral, which underlies the relationship of theologies of the atonement and penal practice.

CHRISTIAN ATONEMENT AND RETRIBUTIVE THEORY

The connection of satisfaction theory with the retributive theory of punishment was a commonplace of late nineteenth-century theology. Perhaps it was the collapse of retributivism, around the turn of the century, and the rise of welfare accounts of penality, which explains why this connection tended to drop out of sight.[52] In fact satisfaction theory emerged, in the eleventh century, at exactly the same time as the criminal law took shape. The two reacted upon each other. Theology drew on legal notions and legal discussion, as the history of satisfaction doctrine makes clear, and law turned to theology for metaphysical justification.

Hart suggests that an, admittedly crude, model of retributive theory will assert first, that a person may be punished only if he or she has voluntarily done something morally wrong; second, that punishment must match the crime; and third, that the return of suffering for moral evil is itself just, or morally good.[53] John Cottingham has pointed out the complexity of the idea, distinguishing nine possible meanings, and concluding that it is not a theory at all but a metaphor based on the root meaning, *retribuo*, to pay back.[54] At its root, therefore, is the intuition that the offender must 'pay' for the crime and that any punishment is 'deserved'. What is meant by saying that offenders must 'pay' for their crime is obscure. Cottingham considers that only what he calls the 'placation theory' gives any account of why offenders ought to suffer. This is the view expressed by Kant's famous remark that even if a civil society were to dissolve itself tomorrow, 'the last murderer in prison must first be executed so that ... blood guilt will not fall on the people'.[55] In Cottingham's view

---

[52] The revival of this penal theory in the 1970s, however, has been followed by atonement theologies which largely rest on its insights, as I shall argue in chapter 10.

[53] H. L. A. Hart, *Punishment and Responsibility* (Oxford, Clarendon Press, 1968), p. 231.

[54] J. Cottingham, 'Varieties of Retribution', in *Punishment*, ed. R. A. Duff (Aldershot, Dartmouth, 1993), pp. 75ff.

[55] Kant, *Rechtslehre*, Part II, 49E.

this would only make sense 'were there a blood thirsty Deity who insisted on punishment'.

Hart argues for a weaker form of retributivism, which he finds already in Bishop Butler, which emphasises the value of an authoritative expression, in the form of punishment, of moral condemnation for the moral wickedness involved in the offence.[56] Both this weaker, as well as stronger, versions of retributivism are distinguished in the first place by the relegation of considerations of deterrence or of reform to secondary status and in the second by the belief that 'Certain things are simply wrong and ought to be punished.'[57] Retributivism, in other words, appeals to a very strong identification between law and morality of the type we have just been considering, and it is partly this which accounts for its appeal to Christian theorists. By the same token, as Cottingham's remark on Kant's theory indicates, theology has provided much of the metaphysical justification for what is otherwise deeply obscure. The rites and symbols of Christianity have been the means by which Western culture has sought to master the intractable features of human existence. These intractable features have included, at their centre, wickedness, guilt and punishment. The practical business of punishing offenders 'takes place within a cultural space which is already laden with meaning and which lends itself easily to symbolic use'.[58] Christianity was wheeled in to validate the legal process through the taking of oaths (on a book which absolutely forbids them, as Tolstoy caustically noted), through assize sermons, and through the ministrations of chaplains at the gallows. In the prison Tolstoy describes in *Resurrection* 'hung the customary appurtenances of all places of barbarity – a large image of Christ, as it were in mockery of his teaching'. The suffering Christ, an icon of the wickedness of judicial punishment, became the focus of its legality, and of the need for the offender to suffer as he did.[59] An image of torture provided the central construal of the cultural space within which punishment took

56 Hart, *Punishment*, p. 255.
57 A. von Hirsch, *Doing Justice* (New York, Hill & Wang, 1976).
58 Garland, *PMS*, p. 274.
59 This was an insight which the despised liberal theologian Hastings Rashdall was far clearer about than his orthodox opponents, with their supposedly deeper understanding of human sin.

place. In the terms elaborated above, it created the 'structure of affect' which guided thinking about punishment. In this way we can begin to see how the mutual reaction of penal theory and atonement theology led to a rhetoric of violence and the creation of a structure of affect where violence was legitimated.

RETRIBUTION AND VIOLENCE

It is above all to Nietzsche and to the French cultural anthropologist René Girard that we owe the insight that the way in which redemption has been understood has itself generated a rhetoric of violence.

In *The Genealogy of Morals* Nietzsche argues that the feeling of guilt, of personal obligation, has its origin in the relation between buyer and seller, creditor and debtor. Religion begins with the sense of debt to the ancestors, who become divinised. The natural means of dealing with the sense of guilt this engenders is aggression, but this is turned inwards. The guilty feeling of indebtedness grew for several millennia until the advent of Christianity, when it reached its height. The notion of irredeemable debt breeds that of irredeemable penance, and Christianity deals with this through the claim that God sacrifices himself for humanity, the creditor for the debtor. What really happens here, however, is that self-torture reaches its most acute pitch of severity:

Guilt before *God*: this thought becomes an instrument of torture to him (the man of the bad conscience). He apprehends in 'God' the ultimate antithesis of his own ineluctable animal instincts; he reinterprets these animal instincts themselves as a form of guilt before God (as hostility, rebellion, insurrection against the 'Lord', the 'father', the primal ancestor and origin of the world); he stretches himself upon the contradiction 'God' and 'Devil'; he ejects from himself all his denial of himself, of his nature, naturalness, and actuality, in the form of an affirmation, as something existent, corporeal, real, as God, as the holiness of God, as God the Judge, as God the Hangman, as the beyond, as torment without end, as hell, as the immeasurability of punishment and guilt.[60]

---

[60] *Genealogy*, 2.22. I follow the translation of Walter Kaufmann (New York, Random House, 1969).

Nietzsche sees that the doctrine of the cross can be envisaged as a 'mystery of an unimaginable ultimate cruelty'. He has no difficulty in showing the violent sub-text in much Christian rhetoric of salvation.[61] In his view it is on the level of punishment and cruelty that law and religion belong together. Religion lies at the origin of culture, in the need for memory, and since memory 'must be burned in', 'all religions are at the deepest level systems of cruelties'.[62] In law, the origin of punishment is in the substitute for a debt. In place of literal compensation for an injury a recompense is made in the form of a kind of pleasure, the right to torture. 'In "punishing" the debtor, the creditor participates in a *right of the masters*: at last he, too, may experience for once the exalted sensation of being allowed to despise and mistreat someone as "beneath him" ... the compensation ... consists in a warrant for and title to cruelty.'[63] The sphere of legal obligations, then, like religion, has its beginnings 'soaked in blood thoroughly and for a long time'. In a brilliant insight he sees that 'even in good old Kant ... the categorical imperative smells of cruelty'.[64]

Nietzsche's account of the origin of law, culture and religion has not commanded any kind of following, but his insights into both law and religion, and in particular into the religion of the cross, are quite indispensable. We do not have to follow either his famous theory of *ressentiment*, that these theories represent the revenge of the weak on their oppressors, or his solution of the return to Dionysian ideas of human well-being, to learn from what he has to tell us. He had insights of crucial significance in understanding atonement theology which constitute him one of Paul Ricoeur's 'three masters of suspicion'. 'The gods conceived of as the friends of *cruel* spectacles – oh how profoundly this ancient idea still permeates our European humanity! Merely consult Calvin and Luther.'[65] Contemporary society, argues Nietzsche, continues to enjoy the infliction of cruelty, even when administered vicariously through the state, and the festival of

---

[61] He appeals principally to Tertullian.
[62] *Genealogy*, 2.3.
[63] ibid., 2.5.
[64] ibid., 2.6.
[65] ibid., 2.7.

cruelty which the penal system lays on for us is validated by religion.

Like Nietzsche's, René Girard's analysis of violence begins with an account of the origin of culture. Girard identifies violence, stemming from the mimesis which is at the root of all human learning, as the fundamental problem in human society. Very early on he believes that a way was found to deal with it – through the scapegoat ritual. Here the hatred and violence of the community were all heaped on one figure, through whose destruction the community was delivered from further violence. Christ's mission, according to Girard, was to uncover the secret of the scapegoat mechanism, to establish a human community based on peace rather than violence. This constitutes the very heart of Christian revelation. Unfortunately, from the very earliest days, from the writing of the Letter to the Hebrews, Christianity betrayed its master, reinstituting Christ as the supreme sacrificial victim. To do this was once again to legitimate the violence of the scapegoat mechanism. According to Girard, 'historical Christianity took on a persecutory character as a result of the sacrificial reading of the Passion and Redemption'.[66]

As with Nietzsche, Girard's thesis is simplistic, and I shall develop criticisms of it in the chapters which follow, but it contains two elements of crucial importance. The first is in the perception of the connection between sacrifice and violence, and the second is in drawing attention to the importance of the scapegoat mechanism within human communities. His thesis is that whilst Christ died to expose the scapegoat mechanism, Christianity very quickly used the passion story, read as 'the sacrifice of Christ', as a *legitimation* of scapegoating. For much of Christian history the Jews functioned as the scapegoat, harried and persecuted throughout Christendom. As we enter the early modern period, however – and here we have to go beyond Girard – a new scapegoat is found: the 'idle', 'vagabonds', the criminal classes – the poor.[67] The rise of the prison as a means of dealing with crime is not simply about a new technology of

---

[66] R. Girard, *Things Hidden Since the Foundation of the World*, tr. S. Bann and M. Metteer (London, Athlone Press, 1987), p. 225.

[67] Jacques Le Goff claims that medieval city culture regularly scapegoated not only Jews,

power, as Foucault argues, but also a classical manifestation of the scapegoat mechanism, which deals with the victim by expulsion, by excluding from the community. Most systems of criminal justice, it has been argued, are forms of social control, heavily punitive, concerned with blaming, scapegoating and exclusion.[68] For eighteenth- and nineteenth-century Christian society the prisoner was the scapegoat. To pay for their sins prisoners needed to be expelled, transported, locked out of sight behind walls, prevented from human contact, hanged. That the answer to violence in the community is the violence of sacrificial death is taught Christian society by its faith. Criminals die to make satisfaction for their sins as Christ died for the sins of all. If we ask why Fletcher and the Wesleys could not see the injustice of the legal system of their day, part of the reason, I suggest, is to be found in their passion theology. The rhetoric of redeeming blood found concrete expression in the London hanged.

The connection between the foundational Christian texts and violence operates at the level of both text and sub-text. At the level of text, there is ambiguity. The story of the slaughter of the Amalekites (1 Sam. 15) could be used by Cromwell to justify the destruction of Catholic communities in Drogheda and Wexford. Jesus' woes concerning the Pharisees (Matt. 23) could justify violent treatment of heretics. The texts as a whole are ambiguous. Where they are used as a quarry for proof texts, without an overriding and clear hermeneutic, they could be used for war as much as for peace. More important still is the sub-text. The story of Christ's death by torture was a story of redemption. Following Girard we can argue that redemption was accomplished by the unmasking of the powers which destroy life, and by putting forgiveness in the place of revenge. What both Nietzsche and Girard have seen, however, is that the story could itself become, subconsciously, an endorsement of violence and cruelty.

To draw attention to the connection between violence and

---

but lepers and foreigners as well. *Medieval Civilization*, tr. J. Barrow (Oxford, Blackwell, 1988), p. 316.

[68] The recent Government White Paper on policing thinks fundamentally in terms of exclusion.

atonement theology is in no way to provide a reductionist account of the atonement. It is a drawback with both Nietzsche and Girard that they believe they offer comprehensive, and even 'scientific', explanations of such theologies. The beliefs and claims embodied in theories of satisfaction and sacrifice are of monumental complexity. We need to try to plumb their depths, not rubbish them. Thus, whilst Nietzsche, Girard and others can help us understand something of what is going on in these theologies, we must beware of the illusion that somehow the mechanics of atonement are now once and for all laid bare. But the lessons we learn from the masters of suspicion also alert us to the value of the alternative tradition of atonement thinking whose spokesmen include Abelard, Socinus, William Law and William Blake. Even more important, perhaps, is that tradition of 'Radical Dissent', frequently (though not necessarily) espoused by the poor and oppressed, which claimed to go back to Jesus, and which surfaces again and again through the centuries.[69] This tradition seems always to have sat very light to conventional atonement theology, and its most articulate spokesman, William Blake, frankly loathed it.

Since the mid nineteenth century the opposition between Anselm and his followers, on the one hand, and Abelard and his followers on the other, has been characterised in terms of an opposition between 'objective' and 'subjective' views of the atonement. The claim has been that the latter tradition is Pelagian, soft on sin, rationalist, inadequately aware of the depths of human evil – analogies with the critique of rehabilitionist theories are clear. As noted earlier in this chapter, the debate has operated on a fundamentally idealist level, and it is the fact that it deals in abstractions which has made such a contrast seem plausible. Jesus of Nazareth was tortured to death after a judicial process which was no more of a mockery than that by which tens of thousands of poor people have been sent to their deaths. If his life and death were salvific in any way, if they constituted good news to the poor, we need to keep the historical reality in mind. When we do so I believe that the orthodox assault on so-called

[69] See C. Rowland, *Radical Christianity* (Cambridge, Polity Press, 1988).

'liberal' theories, usually caricatured and misrepresented, must in many ways be turned on its head.

Before commencing the historical narrative, which I begin with Anselm, the Scriptural basis to which satisfaction theory appealed needs to be outlined. From Anselm onwards satisfaction and sacrifice were read together, and sacrifice was understood as propitiation. Even today such a connection is felt by many Christians to be self-evident, a testament to the power of the intellectual and emotional structures which have reinforced retributive theory. It is no accident that the new retributivism of current penal policy has gone along with the rise of Christian fundamentalism, especially in the United States. Many of the arguments advanced in favour of it resemble those of evangelical Christians in the nineteenth century who believed that prisons ought to be places where criminals made atonement. If we wish to critique such attitudes, and I believe this to be a matter of urgency, much will depend on a rereading of the foundational texts. It is this I attempt in the following two chapters.

PART I

The cultural formation of atonement: biblical sources

CHAPTER 2

Blood which makes atonement

It is blood which makes atonement by reason of the life.

Leviticus

There is no forgiveness of guilt without atonement, just as there can be no reconciliation without the restoration of justice.

Jürgen Moltmann

In December 1994 Myra Hindley, imprisoned for life for her part as accomplice in a series of terrible child murders, broke the silence of thirty years to plead for release. Her press statement read, 'I have paid my debt to society and atoned for my crime.' This plea reaches right back, more than two thousand years, to the texts of the Old Testament. To understand it, and the theological affirmation of retributive theory in general, we need to understand and evaluate these texts. Diverse, numerous, and often heavily edited, they come to us from a period of approximately seven or eight hundred years and speak from very varying social situations. This presents a real problem of interpretation for those who take social context seriously. On the other hand, Brevard Childs' 'canonical criticism' has made the important point that these texts have in fact been read as a unity over the past two thousand years and as such have made a profound contribution to the formation of Western culture. Accordingly my concern is first to understand those texts which fed in to the structure of affect which gathered around satisfaction theory, and second to argue that there are resources in the same texts in which to ground the alternative response to offenders which I shall argue for in the final chapter.

I shall try to tease out the meaning of the extraordinarily difficult concept of expiation, of the related notion of suffering as education, and of the relation of religion and criminal law, drawing especially upon the insights of Durkheim and Girard. In the course of this I shall argue for an understanding of sacrifice which was commonplace in the second century CE, but which was lost sight of in the Western tradition from the eleventh century on. This understanding, I shall argue in the following chapter, was adopted by Jesus and functions to subvert dominant readings of the atonement.

TABOO, PROPITIATION AND ORDER

When looking at our oldest texts we need to distinguish between taboo, command and law. The first, it is maintained, is a pre-personal way of establishing order in society, the second personal, and the third, by virtue of its general formulation, post-personal.[1] The distinction between command and law may, like much Old Testament exegesis, owe more to Lutheranism than to an exact reading of the ancient texts. That between taboo and law, however, has to stand. The earliest accounts of expiatory rites known to us all relate to breach of taboo rather than of law. Such a breach incurs the wrath of God, which has to be appeased. The theme of the omniscient God who punishes the evil deeds of humanity has been shown to be widespread in the history of religions.[2] The early stories all reveal belief in a causal link between suffering and disaster on the one hand and sin and guilt on the other. Where guilt brings disaster, propitiation is needed. We can take three examples of propitiation in the biblical stories, the first of which is the story of the sin of Achan, in Joshua 7.

At the taking of Jericho the whole city, with the exception of Rahab's house, is put under the ban, 'devoted to destruction'. One man, Achan, ignores this ban and takes spoil for himself and so 'the anger of YHWH burned against the Israelites', and a

---

[1]   C. Westermann, *Creation*, tr. J. Scullion (London, SPCK, 1974), p. 91.
[2]   R. Pettazoni, *The All-Knowing God: Researches into Early Religion and Culture*, tr. H. J. Rose (London, Methuen, 1956).

group of scouts are massacred by a Canaanite war band. By using the loot Achan is discovered and he is stoned to death by the whole community and all his possessions burned with fire. The narrative concludes: 'Then the Lord turned from his burning anger' (Josh. 7.26).

Again there is the terrible story of 2 Sam. 21, which begins with Israel in the grip of a three-year famine. When David asks YHWH the reason for this he is told that it is punishment for the bloodguilt which rests on Saul for putting the Gibeonites to death. David asks the Gibeonites: 'What shall I do for you? How shall I make expiation (*kaphar*), that you may bless the heritage of the Lord?' (2 Sam. 21.3). David offers them silver and gold, apparently as 'blood-wit' – but they insist on the principle of life for life (Exod. 21.2). They demand seven of Saul's sons to be impaled 'before YHWH at the mountain of YHWH' (verse 6). The link with ancient fertility rites is clear, as they are impaled at the beginning of the barley harvest. Like Antigone, one of Saul's concubines, Rizpah, then protects the bodies from wild animals. When they are buried, together with the bodies of Saul and Jonathan, 'God heeded supplications for the land.'

Finally, in 2 Sam. 24 we find the story of how David's sin in taking a census is punished by a pestilence which kills seventy thousand people. This is only averted by the purchase of a threshing floor and the offering of oxen. 'David built there an altar to the Lord, and offered burnt offerings and offerings of well being. So the Lord answered his supplication for the land, and the plague was averted from Israel' (2 Sam. 24.25).

We can see from these stories why Driver claimed that 'The dim and at first confused ideas of the nature of sin, of its antagonism to the holiness of God, of its effect in arousing His punitive wrath, and of the need of allaying this, first gave rise to expiatory rites.'[3] Eichrodt characterised such views as products of a 'dynamistic' system of thought 'in which sin is seen as the transgression of the commandment of an alien power which reacts automatically against it, or has the effect of contagious matter, which threatens with destruction even the person who

[3] S. R. Driver in *Hastings Encyclopaedia of Religion and Ethics* (Edinburgh, T. & T. Clark, 1908), vol. v, pp. 653ff.

comes into contact with it unconsciously'.[4] He points out that
ideas of power or mana are implicit in the ancient stories, and
that 'well known media of sympathetic magic', such as golden
mice, are used to drive away plague.[5]

Mary Douglas has taken these and other older scholars to task
for failing to understand what is at stake in the holiness requirements, such as the ban, which underlie these stories. She agrees
with von Rad that 'The unclean was the most basic form in which
Israel encountered what was displeasing to God.'[6] According to
her what is involved in this distinction is wholeness, being 'whole
in body, whole-hearted and trailing no uncompleted schemes'.
What the dietary commands give expression to is a concern for
order rather than confusion.[7] Purity codes are 'a strong language
of mutual exhortation'.

At this level the laws of nature are dragged in to sanction the moral
code: this kind of disease is caused by adultery, that by incest; this
meteorological disaster is the effect of political disloyalty, that the effect
of impiety. The whole universe is harnessed to men's attempts to force
one another into good citizenship.[8]

Pollution rituals, says Douglas, focus 'men's common urge to
make a unity of all their experience and to overcome distinctions
and separations in acts of at-one-ment'.[9] This is to say that such
sacrifices are grounded in the need for *order*. This concern
remains fundamental to the retributive theory of punishment up
to the present day.

THE NEED FOR EXPIATION

Propitiatory sacrifices sought to turn away God's anger. In seeking
to understand the bulk of the texts which deal with this form of

---

4   W. Eichrodt, *Theology of the Old Testament*, tr. J. A. Baker (2 vols., London, SCM, 1967),
    vol. II, p. 382.
5   ibid., vol. I, pp.158–9. From Egypt and Greece he cites the use of golden locusts for
    deliverance from locust swarms, and the sacrifice of red dogs to avert rust on corn.
6   G. von Rad, *Old Testament Theology*, tr. D. Stalker (2 vols., London and Edinburgh,
    Oliver & Boyd, 1962), vol. I, p. 273.
7   M. Douglas, *Purity and Danger* (London, Routledge, 1966), p. 54.
8   ibid., p. 3.
9   ibid., p. 169.

sacrifice we need to bear in mind that the emphasis on rites of atonement characteristic of the Pentateuch derives from the period after the exile, which was the most traumatic event in Israel's history. God had made a covenant with the house of David, and was understood to have made an eternal commitment to Sion. Now Jerusalem was destroyed and the Davidic kingship at an end. What had gone wrong? The answer was that Israel had sinned and was being punished for her sin. In order to avoid another such catastrophe sin must be avoided, but if it could not be avoided, as for example in the case of unintentional sin, then, the Priestly writers believed, sacrifice was available as a means of atonement.

We must not fall into the trap of believing that all sacrifice was always as the Priestly writers describe it. In von Rad's view such rites were not unknown in the pre-exilic cult, but they certainly did not then occupy the dominant place that they do in the Priestly redaction. They correspond to 'the broken and anguished mood of the exilic and post-exilic periods'.[10] For the Priestly writer it is clear that expiatory sacrifice is the most important form, and it is the sin offering (*chattath*) which is the most common. The emphasis on expiatory offerings can be seen in growth, according to von Rad, 'even within the strands of P'.[11] This offering cleanses a person from unintentional sins (Lev. 4.27f.; Num. 15.27f.). There is also a guilt offering (*asham*), mentioned in connection with the ancient story of the capture of the ark (1 Sam. 6), and linked by the Priestly writer with 'holy things' (Lev. 5.14ff.).

The Hebrew word group translated by 'propitiate', 'expiate', or even occasionally 'atone' is grouped around the noun *kopher* – what would later be called satisfaction, or *wergild* – and the verb *kipper*. The verb is, Driver notes, a denominative meaning 'to perform an expiatory ceremony', and is closely associated with 'to be clean' or 'to cleanse' (*taher*). In Anglo-Saxon scholarship it was frequently maintained that expiation meant 'wiping out', 'covering over', but this is uncertain.[12] Such a derivation seems to rest quite largely on

---

[10] Von Rad, *OT Theology*, vol. 1, p. 269.
[11] ibid.
[12] See the remarks in von Rad, ibid., p. 262: 'Attempts to reach the meaning of this important word as it were along the lines of its evolution, that is, by way of its etymology, have not led to any result.' The assumption that it meant 'wiping over'

an appeal to the story of the meeting of Jacob and Esau after their long separation when Jacob, fearful of his brother's anger, says, 'I will cover (*kapper*) his face with a present' (Gen. 32.20) – which certainly refers to an attempt to appease him.

We find, in the literature, a familiar distinction between propitiation, placating an angry deity, and expiation, wiping away the sin and impurity which made the sinner offensive. This distinction has been challenged on many counts. In the sacrificial texts it is often impossible to distinguish propitiation from expiation.[13] It is often implied that God is propitiated (Ps. 106.30; Zech. 8.22). In a number of cases God's anger is clearly averted by sacrifice (Exod. 30.13; Num. 8.19, 31.50).[14] Propitiation seems to be implied by the frequent references to God's wrath, which are found in both early and late strata. The *kipper* word group is often used in relation to God's wrath. The imagery of sacrifices having a pleasing smell for God likewise implies propitiation. However, 'None of this need imply crudely buying off an angry deity with sacrifices; rather God has appointed for his people means of removing evil and of turning away wrath ... The sin sacrifices please Him because of the obedience to his will shown by those who offer them, an obedience expressive of sorrow.'[15]

There is a paradox, found equally in the New Testament, between the condemnation of anger amongst humans and its predication of God. Anger is particularly condemned in the Wisdom tradition (Ps. 37.8f.; Job 36.13; Prov. 27.4; cf. Gen. 49.7). But YHWH is a jealous and angry God (Isa. 30.27f.; Jer. 30.23f.). His anger is not irrational but provoked by unfaithfulness and violation of the covenant. The prophets 'spoke of the divine wrath as a fact, and designated as its proper object their contemporaries' whole way of life, their social and economic attitudes, their political behaviour and, in particular, their cultic

seems to go back to C. H. Dodd, *The Bible and the Greeks* (London, Hodder & Stoughton, 1935), who is taken to have proved this case by Vincent Taylor.

[13]   D. Hill, 'The Interpretation of Hilaskesthai and Related Words in the LXX and the New Testament', in D. Hill, *Greek Words and Hebrew Meanings* (Cambridge, Cambridge University Press, 1967), p. 33.

[14]   The distinction Driver seeks to make between allaying God's anger and averting it is hard to follow.

[15]   R. Brown, *The Epistles of John* (London, G. Chapman, 1983), p. 220.

practice'.[16] God's anger is a reaction to the breach of the covenant, as this is expressed in the law, but also a means of restoring the relationship between Godself and human beings. It is the expression of YHWH's wounded love, which is why God's anger is but a 'moment'. Although it is described in the terrible terms of military conquest and devastation, its purpose is restoration.[17] In the latter part of the Old Testament the picture of an ultimate Day of Judgement, which will be a day of 'ruin and devastation' (Zeph. 1.15; 2.2), looms larger.

W. D. Davies remarks that 'It is doubtful if there was any rationale of sacrifice in the first century', and this must apply to the earlier period also.[18] At best we have hints of a rationale, rather than any developed theory. It is in the highest degree doubtful, therefore, whether our distinction between propitiation and expiation formed part of Israelite understanding. We need to bear this in mind when considering the rituals of the Day of Atonement. This, the high point of the sacrificial cultus, was celebrated on the tenth day of the seventh month (Lev. 25.9). The high priest offered a bull and a goat for his own sins and the sins of the people, took the blood into the Holy of Holies and sprinkled it on the *kapporeth*, thus cleansing Israel from its sins. The noun *kapporeth* (Exod. 25.17f., Lev. 16.14f.), which was translated in the Septuagint by *hilasterion*, and in the Authorised Version by 'mercy seat', means 'an expiating thing or means of expiation'. It is thought to refer to the gold lid on the cover of the ark, which was kept in the Holy of Holies. The significance of the sprinkling of blood was explained in the famous passage in Leviticus 17 where it is stated that 'blood makes expiation by reason of the life', and this is offered as the rationale of animal sacrifice. Israel was, of course, forbidden to eat blood, and this regulation rationalises that prohibition: blood is given for the purpose of making expiation.

Behind such a principle seems to be a view of blood as

[16] Von Rad, *OT Theology*, vol. II, p. 179.
[17] Ezek. 6.11: sword, hunger and pestilence; Jer. 50.13: depopulation; Isa. 9.18f.; 30.27; burning of the land. For restoration see Jer. 4.4; 36.7; Isa. 42.25.
[18] W. D. Davies, *Paul and Rabbinic Judaism* (henceforth *PRJ*) (London, SPCK, 1965), p. 235. Cf. G. F. Moore, *Judaism* (3 vols., Cambridge, Mass., 1927–30), vol. I, p. 500.

containing life force, but also an extension of the principle of equivalence – the notion that in cases other than murder the blood of the animal can take the place of the offender's blood. A Rabbinic comment throws some light on this: R. Simeon b. Yohai said, 'Though blood is despised and serves as food of dogs, God said that we should bring a sacrifice and apply its blood to the horns of the altar in order that the blood might atone for the blood of man.'[19] When sprinkled on the *kapporeth* the blood was therefore the means of bringing it into YHWH's presence on the Day of Atonement. Von Rad notes that in many cases it is not YHWH who is appeased but who, himself, makes expiation:

What was effected in expiation was that ... with persons and objects alike, YHWH removed the baneful influence of an act. He broke the nexus of sin and calamity; and this was as a rule effected by way of channelling the baneful influence of the evil into an animal who died vicariously for the man (or for the cultic object). Expiation was thus not a penalty but a saving event.[20]

What expiation (*kapparah*) does, according to this theory (and bearing in mind the caution about rationales of sacrifice), is to purify, either from sin or from ceremonial defilement. The sacrificial cultus is the means by which the holiness of the community is maintained, and equally, therefore, the means by which God's anger is averted. The Priestly writers have what might be described as a properly sacramental understanding of sacrifice. God has given Israel these forms of sacrifice as a means of wiping out guilt, of turning away its destructive consequences. God ordains that life blood may function in this way, even though there are limits to sacrificial expiation.

SACRIFICE AND THE CRIMINAL LAW

In a way which is extremely important for the development of penal theory in the West, criminal law and the need for

---

[19] Pesikta R 194b, cited in A. Büchler, *Studies in Sin and Atonement* (London, Jews College Publications, 1928), p. 418.

[20] Von Rad, *OT Theology*, vol. 1, p. 271. The passages where God is the subject of expiation are Deut. 21.8; Ps. 65.4; 78.38; 79.9; Jer. 18.23; Ezek. 16.63; 2 Chr. 30.18; Dan. 9.24. Von Rad notes that other gifts too, apart from the sacrificial animal, could effect expiation: money (Exod. 30.15), flour (Lev. 5.11) and jewellery (Num. 31.50).

expiation run together in the Old Testament. In the last four books of the Pentateuch we find cultic, moral and criminal laws tightly interwoven. Thus in Leviticus it is laid down that if someone deceives his neighbour in a deposit or security, or by robbery, or by oppressing his neighbour, or conceals something he finds,

he shall restore what was stolen ... or what was extorted ... or the deposit which was committed to him ... or the lost thing which he found ... he shall give it in full, adding a fifth of its value, to the person to whom it belongs, on the day of his guilt offering. And he shall bring his guilt offering to YHWH, a perfect ram without blemish from the flock. (Lev. 5.20–6)

Here crime, sin and guilt are understood together, and both restitution and sacrifice are needed to restore the person to the community. The importance of this connection for the understanding of punishment in medieval Europe cannot be overestimated.

Canonical criticism follows the principle that 'Redactor is Rabbenu (our teacher).' The redactor of the Pentateuch placed law within the framework of the covenant. The covenant, the terms of which are spelled out in codes of law, refers to 'an actual relationship between two persons ... implying behaviour which corresponds to, or is true to, the claims arising out of such a relationship'.[21] Once we under-stand law codes within the framework of the covenant, we can no longer distinguish between law and command. Because punishment follows breach of the covenant, it is not arbitrary, but reaction to a breach of trust. According to the prophets it is betrayal of the covenant which brings about disaster (Jer. 11.10; Ezek. 16.59; Isa. 33.8). The fact that the entire law, both ceremonial and ethical, is presented as the charter of the covenant with God serves to sacralise the law. To disobey the law is to disobey God. In this way societal bonds are given an ultimate sanction.[22]

José Miranda has vehemently contested the connection

---

[21] Eichrodt, *Theology*, vol. II, p. 240.

[22] For the law in Israel see R. de Vaux, *Ancient Israel*, tr. J. McHugh (London, Darton, Longman & Todd, 1961), pp. 143ff.

between law and covenant.[23] His concern is to insist that it was the *mishpatim*, the 'judgements in the gate', in which the rights of the poor were upheld, which constitute the true theophany of YHWH. Whatever the situation may be as regards the results of source criticism, it may perhaps be granted that covenant theology theorises such a view, rather than removing it into the realm of the cult, which seems to be Miranda's fear. In either case, the Old Testament view of justice is consonant with the idea of community law which I shall be advocating in the final chapter.

As I have noted in the previous chapter, whilst the meanings of sin and crime are not co-terminous, there is a very significant area of overlap. Murder and rape, for example, are crimes within the framework of secular law, but they are also sins in so far as they are understood to be breaches of God's intentions for human society. In a society without an elaborated distinction between secular and sacred (though of course with a distinction between the fane and the pro-fane), every act which we now call a crime would be at the same time a sin. It is important to emphasise this obvious point because it bears on the later interrelationship between atonement and penal theory. Though we can find signs of a sacred–secular distinction as early as the twelfth century, it was not until the sixteenth that it became an accepted part of Christian (Protestant) discourse.

The *lex talionis* is the basic rule for establishing punishments in the case of permanent injury. Far from being a relic of a primitive period, it has been argued that this principle, found also in the code of Hammurabi, was an attempt to enlarge the scope of the criminal law and provide protection for members of the lower classes and equality before the law with respect to acts of physical violence. It functioned to prevent the wealthy from escaping punishment simply by paying a fine.[24] At the same time we have to note that in the oldest text in which we have this law (Exod. 21.23–5) it is preceded by a law which specifies only compensation and medical expenses, for a wound received in a fight (Exod. 21.18–19), and followed by a law which orders the freeing of a

---

23   J. Miranda, *Marx and the Bible* (London, SCM, 1977), pp. 137ff.
24   J. J. Finkelstein, 'Mishpat', cited by B. Childs, *Exodus* (London, SCM, 1974), p. 472.

slave for the loss of an eye or tooth (Exod. 21.26–7). Only murder always involves the *lex talionis*. This crime can be neither commuted nor expiated. 'You shall accept no ransom (*kopher*) for the life of a murderer ... You shall not pollute the land in which you live; for blood pollutes the land, and no expiation can be made for the land, for the blood that is shed in it, except by the blood of the one who shed it' (Num. 35.33. A similar sentiment is expressed in Deut. 32.43). In these texts guilt is understood as pollution, which therefore needs to be dealt with liturgically – a notion which survived, as we have seen, even into the work of Kant. Wergild, the commutation of death by a cash payment, was only allowed if, for example, a man was killed by a savage ox (Exod. 21.30).

In the case of murder 'by persons unknown' expiatory rites had to be performed. In that case, according to Deut. 21.8f., the elders of the town must slay a cow (symbolizing the murdered man), wash their hands in its blood, and say: 'Our hands have not shed this blood, neither have our eyes seen it. Expiate, O YHWH, your people Israel, whom you have redeemed, and do not leave innocent blood in the midst of your people.'

According to Num. 15.30f., expiation does not avail for sins committed with a high hand. Lev. 16.16, on the other hand, seems to imply that all sins could be expiated on the Day of Atonement, but the later commentary in the Mishnah certainly did not take this view, maintaining that such sacrifices were only effectual if accompanied by repentance.[25]

For offences not involving permanent injury various forms of restitution were proposed. Deuteronomy envisages mutilation and shame punishments in some circumstances (Deut. 25.9, 12). According to Eichrodt there was from a very early period an analogy drawn between the legal system and God's activity as 'Judge of all the earth'. 'It was in keeping with the living juristic element in the terms of the covenant ... that men sought to elucidate Yahweh's judicial activity by means of *the fundamental principles of human retributive punishment*. Above all it was by applying the maxims of the talion that they tried to illustrate God's irreproachable righteousness.'[26] Law, in other words, and the

25 Yoma 8, 8–9.
26 Eichrodt, *Theology*, vol. ii, p. 425 (my italics).

activity of judges, becomes a fundamental analogy through which God's activity is understood in the same way in which political images have functioned according to Nicholls. In particular, God was understood to punish human beings for their sins, and, by analogy, the king or his delegates was to punish offenders. The nexus between suffering and punishment, expressed in the early stories of propitiation, remains in force in the later texts but is reinterpreted in a most important way. Suffering does not follow a trespass on God's dangerous holiness, nor is it retribution for wrongdoing, but, the Deuteronomists and the later prophets maintain, it is to be understood as a form of moral education.

God is frequently the subject of the verb 'chastise' (*yasar*) or 'punish' (*paquad*). 'O Lord, do not rebuke me in your anger, or discipline me in your wrath', says the Psalmist.

There is no soundness in my flesh because of your indignation; there is no health in my bones because of my sin. (Ps. 38.3; cf. Ps. 91.10; 106.29)

The interconnection between suffering and punishment follows because, in von Rad's words, 'there is absolutely nothing in the thought of the Old Testament which ... corresponds to the separation between sin and penalty'.[27] Two of the most important words for 'sin' and 'guilt' (*chattah* and *awon*), can mean both guilt, offence, and punishment. 'If you are disobedient', says Moses, 'you will have sinned (*chattatam*) against YHWH, and you will realise that you will meet with your penalty (*chatta*)' (Num. 32.23). When Cain says, after his banishment is pronounced, that 'My *awon* is greater than I can bear' (Gen. 4.13), he means both his guilt and his penalty: the two cannot be distinguished. On the one hand this later served to provide justification for retributive theory. On the other hand both individually and corporately the Hebrew Scriptures understand suffering as part of an *educative* process:

> For whom the Lord loves, he chastens,
> And scourges every son whom he receives.[28]

This is a fundamentally different thought to that of the restoration

---

27　Von Rad, *OT Theology*, vol. i, p. 266.
28　Hebrews 12.6, citing Ps. 94.12 and Ps. 119.67, 75. Cf. Prov. 3.11–12; Job 5.17.

of order, and obviously lays the foundation of the reformative line of penal theory.

THE RITUAL OF THE SCAPEGOAT

The ritual of the Day of Atonement, as recorded in Leviticus 16, involved not only expiatory sacrifice, but also another, very different, ritual. At the start of the ritual there are two goats, one of which is sacrificed for the sins of the people. After the sacrifice the high priest lays his hands on the head of the second goat and confesses the sins of the people over it, 'putting them on the head of the goat, and sending it away into the wilderness . . . The goat shall bear on itself all their iniquities to a barren region; and the goat shall be set free in the wilderness' (Lev. 16.21–2). This scapegoat ritual is not a sacrifice in the same sense, but seems to be the account of another ancient ritual about the absolving and banishing of violence and guilt.

René Girard has made the scapegoat ritual the centre of his understanding of sacrifice.[29] As we have seen, the scapegoat ritual was, according to him, a channelling of collective violence. Violence was checked through a ritual act which was itself an act of violence. Girard's thesis is clearly simplistic in its account of the origin of violence: mimesis is not the only root of conflict, illuminating as it is as a model for understanding the contemporary world. His thesis is also simplistic as an account of sacrifice: as we have seen, not *all* sacrifice can be understood as a rationalisation of violence. Nevertheless, Girard contributes to our theme in two ways. In the first place he illustrates the way in which the scapegoat is, as it were, the reverse side of expiation. If expiation is the *voluntary* addressing or bearing of guilt, scapegoating copes with it by loading guilt on to the other. Thus, in the book which followed *Things Hidden*, Girard shows how the fear and guilt caused by the Black Death in the mid fourteenth century were visited on the Jews as scapegoats.[30] We also need to

[29] In *Violence and the Sacred*, tr. P. Gregory (Baltimore and London, Johns Hopkins University Press, 1977); *Things Hidden Since the Foundation of the World*, tr. S. Bann and M. Metteer (London, Athlone Press, 1987).
[30] *The Scapegoat* (London, Athlone Press, 1986).

take together with Girard's work G. H. Mead's analysis of the public response to criminals. He argues that the righteous indignation felt by the public is a sublimation of people's self-assertive instincts and hostilities. It is the repression of these which allows society to function, but 'the rituals of criminal procedure provide an authorized occasion for their release'.[31] They are a sophisticated form of the scapegoat mechanism.

Girard's second great merit is that he draws our attention to the violence implicit in sacrificial imagery. It is a weakness in Girard's model that it has to focus on the scapegoat ritual, which was a ritual without blood. In fact it is blood imagery, taken up so vividly in the New Testament, which has provided the power of the tradition of satisfaction. It is extremely violent imagery and almost certainly evokes echoes of ritual murder at a subconscious level. This is precisely its strength, and it is in its ability to confront the anger, frustration and violence within us that we are to some extent to understand its continuing significance.

Girard also represents, from the standpoint of cultural anthropology, a rehabilitation of some of the earlier arguments of theological liberalism. According to him we find in the Old Testament 'an increasing subversion of the three great pillars of primitive religion', namely mythology, the sacrificial cult (explicitly rejected by the prophets before the exile), and the primitive conception of the law as a form of obsessive differentiation, a refusal of mixed states that looks upon non-differentiation with horror.[32] Whether or not one accepts this thesis makes a great difference to how the New Testament is read. My own view is that this movement of subversion is indeed discernible, and that we can understand Jesus as picking it up and taking it further. The plausibility of the case is increased by two further 'subversions' of violent sacrifice. In the first place, I shall argue that sacrifice was, from the earliest times, understood as both thanksgiving and obedience. But as well as sacrifice and the scapegoat ritual, *intercession* had a function in expiation. In the dramatic

---

[31] David Garland, *Punishment and Modern Society* (Oxford, Clarendon Press, 1990), p. 64, summarising G. H. Mead, 'The Psychology of Punitive Justice', *American Journal of Sociology*, 23 (1918), 591.

[32] Girard, *Things Hidden*, p. 154.

story of Genesis 18 Abraham strives with God for the life of the people of Sodom. In Exodus 32 we read how Moses stands between Israel and the wrath of YHWH, after the making of the golden calf.

> On the next day Moses said to the people, 'You have sinned a great sin. But now I will go up to the Lord; perhaps I can make atonement for your sin.' So Moses returned to the Lord and said, 'Alas, this people has sinned a great sin; they have made for themselves gods of gold. But now, if you will only forgive their sin – but if not, blot me out of the book you have written.' (verses 30–2)

Samuel, too, intercedes before God either for Israel or for Saul (1 Sam. 7.8f.; 12.19; 15.11). In these stories the ancient writers show us intercession as a complete turning of human beings to God, 'a becoming one with the will of God to the point of self sacrifice, and therefore as something to which God ascribes atoning value sufficient for the removal of guilt'.[33]

EXPIATION AND THE SERVANT

Another subversion of the tradition of sacrificial violence (though Girard himself does not think so) is the fourth Servant Song in Second Isaiah (Isa. 52.13–53.12), the description of the 'Suffering Servant', which has stood at the heart of much thinking on expiation since at least the third century CE. When the Servant appears in this song, it is as one with 'no beauty' (53.2). I follow the text in Westermann's translation:

> He was despised and rejected by men,
> a man of sorrows, and humiliated by sickness.
> He was like one before whom men hide their faces,
> despised – we esteemed him not.
> Yet ours were the sicknesses that he carried,
> and ours the pains he bore.
> Yet we supposed him stricken,
> smitten of God and humiliated.
> Yet he was pierced on account of our sins,
> crushed on account of our iniquities.

[33] Eichrodt, *Theology*, vol. II, p. 450.

> Chastisement that led to our welfare lay upon him,
> and by means of his stripes there was healing for us.

Suffering, we have seen, was evidence of sin, and this ought to have been enough to convict the Servant, and yet what is depicted, Westermann claims, is the violent death of a guiltless person whose life becomes an offering for others. In verse 10 the technical word *asham*, 'guilt offering', occurs:

> Yet YHWH took pleasure in him [who was crushed], and [healed] the one who made his life an offering for sin (*asham*).

In verse 12 we are told that he 'poured out his soul (*nephesh*) to death'. According to Westermann *nephesh* could also be translated 'blood', in which case we have two pointers to an expiatory sacrifice, to which we could add the reference to the lamb, the animal most frequently used for sacrifice, in verse 7. The song concludes, 'he bore the sins of many'. This may well be an allusion to the fate of Moses, who interceded for Israel before God, but whose death before entering the promised land was understood to be the result of his bearing his people's punishment. He therefore not only intercedes but dies a vicarious death. Like Moses, the Servant takes the place of his people and undergoes punishment in their stead. But, 'If a man despised and disfigured by suffering, and his death in shame and his grave with the wicked, can be explained as an expiatory sacrifice, this involves a radical desacralization of sacrifice.'[34] According to Westermann, then, this passage does speak of expiation, but in a way which goes far beyond the possibilities of conventional sacrifice. It represents far-reaching perceptions both about the vicarious nature of human existence and about the role of suffering in corporate life. We have to ask, however, whether such an expiatory reading is obligatory.[35]

In the third century CE, Jewish expositors were claiming that the Servant stood corporately for Israel, whilst Christians maintained that he could refer to no one but Christ.[36] If we understand the Servant to be Israel, this substantially affects our

[34] C. Westermann, *Isaiah 40–66*, tr. D. M. G. Stalker (London, SCM, 1969), p. 268.
[35] See the discussion in M. Hooker, *Jesus and the Servant* (London, SPCK, 1959), chap. 2.
[36] Origen, *Contra Celsum* 1.54–5.

understanding of the poem. Read in the context of the whole of Deutero-Isaiah, and of the rest of Israelite prophecy, it is argued, it must be understood as one among many responses to the problem posed by the exile. Why is God allowing Israel to suffer? Deutero-Isaiah's message is not that Israel still has sin for which atonement must be made. On the contrary, she has already paid double for all her sins (Isa. 40.2)! YHWH is now redeeming Israel, not because someone has atoned for her sin, but because he is YHWH and she is his people, and so that his name may be glorified throughout the earth. Further, the song does not actually say that the Servant offered himself as a vicarious sacrifice. 'It is nowhere said that he consciously accepted the path of pain for the express purpose of saving others.'[37] Girard finds the fourth song ambiguous. The phrase 'we esteemed him stricken' he reads as an acknowledgement that it was not God who smote him, but elsewhere this idea is clearly there:

Throughout the Old Testament, a work of exegesis is in progress, operating in precisely the opposite direction to the usual dynamics of mythology and culture. And yet it is impossible to say that this work is completed. Even in the most advanced texts, such as the fourth 'Song of the Servant', there is still some ambiguity regarding the role of YHWH. Even if the human community is, on several occasions, presented as being responsible for the death of the victim, God himself is presented as the principal instigator of the persecution. 'Yet it was the will of the Lord to bruise him' (Is 53.10).[38]

In other words, Girard finds a development of ideas in the Old Testament, and a conflict between two stages of thought in this one passage. One reading views the Servant as a scapegoat, who delivers the community by bearing its guilt; another reading traces the source of the suffering to God. If that is the case then the suffering of scapegoats, and thus human violence, is ultimately endorsed.

---

[37] Hooker, *Jesus*, p. 46. Hooker points out that the Targum refers the suffering to others whilst the Septuagint, in its use of the passive, emphasises that the Servant is a recipient rather than an actor.

[38] Girard, *Things Hidden*, p. 157.

SACRIFICE AND OBEDIENCE

Robertson Smith pointed out more than a century ago that the Priestly liturgical texts amounted to 'an antiquarian resuscitation of forms which had lost their intimate connection with the national life, and therefore had lost the greater part of their original significance'.[39] We are warned, in reflecting on sacrifice, 'of the extraordinary difficulties, which hardly allow us to reach any certain results in this field'.[40] Both practice and interpretation may have varied from shrine to shrine, and the texts themselves do not offer us interpretations of what is going on.

It is certain that expiatory sacrifices were only one part, and not necessarily the most important part, of the sacrificial system. Tylor believed that the gift offering was the most primitive form of sacrifice, and Robertson Smith the 'communion sacrifice'. He spoke of 'the habitually joyous temper of ancient sacrificial worship', which sprang from its celebration and consumption of the fruits of common labour.[41] The 'sacrifice of thanksgiving' (*Todah*) is also frequently referred to, and was probably at least as ancient and as vital as any other form of sacrifice. The word '*minhah*', gift, is used for vegetable offerings, but also to mean sacrifice in general.[42] As with all forms of sacrifice, we can only speculate on its origin, but it is not wholly implausible to suppose that the need to say 'thank you' for the gift of existence is at least as primitive and far-reaching as the need to appease offended powers. What follows from this is momentous, for the current assumption is that the nineteenth-century theory of a slow 'ethicisation' of sacrifice, which we find both in the Rabbis and in second-century Christian teaching, does not apply to the Israel of either the first or the second Temple. 'In order to understand sacrifice in Judaism, and therefore in Christianity, we need to turn to those ancient and primitive religious systems ... in which sacrifice is unequivocally valued within its own terms of refer-

[39] W. Robertson Smith, *Lectures on the Religion of the Semites*, 2nd edn (London, Black, 1894), p. 216.

[40] Von Rad, *OT Theology*, vol. I, p. 252.

[41] ibid., pp. 258–64. Such observations would certainly fit into sacrificial practice in contemporary Hinduism.

[42] See de Vaux, *Ancient Israel*, pp. 430–1.

ence.'[43] But what are those terms of reference? Von Rad warns
us that prophetic strictures on the cult 'do not in the slightest
imply any "evolution" in the direction of an increasingly intensive
spiritualisation'.[44] The shift in Old Testament scholars' account
of sacrifice in the second half of this century corresponds to an
abandonment of the idea of 'primitive' religion by anthropologists, and an awareness that the cultic might express the ethical
rather than be in opposition to it. What I wish to argue, on the
other hand, is not for an evolution of ideas of sacrifice, but rather
that ethical notions were primitive. The insight that a life of
obedience is the proper form of a sacrifice of thanksgiving is a
perfectly obvious one, and is clearly expressed in the texts. There
is in Scripture a thin but clear tradition which speaks of the
'sacrifice' of obedience.[45] This tradition begins with the story in 1
Samuel 15. The Amalekites have been put under the ban, but
Saul spares the flocks and herds, and their king, Agag. Saul
intends to offer the animals in sacrifice, but Samuel's response is:

Has the Lord as great delight in burnt offerings and sacrifices, as in
obeying the voice of the Lord? Behold, to obey is better than sacrifice,
and to hearken than the fat of rams. (1 Sam. 15.22)

This text, which there is no reason to regard as a late redaction,
stands at the head of a whole tradition of reflection on what really
constitutes sacrifice. We find it echoed in Amos 5.22f., where
sacrifice is rejected in favour of justice and righteousness, and
where the pointed question is put: 'Did you bring me sacrifices
and offerings the forty years in the wilderness, O house of Israel?'
(5.25). Micah asks:

> Will the Lord be pleased with thousands of rams,
> with ten thousands of rivers of oil? ...
> He has told you, O mortal, what is good;
> and what does the Lord require of you

---

[43] B. Chilton, *The Temple of Jesus: His Sacrificial Program within a Cultural History of Sacrifice*
(Pennsylvania, Pennsylvania State University Press, 1992), p. 4.

[44] Von Rad, *OT Theology*, vol. 1, p. 279. This sharp word is directed against Eichrodt, for
whom a rather Kantian view of progress constitutes a fundamental interpretive
framework..

[45] Just as there is a clear but thin line which grounds appeals to natural theology.

> but to do justice, and to love kindness (*chesed*),
> and to walk humbly with your God?   (Mic. 6.7–8)

Hosea insists:

> I desire steadfast love (*chesed*) and not sacrifice,
> the knowledge of God rather than burnt offerings
>
>   (Hos. 6.6)

In Psalm 40 we read:

> Sacrifice and offering you do not desire,
> but you have given me an open ear.
> Burnt offering and sin offering
> you have not required.
> Then I said, 'Here I am;
> in the scroll of the book it is written of me.
> I delight to do your will, O my God;
> your law is within my heart.'   (verses 6–8)

The same question is posed in Psalm 50:

> Do I eat the flesh of bulls,
> or drink the blood of goats?
> Offer to God a sacrifice of thanksgiving,
> and pay your vows to the Most High.   (verses 13–14)

Finally, in Psalm 51 we find:

> You have no delight in sacrifice;
> if I were to give a burnt offering, you would not be pleased.
> The sacrifice acceptable to God is a broken spirit;
> a broken and contrite heart, O God, you will not despise.
>
>   (verses 16–17)

It is quite true that only two of these texts (Hosea 6 and Psalm 40) are picked up in the New Testament, but the insight they express is more widely represented. Moreover, they show that the thesis that 'ethicisation' is necessarily late is unfounded. This discussion goes back very early indeed, perhaps to the very beginnings of sacrifice. The claim, then, is not that sacrifice as such was rejected, but that this line of Old Testament thinking insisted on pointing beyond the signifier to the signified, beyond the sacrament to the life of obedience and thanksgiving which was in fact demanded. From the very earliest period animal sacrifice was above all a metaphor for total commitment to God. Such an understanding sat uneasily alongside the tradition of expiatory, or propitiatory, sacrifice which gained such prominence after the exile.

EXPIATION, CRIME AND COMMUNITY

Under the head of 'expiation' we have so far encountered the following cluster of ideas: propitiation and appeasement; sacramental purification ordained by God through the sacrificial cultus; intercession, and the creative offering of suffering for others. By way of throwing light on this whole complex of ideas, especially its connection with crime and punishment, it is important to look not only to anthropology, but also to sociology, and in particular to the work of Emile Durkheim. He worked out the framework of his sociology against the background of Comptean positivism and the biologistic work of Herbert Spencer. He had a positivist antipathy to metaphysics, and sought to replace Kant's speculative and individualistic appeal to a 'categorical imperative' with something more scientific. This he found in the notion of social solidarity. 'We may say that what is moral is everything which is a source of solidarity.'[46] Society is not an aggregate of individuals, all of whom bring with them their own intrinsic morality. On the contrary, 'Man is only a moral being because he lives in society, since morality consists in solidarity with the group, and varies according to that solidarity.' He also discerns no tension between law and morality, because law is the visible symbol – a sort of sacrament – of social solidarity. 'Social life, wherever it becomes lasting, inevitably tends to assume a definite form and become organised. Law is nothing more than this very organisation in its most stable and precise form.'[47] Law reproduces the main forms of social solidarity, and these are of two kinds, 'mechanical' and 'organic', which correspond to the division between penal and civil law. Durkheim's understanding of crime, punishment and expiation naturally follows from this

[46] E. Durkheim, *The Division of Labour in Society*, tr. W. D. Halls (London, Macmillan, 1984), p. 331.
[47] ibid., p. 25.

account of law and morality. A *crime*, for Durkheim, is a socially deviant act: 'Crime disturbs those feelings that in any one type of society are to be found in every healthy consciousness.'[48] The totality of beliefs and sentiments common to the average members of a society forms a determinate system with a life of its own. This is the collective or common consciousness (*conscience collective*). It does not change with every generation, but links successive generations to one another. The values of this collective consciousness are symbolised in laws. When these are broken social cohesiveness is more or less acutely threatened, and this produces outrage. Crime is an injury to an authority which is in some way transcendent, for 'experientially speaking, there exists no moral force superior to that of the individual, save that of the collectivity'. Durkheim explained religion, like morality, in terms of the collective consciousness. Like laws, gods are symbols of the transcendence of the collective over the individual. This explains why he is able to say that penal laws are in origin religious and that they always retain this religious dimension. This naturally affects the account of punishment.

Punishment, for Durkheim, is essentially a defence mechanism on the part of society. 'Punishment constitutes essentially a reaction of passionate feeling, graduated in intensity, which society exerts through the mediation of an organised body over those of its members who have violated certain rules of conduct.'[49] However, it is not just vengeance but, on the part of the criminal, *expiation*. Behind the notion of expiation is the idea of a satisfaction rendered to some power, real or ideal, which is superior to ourselves. 'When we demand the repression of crime it is not because we are seeking a personal vengeance, but rather vengeance for something sacred which we vaguely feel is more or less outside and above us.'[50] Penal law always has a stamp of religiosity because the collective sentiments represent not us but society. It is society and not ourselves we are avenging. 'We are therefore wrong to impugn this quasi-religious characteristic of expiation ... on the contrary it is an integrating element in

48   ibid., p. 34.
49   ibid., p. 52.
50   ibid., p. 56.

punishment.' Punishment does not exist, therefore, to reform or deter but to 'maintain inviolate the cohesion of society by sustaining the common consciousness in all its vigour'. It is a sign indicating that the sentiments of the collectivity are still unchanged, that the communion of minds sharing the same beliefs remains absolute, and in this way the injury that the crime has inflicted upon society is made good. 'This is why it is right to maintain that the criminal should suffer in proportion to his crime, and why theories that deny to punishment any expiatory character appear, in the minds of many, to subvert the social order.'[51] Suffering is attached to expiation not because of some mystic strength deriving from it, which either redeems the individual or avails for others, but because 'it cannot produce its socially useful effect save on this one condition'.

The weaknesses of this account are clear enough.[52] In the first place the collective consciousness is a given which is not explained. Durkheim's epistemology seems to be Kantian: below the observed phenomena of social facts such as law lies the noumenal reality of the collective unconscious. 'Durkheim simply presents us with this concept, unargued, unexplicated and unabashed, as if it were self evident that "society" is centred, unitary and devoid of contradiction, discontinuity or social division.'[53] This *methodological* problem raises a much more serious *substantial* one. By this move Durkheim sidesteps the question of vested interest. If we take the eighteenth century as an example, for instance, then is it Fletcher and the Wesleys who represent the collective consciousness which cries out for punishment, or is it Wilkes, and those thousands like him who went to the gallows or were transported? Durkheim's theory is wide open to the Marxist critique of ideology. What he calls a 'collective' consciousness, we could say, is but the expression of the will of the ruling class. His theory does not allow for class conflict. The other objection, which will not concern us so closely, is that punishment does not have an essence of the kind Durkheim imagines, but refers rather

---

[51] ibid., p. 63.
[52] I follow David Garland, 'Durkheim's Theory of Punishment: A Critique', in *The Power to Punish*, ed. D. Garland and P. Young (Aldershot, Ashgate, 1992), pp. 37–61.
[53] ibid., p. 51.

to a 'differentiated field' of practices such as suspended sentences, reformatories, inebriate asylums, and so on.

In Garland's view the principal importance of Durkheim is that he recognises the *positive* aspect of punishment, and refuses to understand it as simply reactive. It both defines what crime is ('"crime" designates any act which ... provokes ... the characteristic reaction known as punishment'[54]) and notes its positive social effects in the reinforcement of solidarity, the release of collective emotion, and the symbolic display of collective sentiments.[55] For the theologian, however, his main interest is in making a clear link between atonement and penal theory, and in giving an account of expiation. The need for atonement and expiation, according to Durkheim, is the need to appease the outraged collective conscience. The offender's suffering, in other words, is a form of propitiatory offering. That the background to such a retributive view is vengeance is clear.[56]

Girard's debt to Durkheim is plain. In place of the collective outrage which leads to punishment we have the venting of the entire community's violence on the scapegoat. Where Durkheim understands the force of expiation in terms of the maintenance of social solidarity, Girard understands this in turn as a matter of dealing with the violence which threatens to tear a society apart. Both of these perspectives have something essential to offer in seeking to understand expiation. For the one expiation is demanded by society, and willingly borne by the offender who understands what society really is – that collective structure which makes life possible. For the other 'expiation' is an ideological rationalisation of collective violence, the attempt to give moral cover to an intrinsically immoral act. Both perspectives are extremely illuminating in an attempt to understand John 18 and 19, for example – the Johannine account of Jesus' trial and passion.

We need in addition to try to understand the connection between expiation and voluntary suffering hinted at in the fourth Servant Song. For Israel all suffering had to be understood

54　Durkheim, *Division*, p. 31.
55　Garland, 'Durkheim's Theory', p. 59.
56　Durkheim, *Division*, p. 86.

against the belief that God is both just and loving, and controls all events: this framework was non-negotiable. Since neither the fact of suffering nor the belief in God's lordship could be surrendered, the number of options was limited: one was to say that God is using suffering to educate us (the solution of the Deuteronomist). The second was to say that God has provided the means by which we can wipe away our sin and so avert suffering (the solution of the Priestly redactors). A third response, hinted at in the Servant Songs, appeals to the intuition that suffering as it were pays debts, or even more that it can in itself be creative for others. This idea was taken up by the authors of Maccabees, whose martyr theology attributes a creative function to the suffering of the just (2 Macc. 7.38). The view that the suffering of the martyrs turns away God's wrath from Israel, however, picks up ideas of the violence of God which belong to the earliest period and which, in Girard's terms, the Old Testament was slowly moving away from.

The complexity of ideas involved in Old Testament ideas of expiation makes it self-evident to us that we cannot speak simply of a 'biblical theology of sacrifice'. No such thing was self-evident to any Christian prior to the close of the eighteenth century. These texts, read as God's Word in the *lectio divina*, providing the very identity of Protestant individuals like John Bunyan and communities like Calvinist Holland or New England, shaped both theologies and sensibilities. When communities framed their laws, it was to these texts that they turned. Bishops were still appealing to the text of Numbers, which denies the possibility of commutation for murder, in the nineteenth-century House of Lords. Needless to say, it was these texts through which the early Christian communities struggled to understand the significance of Jesus of Nazareth.

CHAPTER 3

Accounting for the cross

We speak God's wisdom, secret and hidden, which God decreed before the ages for our glory. None of the rulers of this age understood this; for if they had, they would not have crucified the Lord of glory. 1 Cor. 2.7–8

A social style characterized by the creation of a new community and the rejection of violence of any kind is the theme of New Testament proclamation from beginning to end. John Howard Yoder

The story of the crucifixion, I have argued, plays an indisputably important role in shaping the mentalities and sensibilities of Western culture. As such it has also helped shape Western attitudes to the punishment of offenders. The interpretive lens through which Jesus' execution was understood by the earliest Christian community was provided by the writings of the 'Old Testament'. In the previous chapter I argued that texts which have been used for centuries to legitimate retributive ideas of punishment can be understood in a very different way. Continuing this argument I shall try to show that the New Testament, far from underscoring retributivism, actually deconstructs it.

For many Christians the 'meaning of the cross' is simply self-evident. They do not reflect that they have been taught to understand it through hymns and paintings, and through the way it is described in the liturgy – 'a full, perfect and sufficient sacrifice, oblation and satisfaction'. In the narrative I take up in the following chapter it will become clear that there have been majority and minority understandings of the atonement for at least a thousand years of the church's history. The majority view has appealed to retributivist assumptions, the minority, implicitly, to a different account of penality. I shall seek to show that the minority view is more truly rooted in the New Testament than the majority. If, as I contend, Christianity has had a vital bearing on our thinking about crime and punishment, we need to re-examine the founding texts before it can contribute constructively to the formation of alternative ways of thinking and structures of affect. The outline of such an alternative reading is the task of this chapter.

THE PROBLEM OF THE CROSS

Exegetes of every school are agreed that a judicial execution, using torture reserved for slaves or guerrillas, stands at the centre of the entire New Testament. This fact posed a considerable problem for the first Christians. Mostly Jewish, and working at first within Jewish communities, they had to try and convince people that Jesus, who had died in a way which signified being cursed according to the Torah, was the long-awaited Messiah. Not only did death by crucifixion seem to disqualify any such claim, but people were mostly looking for a very different Messiah. The struggle against Rome was a vital issue, leading to bloody conflicts both in 66 CE and again between 132 and 135 CE. The second revolt was led by someone, Bar Kochba, who was proclaimed Messiah. In other words, the idea of the Messiah as a warrior prince who would lead a successful struggle against Rome was very powerful. The solution of the early community, in the face of these two difficulties, was to look to a quite different picture of Messiahship, taking up Priestly, prophetic and Wisdom strains of Old Testament teaching. No doubt it had its roots in the teaching of Jesus himself. Whatever they argued had to be 'according to the Scriptures' (1 Cor. 15.33). Combing these they found a great deal of material which could illuminate Christ's death and help them to understand God's purposes through it. Much of this used sacrificial imagery. To say this is not yet to say that either a vicarious atonement, or 'justification' (to use Luther's watchword), was at the heart of their reading. As I have already noted, many centuries of argument have accustomed us to believe

that there is something which can properly be called 'the atonement in New Testament teaching'. What this is supposed to mean
can be taken from Vincent Taylor's book of that name: 'sin' is
what makes fellowship with God impossible. The atonement,
effected by the death of Christ, is concerned with anulling sin,
destroying its roots and removing its stain, and therefore making
such fellowship possible again.[1] I do not deny that this might be a
proper reading of the New Testament, but I do not want to begin
by assuming it. Instead I want to ask why the various writers of
the New Testament believed Jesus' life to be significant, and in
particular why they thought that Jesus' judicial execution could
be understood in a creative way.

CROSS AND DISCIPLESHIP IN THE SYNOPTIC GOSPELS

If we begin with *the Synoptic Gospels*, we must first observe their
structure before looking at details. Martin Kähler described them
famously as 'passion stories with an extended introduction'. This
description justifiably draws attention to the proportion of material in the gospels which deals with Christ's death, but it does a
disservice if it leads us to neglect the significance of the ministry of
teaching and healing, the calling and instruction of the disciples,
and the resurrection stories. Jesus comes preaching the kingdom,
and his teaching is directed to a new way of conceiving and
practising human relationships. There is little in this which relates
directly to the concerns of later theologies of the atonement with
expiation or vicarious sacrifice.

Was Jesus himself concerned about sacrifice? According to
Matthew he twice cites what I have called the alternative tradition
about sacrifice. In dialogue with the Pharisees Jesus quotes Hos.
6.6:

, Go and learn what this means, 'I desire mercy, not sacrifice.' For I have
come to call not the righteous, but sinners. (Matt. 9.13)

The same text is cited in Matthew's account of the sabbath
controversy:

---

[1]   V. Taylor, *The Atonement in New Testament Teaching* (London, Epworth, 1940), p. 249.

Have you not read in the law that on the sabbath the priests in the temple break the sabbath and yet are guiltless? I tell you, something greater than the temple is here. But if you had known what this means, 'I desire mercy and not sacrifice', you would not have condemned the guiltless. (Matt. 12.6–8)

These arguments are consonant with Rabbinic understandings of sacrifice. For the Rabbis sacrifice is important because God has commanded it, as a form of obedience to Torah, and not in itself. Johanan ben Zakkai explains the efficacy of the ashes of the red heifer in terms of the divine decree: 'God has decreed. A Statute I have ordained and an institution I have established and it is not permitted to transgress the Law.'[2] It is true that at the time of Jesus the sacrificial cultus was vigorous, and scrupulous people 'longed for some special opportunities for bringing sin offerings and for that purpose undertook repeatedly the vow of the Nazirite'.[3] On these grounds it has been argued that the Rabbinic views just cited reflect the new situation after the destruction of the Temple. In the light of the Matthaean texts, however, is it not possible that they represent a development within Judaism which had been long in process, and which Jesus is part of?[4] Jesus' cleansing of the Temple could also be read as an implicit rejection of sacrifice, rather than as expressing a desire for a stricter sacrificial cultus.[5] The destruction of the Temple in 70 CE was certainly regarded as a disaster, but on the other hand, 'the facility with which the Rabbis adapted themselves after the destruction of the Holy Temple to the new conditions must impress one with the conviction that the sacrificial system was not considered absolutely indispensable'.[6] The famous story of Johanan ben Zakkai's reaction significantly cites the same text

[2]   Numbers Rabbah 19.8.
[3]   A. Büchler, *Studies in Sin and Atonement* (London, Jews' College Publications, 1928), p. 429. Cf. B. Chilton, *The Temple of Jesus: His Sacrificial Program within a Cultural History of Sacrifice* (Pennsylvania, Pennsylvania State University Press, 1992).
[4]   Bruce Chilton argues that Jesus was indeed concerned with cultic purity and that the 'cleansing of the Temple' was designed to purify the sacrificial cultus. His view of sacrifice changed when that failed. Thereafter he understood social purity as the true sacrifice. Though the argument is designed to do justice to the importance of the sacrificial cultus in second-Temple Judaism he ends up by making Jesus agree with the Rabbis.
[5]   See C. Myers, *Binding the Strong Man* (New York, Orbis, 1990), p. 301.
[6]   S. Schechter, *Some Aspects of Rabbinic Theology* (London, Macmillan, 1909), p. 208 n. 3.

from Hosea as does Matthew. When another Rabbi lamented the fact that the place where atonement was made was destroyed, he replied: 'Do not grieve, my son, for we have an atonement which is just as good, namely deeds of mercy, as the Scripture says, "For I desire mercy and not sacrifice." '[7] The strongest emphasis was put on the need for repentance, as a precondition for sacrifice, and on the need to make restitution to anyone injured by the offerer.[8] It is highly likely that the Essenes had already abandoned sacrificial practice.[9] The growth of the Synagogue liturgy, which was entirely non-sacrificial, must have had an effect on the understanding of worship. And the fact is that, as we saw in the previous chapter, an ethical reading of sacrifice, which was picked up by Jesus, had the deepest roots in Israel's religion.

The principle behind the second Matthaean passage is also important. There is an assumption, perhaps mirrored in the charges brought against Jesus at his trial, that the function fulfilled by the Temple before Jesus came is now fulfilled by him. This becomes the central argument of the Letter to the Hebrews, where it is applied to mediation, the law, priesthood and sacrifice. In seeking to interpret Jesus to their Jewish contemporaries the first Christians took all the central categories of their religion and claimed to find them fulfilled in Jesus. The argument took the form: 'previously you needed this (sacrifice, or whatever), but the function of that institution has now once and for all been fulfilled'. The question we then have to ask is whether that was in any way anticipated in Jesus' teaching. That Jesus offered a reinterpretation of Messiahship is very plausible, and this would have involved reinterpretation of other categories at the same time.

In seeking an expiatory theology within the Synoptic Gospels attention is drawn to the so-called 'passion predictions' (Mark 8.31; 9.31; 10.33 and par., cf. Mark 9.12). These, so it is said, show that Jesus believed that his death lay 'deep in the Providence of

---

[7]   *Aboth de R. Nathan,* ed. S. Schechter (Vienna, 1887), p. 21.

[8]   'Repentance is ... the *conditio sine qua non* of the remission of sins.' G. F. Moore, *Judaism* (3 vols., Cambridge, Mass., 1927–30), vol. I, p. 498; cf. M. Yoma 8.8. On the need for restitution: Moore, *Judaism,* vol. I, pp. 408f., 418; cf. Lev. 5.23.

[9]   Philo, *Quod Omnis Probus Liber Sit* 12, *Opera,* ed. L. Cohn and P. Wendland (Berlin, Geo Reimer, 1896–1930), vol. VI, pp. 21ff.

God'.[10] That Jesus reckoned with his death from an early stage is beyond question, but the *dei*, the necessity of the death, may have less to do with providence than with the fate of anyone who critiques the ruling powers. John the Baptist, with whom Jesus was compared, had been executed, and Jesus must have seen the writing on the wall:

According to the understanding of Peter, 'Messiah' *necessarily* means royal triumph and the restoration of Israel's collective honour. Against this, Jesus argues that 'Human One' *necessarily* means suffering. This is so because, as the advocate of true justice, the Human One ... *necessarily* comes into conflict with the 'elders and chief priests and scribes' (Mk 8.31). In other words, this is not the discourse of fate or fatalism, but of political *inevitability*.[11]

Another corner stone of traditional atonement teaching is the so called 'ransom saying' of Mark 10.45: 'the Son of Man came not to be served but to serve, and to give his life as a ransom for many'. This passage, we are told, must be read in the light of the Suffering Servant of Isaiah 53.[12] There are two problems with this interpretation. The first is that it misses a more obvious reading given by the context. The saying comes at the end of a discourse about power and greatness, about the normal way of exercising that power and the alternative practice of the disciples. The 'Son of Man' comes as the embodiment of a different kind of order. According to Myers the saying should be understood in the light of Gandhi's saying that the way of non-violence will be proved 'by persons living it in their lives with utter disregard of the consequences to themselves'.[13]

Second, however, the traditional reading rests on making a connection between the 'ransom' (*lutron*) Jesus speaks of and the 'guilt offering' (*asham*) of Isa. 53.10. According to Hooker 'there is not the slightest evidence' that these two terms were ever connected. The *lutron* was the redemption of a person or thing by purchase, whereas the *asham* was the repayment of something wrongfully withheld, together with a guilt offering by means of

[10]   So Taylor, *Atonement*, p. 19.
[11]   Myers, *Binding*, p. 244.
[12]   Taylor, *Atonement*, p. 19.
[13]   Myers, *Binding*, p. 279.

expiation.[14] Hooker concedes that the idea of God as Redeemer is important in Second Isaiah, where the verb *gaal* is translated by *lutro-o*. The traditional argument then runs: 'And Jesus saw that humankind needed above all to be delivered from sin, and he used the ancient imagery of redemption to refer to this.' But there is nothing in the rest of Jesus' teaching to say that he *did* make such a transposition. The phrase 'to give his life as a ransom for many' does not introduce a sacrificial concept into an exhortation to serve others.

For the willingness to give one's life is not only the supreme example of service for others, but is in this case the culmination which gives meaning to the whole of that service. So Jesus, who has spent his whole life in the lowly service of others, now gives that life itself in the supreme act which, he believes, will complete the act of redemption.[15]

Much of the case for reading vicarious significance into the sayings of Jesus in the gospels comes from the habit of reading them through Isaiah 53. Hooker has pointed out that on the few occasions where this is quoted explicitly in the New Testament it is never related to the theme of expiatory suffering. Where it occurs, in 1 Peter, for example (1 Pet. 2.21f.), it is in the context of ethical exhortation, urging Christians to imitate Jesus' humility. She concludes that 'There is ... no certain reference to the Songs themselves, which in any way suggests that Jesus was identified with a Messianic interpretation of the "Servant", or which is concerned with the significance of his suffering and death.'[16]

It is, however, above all the Last Supper discourses which have been pressed into service to yield an expiatory reading of the atonement. For Denney, at the beginning of the century, the 'sacraments, but especially the sacrament of the Supper, are the stronghold of the New Testament doctrine concerning the death of Christ'.[17] At the last meal Jesus shares with his disciples he speaks of his blood 'of the covenant, poured out for many' (Mark 14.24). Matthew adds the commands to eat and drink, and the

14   M. Hooker, *Jesus and the Servant* (London, SPCK, 1959), p. 77.
15   ibid., p. 78.
16   ibid., p. 149.
17   J. Denney, *The Death of Christ* (London, James Clarke, 1950), p. 278.

phrase 'for the forgiveness of sins'.[18] Many difficulties attend the interpretation of these words. Jeremias maintains that the phrase 'This is my blood of the covenant' is impossible in Aramaic and proposes to omit 'of the covenant' as a later gloss.[19] Hooker prefers to omit 'my' and keep 'blood of the covenant', which would parallel Zech. 9.11, 'the blood of thy covenant'.[20] In any event the emphasis seems to be more on the ratification of the covenant than on expiation (cf. Exod. 24.8). The saying then goes together with the vow to eat and drink no more 'until the kingdom of God comes' (Luke 22.14–18; Mark 14.25). The words speak of Jesus' self-offering to the uttermost for what he discerns to be God's purpose – the kingdom.[21] Davies, who believes that for Paul the Last Supper was a New Passover, concludes that the idea of community is more prominent than that of the expiation of sin.[22] The shared cup signifies the suffering which those who commit themselves to a new vision of human community will have to undergo. Since it is these narratives which frame the crucifixion, and offer an interpretation of them, such an alternative reading offers a different, non-expiatory, account of the 'passion'.

It is worth asking whether, if we had *only* the Synoptic Gospels, and not the rest of the New Testament, we would have arrived at the atonement theology predominant in the West from the eleventh century onwards. I find it unlikely. For a start, Kähler represents a whole tradition of Lutheran exegesis which reads the gospels as it were through the passion chorales of Bach. But, at least in Luke's case, one could equally well represent them as *resurrection stories* with extended introductions. The concentration on creative suffering has been at the expense of that element of hope for the future which we are given by the narratives of the resurrection.

---

[18] In Luke there is a shorter and a longer reading, the first of which stresses only the sharing of the cup, and the second the wine as 'poured out'. In Paul's account we read: 'This cup is the new covenant in my blood' (1 Cor. 11.25).

[19] J. Jeremias, *The Eucharistic Words of Jesus* (London, SCM, 1955), pp. 133f.

[20] Hooker, *Jesus*, p. 81.

[21] See Myers, *Binding*, p. 363.

[22] W. D. Davies, *Paul and Rabbinic Judaism* (henceforth *PRJ*) (London, SPCK, 1965), p. 252.

Second, Jesus does not present himself in these gospels as coming to expiate or atone for 'sin'. There is no hint in the Synoptic Gospels of the doctrine of a Fall which needs to be redeemed by a once-for-all sacrifice. In fact, as a number of recent exegetes have argued, the most natural reading of the gospel material as a whole understands the cross and passion, and Jesus' overall significance, quite differently. Luke's gospel begins, for example, with a hymn, the Magnificat, the preoccupations of which are not cultic or doctrinal, but social and political. The temptations are to various kinds of power. Jesus begins his ministry by proclaiming the Jubilee year, and remission of debt, the key part of that, is at the heart of the prayer he teaches his disciples. In the parable of the ruthless creditor (Matt. 18.23ff.) what we owe to God (our 'debt') is bound up with real financial debts. Our debt to God, which in the Levitical economy is paid by sacrifice, is thus paid by remitting the debts of our neighbours. The disciples are required to follow Jesus in a way not conformed to 'this world', but as those who serve. Their distinctness is not that of cultic or ritual separation but 'a nonconformed quality of ("secular") involvement in the life of the world'. The cross they are required to take up is not an instrument of propitiation; it is 'the political alternative to both insurrection and quietism', the price of social nonconformity.[23] Jesus comes preaching the imminence of a new regime which involves visible socio-economic restructuring of human relations, the realisation of the Jubilee programme. He liberates people from their illnesses, many of which may be metaphors for other forms of oppression. The most convincing reading of the story of Legion understands it as speaking of deliverance from Roman oppression, though not by armed struggle.[24] He emphasises that the law (of the sabbath, for example Mark 2.27) exists for people, and not people for the law. When people's 'sins' are forgiven this happens prior to the passion, and is done in the name of the God who seeks life for all his creatures. Guilt is shriven, not expiated. It is likely, then, that if we had only the

[23] J. Howard Yoder, *The Politics of Jesus* (Grand Rapids, Mich., Eerdmans, 1972), pp. 43, 47.
[24] See Myers, *Binding*, pp. 190ff.

gospels the emphasis on vicarious, expiatory sacrifice in Western theology would be much less.

The same would apply were we to extend the canon to include the second volume of Luke's work, the Acts of the Apostles. With regard to Acts even Taylor has to admit that it contains 'no teaching of the Atonement'.[25] Instead, Acts is the story of how Christian communities were established by Paul around the Mediterranean, and finally in the heart of empire, Rome. If Acts were our principal interpretation of the Synoptic Gospels, our attention would focus not on vicarious suffering but more on the new inclusive community which took the place of a largely racially determined Israel, a community characterised by its sharing of all its resources. Hints at a vicarious sacrificial reading are few and far between. In Peter's Pentecost sermon it is said that Jesus was 'delivered up by the determinate counsel and foreknowledge of God' (2.23), but the reason for this is not spelled out. We are told that through Jesus remission of sins is preached to us, so that 'by him everyone who believes is justified from all things, from which you could not be justified by the law of Moses' (13.39). This seems to be an echo of Pauline teaching on justification, which certainly does not have to be read in an expiatory way. The only clear sacrificial allusion is in Paul's speech at Miletus, where he refers to Jesus as the one who 'purchased [the church] with his own blood' (20.28).

Not only is there little evidence for expiatory theology in the gospels and Acts, but, in a remarkable rereading, Girard finds in the Synoptic Gospels the heart of his case. He begins with the most terrible of the curses against the Pharisees in Matthew 23, upon whom will come 'all the righteous blood shed on the earth, from the blood of innocent Abel to the blood of Zechariah the son of Barachiah, Whom you murdered between the sanctuary and the altar' (Matt. 23.35). When he looks at Luke's version of this he finds it includes the expression, 'the blood of all the prophets, shed from the foundation of the world – *apo kataboles kosmou*'. But this expression occurs in another passage in Matthew, where Jesus says:

---

[25] Taylor, *Atonement*, p. 24.

I will open my mouth in parables, I will utter what has been hidden since the foundation of the world. (Matt. 13.35)

What is this secret? It is a legitimate question, because the conventional commentaries have no convincing answer. Girard's answer is that it is the truth of the founding murder which lies at the origin of culture. What Jesus reveals is the secret of human violence.

Religion is organized around a more or less violent disavowal of human violence. That is what the religion that comes from man amounts to, as opposed to the religion that comes from God. By affirming this point without the least equivocation, Jesus infringes the supreme prohibition that governs all human order, and he must be reduced to silence.[26]

The passion of Christ, as many anthropologists have noted, has an archetypal significance. The passion redeems through transference – our violence is heaped on the victim, and the community is exonerated. However, after Christ no further sacralisation is possible.

No more myths can be produced to cover up the fact of persecution. The Gospels make all forms of 'mythologizing' impossible since, by revealing the founding mechanism, they stop it from functioning.[27]

By submitting to violence Christ reveals and uproots the structural matrix of all religion. But if this is the case, then the sacrificial interpretation of Christ's death is an 'enormous and paradoxical misunderstanding'. The essential theme of the gospels is – and here again the cultural anthropologist rehabilitates the liberalism of the early part of this century – that reconciliation with God can take place 'unreservedly and with no sacrificial intermediary through the rules of the kingdom'.

This reconciliation allows God to reveal himself as he is, for the first time in human history. Thus mankind no longer has to base harmonious relationships on bloody sacrifices, ridiculous fables of a violent deity, and the whole range of mythological cultural formations.[28]

[26] R. Girard, *Things Hidden Since the Foundation of the World*, tr. S. Bann and M. Metteer (London, Athlone Press, 1987), p. 166.
[27] ibid., p. 174.
[28] ibid., p. 183.

DEATH AND ATONEMENT IN FIRST-CENTURY JUDAISM

Such a reading of the New Testament is in line with the teaching of the Dead Sea Scrolls community. Good deeds substitute for sacrifices as acts of atonement. Although the suffering of the select fifteen in this community, and their practice of justice, is vicarious, the idea of expiatory suffering does not have the significance for this community which it has in the Tannaitic literature. Sanders comments: 'it must be remembered that it was only after the destruction of the Temple that the view that suffering atones came to full and systematic expression'.[29] In that case we have a parallel with the experience of the Old Testament, namely that it was after the catastrophe of the exile that expiatory views came to the fore.

The Tannaitic literature is broadly Rabbinic material which dates from the period between 200 BC and 200 CE. Although the documents involved are difficult to date precisely, it is generally granted that this literature can be reliably used to give the background for Paul. In this literature atonement and expiation is certainly an issue. We find in it a 'universally held view' that God has appointed means of atonement for every transgression except the intention to reject God and the covenant. According to Jeremias four chief means of atonement were known: repentance (which atones for sins of omission); the sacrifice of the Day of Atonement (repentance and sacrifice atone for the transgression of a prohibition); suffering (repentance and sacrifice and suffering atone for a transgression which merits destruction at God's hand); and death (repentance and sacrifice and suffering and death are together necessary for atonement when a person has profaned the name of God). He argues that there were stages in the atoning power of death. Any death, even that of a criminal, had the power to atone if it was bound up with repentance. The death of a righteous man was to the advantage of others. The death of innocent children atoned for the sins of their parents. The death of the high priest meant that murderers could leave the cities of refuge. The death of a martyr brings God's wrath upon Israel to

[29] E. P. Sanders, *Paul and Palestinian Judaism* (henceforth, *PPJ*) (London, SCM, 1976), p. 304.

a standstill and is an *antipsuchon* ('substitute'), *katharsion* ('means of cleansing'), and *hilasterion* ('means of atonement') for Israel. The Maccabean martyr Eleazar prays 'Let my blood serve to cleanse them [the people of God]. Take my life in place of theirs.' But in the Palestinian milieu too, it could be said that martyrdoms would usher in the end, that the martyrs were intercessors and worked atonement for Israel.[30]

Jeremias' summary fails to draw attention to the fact that there was an energetic debate amongst the Rabbis about how many means of atonement there were – whether two or four – and whether there were transgressions which could not be atoned for, and if so, which. Paul, and the other New Testament authors, enter into this *debate*. Sanders finds two reasons why suffering is redemptive in the Rabbinic teaching. The first is that it leads you to repent and seek God. The other is the retributivist idea taken to be implied by the justice of God: 'If God is just and if man sins, it is not possible that no payment will be exacted for transgression. Sacrifices may atone, or even a ransom paid in money, but suffering is more effective and atones for more serious sins, because it is costlier.'[31] From here it is but a short step to saying that death atones. Death counts as paying one's account with God:

The view that death as such atones for sin was developed after the destruction of the Temple ... while the Temple stood, the prescribed sacrifices atoned for transgressions against God, while the punishment of the court and the restitution required by the law atoned for offences against one's fellow ... The view that death in general atones for sins developed from the idea that death at the hands of a court atoned for sin, provided that the one being executed repented.[32]

There was an opinion that death could atone for all but the most serious sin even without repentance. On the other hand, repentance accompanies the other means of atonement as a general rule, so that it is not actually a fourth means but an attitude always necessary to God's forgiveness.[33] Suffering and death

[30] J. Jeremias, *New Testament Theology* (London, SCM, 1971), pp. 287–8.
[31] Sanders, *PPJ*, p. 170.
[32] ibid., p. 173.
[33] ibid., p. 174.

could be understood vicariously, as in the text from 4 Maccabees where we read that 'through the blood of those devout ones and their death as an atoning sacrifice (*hilasterion*), divine Providence preserved Israel that previously had been mistreated' (4 Macc. 17.22). The same text also works with ideas of propitiation:

You know, O God, that though I might have saved myself, I am dying in burning torments for the sake of the law. Be merciful to your people and let our punishment suffice for them. Make my blood their purification, and take my life in exchange for theirs. (6.27–8)

In Tannaitic teaching an important place was given to the scapegoat:

For uncleanness that befalls the Temple and its Hallowed Things through wantonness, atonement is made by the goat whose blood is sprinkled within [the Holy of Holies] and by the Day of Atonement; for all other transgressions spoken of in the Law, venial or grave, wanton or unwitting, conscious or unconscious, sins of omission or of commission, sins punishable by Extirpation or by death at the hands of the court, the scapegoat makes atonement.[34]

This emphasis on atonement certainly forms the background to Paul, and, in a very different way, to Hebrews.

PAUL: THE DEATH OF CHRIST AND REDEMPTIVE COMMUNITY

Paul has been the main source for theologies of vicarious atonement, and it is indisputable that he draws to some extent on sacrificial imagery. In the famous passage in Romans Paul speaks of the *hilasterion*, which translates Hebrew *kapporeh*:

For there is no distinction, since all have sinned, and fall short of the glory of God; they are now justified by his grace as a gift, through the redemption that is in Christ Jesus, whom God put forward as a sacrifice of atonement (*hilasterion*) by his blood, effective through faith. (Rom. 3.25)

It seems that here the old vocabulary of expiation is now applied to the death of Christ, understood as an expiation for sin. This blood imagery is used in a catena of other famous texts which became the mainstay of satisfaction theory. A little later in

---

[34] Shebuoth 1.6f., cited in Sanders, *PPJ*, p. 158.

Romans we are said to be justified by Christ's blood (Rom. 5.9). Colossians (which may be pseudo-Pauline) speaks of the forgiveness of sins obtained by the 'redemption through his blood' (1.14) and speaks of Christ 'making peace through the blood of his cross' (1.20). Ephesians (more widely agreed to be pseudo-Pauline) repeats the phrase about redemption through blood (1.7), and tells the Gentiles that they are 'drawn near to God' by the blood of Christ (2.13). In 1 Corinthians Christ is described as the passover sacrificed (*etuthe* from *thuo*) for us (1 Cor. 5.7). Paul frequently asserts that Christ's death took place 'for us', or 'for our sins', without spelling this out further, and this has usually been read in a sacrificial way (for example 1 Thess. 5.9; 1 Cor. 15.3). In the second letter to Corinth we are told that Christ is 'made sin on our behalf' (2 Cor. 5.14, 21). In Galatians Paul speaks of Christ who 'gave himself for our sins' (1.4) and who 'became a curse for us' (3.13). Christ was 'delivered up for our trespasses' (Rom. 4.25, cf. Rom. 8.32).[35] In Ephesians we read that Christ 'loved us, and gave up himself for us, an offering and a sacrifice to God for an odour of a sweet smell' (5.2).

The element of propitiation is not missing. There is a link implied between the anger of God and the anger of men. On the whole anger is condemned (Eph. 4.31; Col. 3.8), but 'if anger is ruled out a limine, what is said about God's wrath has to be explained away. Conversely, when this is taken seriously, a limited anger has to be accepted in the human sphere too.'[36] Thus Paul describes the ruler of the secular state as 'the servant of God to execute his wrath on the wrongdoer' (Rom. 13.4). The wrath of God is directed against unrighteousness, transgression of the law or irreverence (Rom. 1.18). We can choose to remain 'under God's wrath' (1 Thess. 2.16; Rom. 9.22) or turn to Christ and be freed from the wrath (Rom. 5.8f.; 1 Thess. 1.10). 'God continues to be the Judge, and Christian faith in the grace of God does not consist in the conviction that God's wrath does not exist or that there is no threateningly impending judgement

---

[35] In these passages, it is pointed out, he uses *huper*, 'on behalf of', and not *anti*, 'instead of', so he cannot be thought to support a substitutionary view.
[36] G. Stählin, *TDNT* v.419.

(2 Cor. 5.10), but in the conviction of being rescued from God's wrath.'[37]

On the basis of passages such as these Taylor can outline the atonement theology of Paul under such heads as 'the vicarious aspect' of Christ's death, or its 'sacrificial significance', or 'faith union with the crucified'.[38] Bultmann, too, though his critical assumptions are at the other end of the spectrum from Taylor's, agrees. He finds the ideas of both propitiatory and vicarious sacrifice in Paul, both of which derive from Jewish sacrificial practice and 'the juristic thinking that dominated it'.[39] W. D. Davies' conclusions are more reticent. Whilst acknowledging Paul's use of sacrificial terms he believes that Paul leaves them 'inchoate'. In the light of Rabbinic attitudes to the sacrificial cultus he maintains that sacrificial categories are only of minor importance in Paul's interpretation of the death of Jesus.[40] Krister Stendahl reinforces this conclusion from another direction. Paul's concern, he argues, was not 'sin' in the abstract but overcoming the hostility between Jews and Gentiles.[41] We have learned to read Paul through Augustine and Luther:

Once the human predicament – timeless and exercised in a *corpus christianum* – became the setting of the church's interpretation of Paul's thought, it also became less obvious that there was in fact a great difference of setting, thought, and argument between the various epistles of Paul ... It was possible to homogenize Pauline theology since the common denominator would easily be found in generalized theological isues, and the specificity of Paul's arguments was obscured.[42]

Paul's preoccupation was not 'justification by faith', in the sense in which Luther understood it. That understanding represents a preoccupation with the ego which begins with Augustine and reaches its climax with Freud, but from which Paul was happily free. A particular way of preaching the gospel of sin and atonement, illustrated vividly in our opening story from John

---

[37]   R. Bultmann, *Theology of the New Testament*, tr. K. Grobel (2 vols., London, SCM, 1952), vol. 1 p. 288.

[38]   Taylor, *Atonement*, pp. 83ff.

[39]   Bultmann, *Theology* vol. 1, pp. 295f.

[40]   Davies, *PRJ*, pp. 242, 259.

[41]   K. Stendahl, *Paul among Jews and Gentiles* (London, SCM, 1977).

[42]   ibid., p. 5.

Fletcher, is part of this tradition of introspection. I am sunk in darkness, bound in the chains of sin, and I then realise that Christ has died for *me*, and at that moment my heart is strangely warmed and my chains fall off. But, Stendahl maintains, Paul's use of 'justification' must be understood against the background of the Septuagint's use of the *dikaio-o* word group, where it translates *tsedequah*, God putting things right, vindicating Israel. In the same way, we can argue, to draw up a scheme of representative suffering, vicarious punishment and so forth is to do impossible violence to Paul's arguments. The concern with 'sin' in the first eight chapters of Romans must be understood in the light of the argument of the second eight, and especially Romans 9–11. What Paul is able to demonstrate is that Jews and Gentiles are in the same boat, and that Abraham is the father 'in faith' of both.

E. P. Sanders is equally critical of the traditional Protestant reading of Paul, but from a different perspective. According to him, Paul's gospel was that Christ had died and God had raised him from the dead, that Christ is Lord, that the Lord will return, that the *apistoi* will be destroyed (2 Cor. 4.3), and that the believers will be saved.[43] The notion of expiation should not be excluded from Paul's account of the means of salvation, but 'the emphasis unquestionably falls elsewhere'. Moreover, whilst we may theoretically distinguish expiation, propitiation and substitution, 'it is not clear that such distinctions were made in the first century or are relevant to Paul'.[44] The heart of Paul's atonement theology is not expiation but participation. It is a theology of transfer – from one lordship to another. By sharing in Christ's death one dies to the power of sin, with the result that one belongs to God. He sums up:

Paul did accept the common Christian view that Christ's death was expiatory ... but the main conviction was that the real transfer was from death to life, from the lordship of sin to the lordship of Christ ... Man's problem is not being under Christ's lordship. Since this is the real problematic, the traditional language of repentance and forgiveness is almost entirely missing, the language of cleansing appears primarily in

[43] Sanders, *PPJ*, p. 446.
[44] ibid., p. 465.

hortatory passages (1 Cor. 6.9–11), and the discussion of transgression is used only rhetorically to lead to the conclusion that everybody needs Christ (Rom. 1–3).[45]

The theme of participation is found in the idea of the body of Christ; in the notion of sharing in one Spirit; in being one together 'in Christ'; in the idea that we are 'Christ's'. Salvation, for Paul, works by being incorporated into Christ, rather than by expiation. It is not clear that all the references to Christ's dying 'for us' should be taken as referring to his sacrificial death for past transgressions. For example, 2 Cor. 5.14:

For the love of Christ controls us, because we are convinced that one has died for all, therefore all have died. And he died for all, that those who live might no longer live for themselves but for him who for their sake died and was raised.

Sanders points out that the 'huper panton' here is not expiatory. 'Paul uses categories of participation to explain his meaning: "therefore all have died", not "therefore all have had their sins expiated".'[46] One dies to the power of sin, and does not just have sins atoned for. The real bite of Paul's theology, then, is not in juristic but in participatory categories. The goal of religion is to be found in Christ, and it is by suffering and dying with him that we attain the resurrection.

A more radical reading insists that Paul's use of sacrificial imagery has to be read together with his critique of the law. As a Jew who accepts that God's will is revealed in Torah, Paul has to come to terms with the fact that Jesus was crucified after due legal process. Christ redeemed us from 'the curse of the law', by dying under its curse (Gal. 3.13). Jesus had placed human life above the law, and Paul follows him in this. Law, says Paul, is transcended in love, bearing the burdens of others (Gal. 5.14; 6.2). Love is the criterion by which we assess the legitimacy of law. When Jesus dies 'legitimately', law destroys itself. Law is revealed, in the death and resurrection of Christ, as 'the strength of sin' (1 Cor. 15.56). If the 'bond' of Col. 2.14 is the law, we have to say that the principalities and powers work through law to accomplish the

[45] ibid., p. 500.
[46] ibid., p. 464.

death of Jesus. The bond (*cheirographon* – written document) is 'nailed to the cross', and instead forgiveness is freely proclaimed. The legitimacy of the rulers is thus exposed – a 'public example' is made of them. The cross therefore demonstrates that seeking justice through the observance of law leads to and exacts human sacrifices. Jesus' death brings such sacrifices to an end by exposing their hollow and bogus nature.[47]

The claim is not, then, that Paul does not use sacrificial metaphors. He speaks of Christ's death averting God's wrath in a way which has parallels in 4 Maccabees. So in the famous passage in Romans 5:

God proves his love for us in that while we were still sinners Christ died for us. Much more surely, then, now that we have been justified by his blood, will we be saved through him from the wrath of God. For if while we were enemies, we were reconciled to God through the death of his Son, much more surely, having been reconciled, will we be saved by his life. (Rom. 5.8–10)

However, we have to put Paul's sacrificial language in the context of his overall strategy. He did not, like some proto-gnostic, have a formula to impart which, if followed, would bring salvation: 'believe that Jesus died for your sins and be saved'. What he sought to do was to constitute communities of Jews and Gentiles which he spoke of as the 'body of Christ'. It was through this body that reconciliation was worked out in practice – through the strong accommodating the weak (Romans 14), through the wealthier churches supporting the poorer (2 Corinthians), through masters learning to accept their slaves as brothers (Philemon). Whether or not Ephesians is by Paul, it continues essentially this thought. What 'the blood of Christ' has done is to bring Jews and Gentiles together. It is clear that Christ's death was not, for Paul, simply a good example of radical love. He interprets Jesus' death sacrificially, as we would expect from someone familiar with the Rabbinic discussion of the time. But it is equally clear that his death had brought about not a new *doctrine* but a new *movement* in which alienated human beings were to be

---

[47]   F. Hinkelammert, following E. Tamez, *Contra toda condena: La justificación por la fe desde los excludos* (DEI (Ecumenical Department of Research), Costa Rica, 1991), pp. 196ff.

caught up and reconciled. It is the *community* which has 'the ministry of reconciliation' (2 Cor. 5.18). This work of reconciliation can appeal to sacrifice in a way congenial to what I have called the 'second tradition'. So, after establishing finally the equality of Jews and Gentiles before God, Paul goes on:

I appeal to you, therefore, brothers and sisters, by the mercies of God, to present your bodies as a living sacrifice, holy and acceptable to God, which is your spiritual worship. Do not be conformed to this world, but be transformed by the renewing of your minds, so that you may discern what is the will of God. (Rom. 12.1–2)

Ultimately the work of God is effected by reconciliation, which in turn demands the 'sacrifice' of obedience, which works itself out in community life. For Paul it is true that 'the primary social structure through which the gospel works to change other structures is that of the Christian community'.[48] As we shall see in the final chapter, this has great significance for an understanding of penal practice.

CHRIST THE PIONEER IN HEBREWS

Hebrews has, even more than Paul, been read as a tract about the sacrificial significance of Christ's death. According to Girard it is this letter which begins once again the sacrificial reading of Christ's death. It is true that according to this author Christ 'tastes death' for all (1.9). He is the only New Testament writer to use the verb *hilaskomai*, which translates the Hebrew *kipper*:

Therefore he had to become like his brothers and sisters in every respect, so that he might be a merciful and faithful high priest in the service of God, to make a sacrifice of atonement (*eis to hilaskesthai*) for the sins of the people. (Heb. 2.17)

It is 'through his own blood' that he has attained redemption. The crucial question, however, is how Christ's death is interpreted, and here at the very heart of the letter the author cites Psalm 40:

> Sacrifices and offerings you have not desired,
> But a body you have prepared for me;

[48] Yoder, *Politics*, p. 157.

> In whole burnt offerings and sin offerings you have
> taken no pleasure,
> Then I said, 'See, God, I have come to do your will O
> God.'　　　　　　　　　　　　　　　　　　　(Heb. 10.5–7)

What Christ offers is the sacrifice of *obedience*. More clearly than in other parts of the New Testament 'blood' here is a metaphor for obedience to God carried all the way. It is this which constituted him our pioneer (*archegos*), the one who has gone ahead of us when we face the final trial of martyrdom, referred to as 'shedding blood'. The whole point of the author is that Christ's sacrifice is quite different from that of earlier sacrifices. Thus, far from reintroducing the theme of violent, cultic sacrifice, Hebrews seeks to shift the discourse to an entirely different level.

REDEMPTION IN THE JOHANNINE WRITINGS

In the 'Johannine corpus' we have the three very different documents of the gospel, the epistles, and Revelation. The theology of redemption in the gospel is not centrally dominated by expiatory ideas. The only text which uses specifically sacrificial imagery is 1.29: 'Behold, the Lamb of God who takes away the sin of the world'. A number of passages emphasise the vicarious nature of Christ's death: 'The good shepherd lays down his life for (*huper*) the sheep' (10.11). 'Greater love has no man than this, that a man lay down his life for (*huper*) his friends' (15.13). It is probably significant that John mentions all the major Jewish festivals except the Day of Atonement. The reason may well be that the tradition of reflection about the atoning significance of death which had grown up since the time of the Maccabees is now applied to the death of Jesus. Otherwise the death of Jesus is seen more from the point of view of triumph and glorification than of sacrifice.[49] Richter finds in the story of the footwashing an anticipation of an Abelardian soteriology. According to him this story adumbrates a theology whereby the death of Jesus is an act of love which establishes an example to be imitated.[50]

---

[49]　12.27–32; 13.1; 14.30–1; 16.10–11; 17.1.
[50]　G. Richter, *Studien zum Johannesevangelium*, Biblische Untersuchungen 13 (Regensburg, Pustet, 1977).

Girard finds his thesis adumbrated in John in the triple correspondence between Satan, the original homicide, and the lie (John 8.43–4). The lie in question is the lie which covers homicide. In the Temptation stories we see that Satan is identified with circular mechanisms of violence, with our imprisonment in cultural or philosophical systems that maintain the *modus vivendi* with violence.

Satan is the name for the mimetic process seen as a whole; that is why he is the source not merely of rivalry and disorder but of all the forms of lying order inside which humanity lives. That is the reason why he was a homicide from the beginning; Satan's order had no origin other than murder and this murder is a lie. Human beings are sons of Satan because they are sons of this murder.[51]

John has for centuries been read as a 'hellenistic' gospel in which Jesus redeems us through revelation. Girard offers us a variation on this theme. It is by unmasking the lie which cloaks human violence that Jesus helps us.

The First Epistle of John is polemical, directed against those who have once been members of the group and are now so no longer. The group concerned most probably derived from the community from which the fourth gospel came. The opening verses of the letter have led many to suppose that the opposition group has a docetic Christology, putting all the emphasis on triumph, and on knowledge at the expense of love. The letter accordingly stresses the need for love to take flesh, and such love is adumbrated by Christ's death: 'Hereby we know love, because he laid down his life for (*huper*) us' (1 John 3.16). The word *hilasmos*, which translates *kopher*, is used twice: Jesus is the *hilasmos* (usually translated 'expiation') for the sins of the whole world (1 John 2.1; 4.10). His blood 'cleanses us from all sin' (1.7). Jesus was 'manifested' 'to take away sins' (3.5). On the basis of these texts a doctrine of expiatory atonement can be cogently argued for from the letter. However, it has to be said that expiation is not the central focus of the letter: that is rather that members of the community should love one another, and that that love should find tangible expression. Moreover, the fact that Christ laid down

[51] Girard, *Things Hidden*, p. 162.

his life for us is offered as a fundamental *example* for our own behaviour (3.16). When the blood of Christ is spoken of it sometimes seems to refer more to Christ's total self-offering than to expiation (5.6; perhaps 1.7 should be read in this way). The eschatological hope grounded in Christ's coming is also spoken of as the source of purification. Whilst an expiatory theology may very plausibly be taken from the letter, therefore, we cannot say that it is the sole legitimate reading of the text.

THE LAMB SLAIN IN REVELATION

The theme of blood is yet more important in Revelation. There Jesus is 'the one who loves us and has freed us from our sins by his blood' (Rev. 1.5). Christ is the one who was slain 'and by your blood ransomed men for God' (5.9). The elect are those who 'have washed their robes and made them white in the blood of the Lamb' (7.14). It is in Revelation that we have the highest number of references to the wrath of God.[52] In Revelation the anger of the Dragon is opposed to the anger of God (Rev. 12.17). Those who destroy the earth will be brought to destruction (Rev. 11.18; cf. 6.16). In trying to assess this language we need to take account of what Fiorenza calls the 'rhetorical strategy' of Revelation. The book is written to encourage Christians to resist in the face of persecution and possible death. The language about wrath is not to be understood timelessly, but is rather a way of affirming that God still rules in righteousness. It is written with a 'jail house' perspective, 'asking for the realization of God's justice and power. It therefore can only be understood by those "who hunger and thirst for justice".'[53] Girard's contention that the apocalyptic passages of the New Testament speak only of human, and never of divine, violence is too strong, and yet we cannot simply read them as portrayals of the violent, vindictive God either. To do this is to fail to respect their context.

---

[52]   Though this is found also in John, Paul and Hebrews. Cf. Rom. 1.18; 2.5; 5.9; Eph. 5.6; Col. 3.6; 1 Thess. 1.10; Heb. 3.11; 4.3; John 3.36; cf. Rev. 6.16–17; 11.18; 16.19; 19.15.
[53]   E. Schussler Fiorenza, *The Book of Revelation* (Philadelphia, Fortress, 1985), p. 198.

CONCLUSION: EXPIATION AND THE FLIGHT FROM THE JUBILEE

If the New Testament were quite unambiguous, there would be no argument. Most commentators wish to hold both that Jesus preached a gospel of non-retaliation, of love for the enemy, *and* that he died a vicarious death. The problem is that, to the extent that notions of vicarious suffering presuppose scapegoating, then they presuppose violence. The New Testament can certainly be read as supporting satisfaction theory. What I have tried to argue is that it does not *have* to be read in this way, and that there is much which points in other directions. Suspicions about the conventional reading are raised both by the fact that it did not form a part of the understanding of the early Church Fathers, and also by the way it functions.

According to this argument, the Father of Jesus is still a God of violence, despite what Jesus explicitly says. Indeed he comes to be the God of unequalled violence, since he not only requires the blood of the victim who is closest to him, most precious and dear to him, but he also envisages taking revenge upon the whole of mankind for a death that he both required and anticipated.

In effect, mankind is responsible for all of this. Men killed Jesus because they were not capable of becoming reconciled without killing.[54]

Despite the acknowledged weaknesses of Girard's account, he has put his finger on a profound truth about the way in which this interpretation of the crucifixion has functioned. Not only were the scapegoat and sacrificial themes amalgamated, but these were read *politically* in conjunction with a series of texts (Romans 13, 1 Peter 2, Titus 3) which taught that 'the powers that be are ordained of God'. The judicial arm of the state, exercised above all in capital punishment, was understood, quite explicitly by Luther, as the exercise of God's rule. Thus a story which was a unique *protest* against judicial cruelty came to be a *validation* of it. The community which was supposed not to be conformed to the world now underwrote its repressive practice. That this could happen, and not be perceived, was due not just to the ambiguity of the New Testament texts, but to the fact that profound and

54 Girard, *Things Hidden*, p. 213.

necessary truths about suffering and vicarious love are concealed within the conventional interpretation. The justification of retributivism by Christianity does not represent the intrusion of an 'alien element' but, like the justification of crusading, is a deformation of biblical faith. The church has contributed both to the mentality in which people make war, and to vengeful attitudes towards offenders. It is this which makes the work of exegesis on the founding texts so important.[55]

Are we left, then, with irreconcilable interpretations, equally justified in terms of appeal to the founding texts? I believe not. Our fundamental hermeneutic principle must be derived from the overall *direction* of the New Testament documents. The central story they tell speaks of God's movement 'downwards and to the periphery, his unconditional solidarity with those who have nothing, those who suffer, the humiliated and injured'. This represents a diametrically opposite perception to the Roman view which assumed that, as Caesar once said to his rebellious soldiers, 'as the great ordain, so the affairs of this world are directed'. The crucifixion of Jesus, on the other hand, constitutes 'a permanent and effective protest against those structures which continually bring about separation at the centre and the margin'.[56] It is this protest, I contend, rather than an endorsement of expiatory sacrifice, which is the heart of the New Testament witness. Turning Christianity into a cult centred on an expiatory death achieved long ago, and honoured in the present by other- or inworldly asceticism, represented an easy option, a refusal of the costliness of the gospel ethic, of a realisation of the Jubilee prescriptions. The recovery of a text of protest and critique would serve to create quite different mentalities and structures of affect from those avowed by Christendom, and it is these I shall argue for in my account of the present debate on penality. Before coming to that, however, I must turn to my narrative, which begins with Anselm.

[55] I am alluding to Yoder, *Politics*, p. 247.
[56] K. Wengst, *Pax Romana*, tr. J. Bowden (London, SCM, 1987), pp. 140–1.

PART II

Making satisfaction: atonement and penalty
1090–1890

CHAPTER 4

The ladder of all high designs

The false God changes suffering into violence. The true
God changes violence into suffering.

Simone Weil

Almost everything we call 'higher culture' is based on the
spiritualization of *cruelty*, on its becoming more profound:
this is my proposition.

F. Nietzsche

Anselm of Canterbury (1033–1109) came from Aosta, in the
foothills of the Alps, but by the age of twenty-six had settled at
the monastery of Bec, in Normandy, drawn by the fame and
energy of Lanfranc. He arrived during what may be regarded as
the peak of Norman expansion and achievement. Eleventh-
century France contained a number of powerful dukedoms, all
expanding and given to brutal military conquest, and the
Normans were probably the most successful of these. 'The
arrogant self-confidence of these rulers' aggressive campaigns',
writes David Bates, 'as well as the essential instability of French
society at this time, are contextual matters which cannot be over
emphasised.'[1] Seven years after Anselm's arrival at Bec, William,
Duke of Normandy, invaded England. William was well known
for cruelty even in an age of cruelty, and the 'harrying of the
North' in the winter of 1069/70 was condemned by contemporaries.[2] At the same time he took his responsibilities as a

---

[1] D. Bates, *William the Conqueror* (London, G. Philip, 1989), p. 9.
[2] 'I declare that assuredly such brutal slaughter cannot remain unpunished. For the
Almighty Judge watches over high and low alike. He will weight the deeds of all in a
fair balance, and as a just avenger will punish wrongdoing, as the eternal law makes
clear to all men.' Orderic Vitalis, *Ecclesiastical History*, ed. and tr. M. Chibnall (6 vols.,
Oxford, Oxford University Press, 1969–80), vol. II, p. 233.

Christian ruler with great seriousness. He is said to have attended mass every day. The church prescribed one year's penance for each person killed in battle. William, who probably lacked the necessary longevity, built abbeys as a penance instead, endowing them, as well as existing establishments, with land and wealth. Noting that William's religious patronage was especially generous at difficult times, Bates comments: 'These are the actions of a man trying to propitiate a demanding deity, aware that his violent way of life placed him in danger of being despatched to hell.' He then goes on, significantly for our understanding of Anselm, 'We have to see him as cut off from all notions of a reconciling and loving God, rarely able to forget that he would one day be judged.'[3] William was concerned with church reform, at least to the extent of trying to suppress clerical wives and mistresses. He was also responsible for a vast explosion of church building. More cathedrals and abbeys were built during Lanfranc and Anselm's lifetime than castles, and these constitute the primary artistic legacy of the Normans.

The violence which accompanied William's conquests did not go quite unchallenged. According to Orderic Vitalis, writing in the next century, one Guitmund was offered an English see by William, but refused it, saying that he could find no authority in Scripture for the imposition on Christians of a pastor chosen from amongst their enemies. 'I deem all England the spoils of robbery', he said, 'and shrink from its treasures as from consuming fire.'[4] Although Lanfranc pined for the monastery, he seems to have made no such protest, and Anselm's difficulties with William Rufus and Henry I were over quite other matters. He was more worried about sodomy at the court than about the forest laws which provoked the indignation of William of Malmesbury or John of Salisbury.[5] He became archbishop in 1093, in rather

3 Bates, *William*, p. 152.
4 Orderic Vitalis, *History*, vol. II, p. 273.
5 John of Salisbury, *Policraticus*, ed. C. Webb (2 vols., Oxford, Clarendon Press, 1909), vol. I, pp. 390ff. 'Presumptuous men dare, even in the sight of God, to claim as their private property and enclose within their encircling net things that were by nature wild and should belong to all possessors of land. Even more remarkable, it had become a crime punishable by loss of property or of limbs, or of life, to set snares for birds, knot nooses, entice by music, or lay any sort of trap. There were men who, to avenge a wild beast and for the sake of an animal, subjected those made in the likeness

melodramatic circumstances, at the insistence of William Rufus. By talent and inclination he was a monk and an intellectual, not an administrator and man of action like his predecessor, Lanfranc, and the scope of his major works reveals this. Nevertheless, the profound integration of church and state, secular and sacred, at this period means that he must be recognised, even in his theology, as one of the most important spokesmen of the ruling class of his day.

'It can scarcely be too strongly emphasized', writes Anselm's most recent biographer, 'that the span of Anselm's life covered one of the most momentous periods of change in European history, comparable to the centuries of the Reformation or the Industrial Revolution.'[6] Perhaps it might be more accurate to say that Anselm witnessed the birth of a new world, a fact recognised in the old cliché that he was the last of the Fathers and the first of the Scholastics. Intellectually he was an innovator, originating theological lines of thought still under debate today. The world his work reflects, however, is vanishing. 'By the end of his life', Richard Southern also concedes, 'Anselm was already old fashioned.'[7] This applies especially to the field of law, which supplied Anselm with the central analogy of his theology of redemption. In this area the great changes to which Southern refers, and which had obvious bearing on theology, took place for the most part in the century and a half after Anselm's death.

That Anselm was familiar with the law of the day cannot be doubted. Lanfranc, his great mentor, was a lawyer of European fame. He was a native of Pavia, and the lawyers of Pavia had been harmonising, digesting and modernising the ancient statutes of the Lombard kings for generations. His legal precocity passed into legend. He knew Lombard, Roman and canon law, and when he accompanied William to England he mastered English law so thoroughly that he carried all before him, even when talk

---

of God to exquisite tortures, and did not shrink from shedding the blood of one whom the Only-begotten Son had redeemed with his own precious blood.' Cf. the remarks in William of Malmesbury, *Chronicle of the Kings of England*, tr. J. A. Giles (London, Bohn, 1847), p. 307.

6 R. Southern, *Anselm, A Portrait in a Landscape* (Cambridge, Cambridge University Press, 1990), p. 4.

7 ibid., p. 457.

was of *sake* and *soke* – tenancy rights.[8] It is inconceivable that law had not formed part of the discussion between master and pupil.

The definition of feudalism is one of the most contentious issues amongst medieval historians, but all are agreed that England became properly feudal under Norman rule. By this I mean in the first place a society characterised by the subordinate relation of vassal to lord, and in the second, a system of society based on dependent and derivative land tenure.[9] In such a society there is no distinction between public and private, for society forms a perfect whole:

Just in so far as the ideal of feudalism is perfectly realized, all that we call public law is merged in private law; jurisdiction is property, office is property, the kingship itself is property; the same word '*dominium*' has to stand now for 'ownership' and now for 'lordship' ... Any such conception as that of 'the state' hardly appears on the surface of the law; no line is drawn between the king's public and private capacities, or it is drawn only to be condemned as treasonable. The king, it is true, is a highly privileged as well as a very wealthy person; still his rights are but private rights amplified and intensified.[10]

In such a community all wrongdoing is an attack on the community. Social status determined severity of punishment. Thus, in the new forest laws introduced into England by Anselm's Norman masters, the penalty for a freeman resisting a forest Verderer was loss of freedom, but for a villein the loss of his right hand. If a deer was hunted till it panted, there was a fine of 10 shillings: 'If he be not a free man, then he shall pay double. If he be a bound man, he shall lose his skin.' The penalty for a serf killing a deer was death.[11] In Anselm's time outlawry was still a valid punishment. If the court declared *Caput gerat lupinum*, it meant that the outlaw could be hunted down without mercy. He was no longer a member of the community, but a wild animal, a wolf. However, from the times of King Ine (688–726) and Alfred (871–899) a system of

[8]   F. Pollock and F. W. Maitland, *The History of English Law before the Time of Edward I* (2 vols., Cambridge, Cambridge University Press, 1895), vol. 1, p. 54.
[9]   Land tenure developed only in the twelfth century according to some historians.
[10] Pollock and Maitland, *History*, vol. 1, pp. 208–9.
[11] D. M. Stenton, *English Society in the Early Middle Ages* (Harmondsworth, Penguin, 1965), p. 111.

compositions had been the favoured way of dealing with disputes, as opposed to either outlawry or the blood feud.[12] An offender could buy back the peace he had injured by a system of fines, by paying *bot* (betterment) to the offended party and *wite* to the king. A tariff existed for all kinds of offence. Homicide was emendable by the payment of *wergild*, calculated in accordance with the social status of the slain. When Anselm came to England the *wer* (worth) of the *ceorl* or *villanus* was £4, of a thegn, £25. Cutting off an ear incurred a fine of 30 shillings, knocking out an eye 66 shillings and rape 60 shillings if the woman was a virgin and 16 if she was not.[13] The system had been encouraged by the church to avoid the death penalty, but had far-reaching social efects. Those who could not pay were either outlawed or sold as slaves:

From the very first it was an aristocratic system; not only did it consecrate the barriers between classes, making a distinction between those who were 'dearly born' and those who were cheaply born, but it raised those barriers by impoverishing the poorer folk. One unlucky blow resulting in the death of a thegn may have been enough to reduce a whole family of ceorls to economic dependence or even to legal slavery. When we reckon up the causes which made the bulk of the nation into tillers of the lands of lords, *bot* and *wite* should not be forgotten.[14]

In Roman law, just being rediscovered in the schools of Pavia and Bologna, *satisfactio* referred to compensation to an injured person other than by direct payment. The use of this term for these commutations was obvious. It is against this background that we must understand Anselm's introduction of a new metaphor for understanding the work of Christ – satisfaction.

When Anselm finally turned over *Cur Deus Homo?* to the copyist in an attempt to forestall problems which might arise from pirated editions, probably in the closing years of the eleventh century, he started a line of theological argument of immense

---

[12] D. Roebuck, *The Background of the Common Law* (Oxford, Oxford University Press, 1988), p. 29.
[13] J. Greenberg, 'The Victim in Historical Perspective: Some Aspects of the English Experience', *Journal of Social Issues*, 40 (1984), 79.
[14] Pollock and Maitland, *History*, vol. II, p. 458.

significance.[15] Both Calvinist and Catholic defenders of the satisfaction theory have claimed that it has been the central expression of the theology of the atonement from the very beginning, but this is certainly mistaken. They have cited references in Tertullian, but he uses the term to refer to the penitence of the believer, and never applies it to the death of Christ.[16] Similar uses are found in Cyprian, Lactantius and Ambrose, but these scattered references do not constitute a theology.[17] Harnack makes the point that the theory and practice of penance reacted on the conception of Christ's work, but to all intents and purposes the theology of satisfaction begins with Anselm.[18]

Anselm is writing partly in response to non-Christian objectors, widely agreed to be Jews, who felt that ideas of incarnation and crucifixion meant a dishonouring of God, and partly in reaction to theories of redemption, current since at least the fourth century, which seemed to imply that the devil had rights over human beings. How absurd and improper to believe that God should take on the indignities of the human condition, said the 'unbelievers', especially when this involved death by torture. Why could we not be redeemed simply by an act of divine forgiveness? Why was the death of the Son of God necessary? The school of Laon, a rival to the Benedictine school at Bec, answered this

---

[15] Anselm tells us that he was compelled to hurry the completion of the book during his exile, because pirated editions of the first volume were already circulating (*Cur Deus Homo?*, Preface). Anselm was exiled from 1097 until September 1100, so we can assume that the official version appeared during those years.

[16] Tertullian speaks of those 'who, through repentance for sins, had begun to make satisfaction to the Lord' but who will, by further lapses, 'make satisfaction to the devil' (*De Poenit.* 5). Later he says we confess our sins to God, not because God is ignorant but 'inasmuch as by confession satisfaction is settled, of confession repentance is born; by repentance God is appeased' (ibid., 9). In Roman law 'satisfaction' meant making compensation to an injured person other than by direct payment, and for Tertullian it is obviously penitence which plays this role. In the same pamphlet *On Penitence* we find the root of much medieval thinking on merit. 'A good deed has God as its debtor', he writes, 'just as also an evil one, because a judge is a rewarder of every cause' (*De Poenit.* 2).

[17] Ambrose, *De Fide* III.5; Hilary, on Ps. 53.12. The point in these passages is Christ's sacrificial role.

[18] A. Harnack, *History of Dogma*, tr. J. Millar (7 vols., London, Williams & Norgate, 1897), vol. III, p. 312. Cf. J. McIntyre, *St Anselm and his Critics* (London, Oliver & Boyd, 1954). He insists that Anselm is not determined by his predecessors. 'He builds up his own interpretation of it as the work proceeds, so that in the end we have an entirely new conception', p. 87.

question by restating a prominent theme of patristic teaching in finding the rationale of the incarnation in the need to deceive the devil. The devil acquired rights over humankind at the Fall, but when he exercises these rights over a perfectly sinless creature he goes beyond appointed limits and forfeits his due. Anselm will have none of either the objections or this response, and therefore sets out to prove, *remoto Christo*, the intrinsic fitness and inner necessity of the incarnation as that without which God's purposes would be frustrated.

Cur Deus Homo? has three distinct arguments. In the first place Anselm needs to clear the ground. He establishes that aesthetic arguments alone, though compelling to the Christian, will not serve.[19] He demonstrates that a mere man could not save us, because we would then become servants of him rather than of God (as the English became servants of William rather than of Harold). Finally, he disposes of the theology which explains the incarnation in terms of the devil's rights in two chapters ascribed to Anselm's friend and philosophical interlocutor, Boso.[20] The devil is only a creature, he argues, and no creature can have a claim against God. Moreover, the devil knows no justice, and so there is no reason why God should not use his power against him.[21] This ancient theory, Anselm implies, rests on an entirely inadequate theology of creation. When we truly understand God's lordship in creation we cannot trifle with it even for a moment.[22]

Having cleared that ground, Anselm turns to the elaboration of a new theory. Again we begin from God's purposes in creation. Human beings were created to love the highest good for its own sake and nothing else, for which they need to be both rational and holy.[23] This purpose they frustrate by sin, which Anselm

---

[19] *Cur Deus Homo?* 1.3, 4; I follow for the most part the translation in S. N. Deane, *St Anselm, Basic Writings* (Open Court, La Salle, Ill., 1962).

[20] 1.6, 7.

[21] 1.7.

[22] It is true that the argument was not immediately despatched, and recurs amongst the twelfth-century Schoolmen, but its power was really broken. When Gustav Aulen sought to repristinate it in *Christus Victor* (tr. A. G. Hebert (London, SPCK, 1932)) he was, of course, doing something quite different from the theologians of Laon with whom Anselm was arguing.

[23] 2.1.

famously defines as 'failure to render God his due'.[24] The implications of God's lordship in creation lie behind this, for this means, according to Anselm, that I owe God everything.[25] 'In the order of things, there is nothing less to be endured than that the creature should take away the honour due the Creator, and not restore what he has taken away.'[26] To follow the argument further we need to refer to Anselm's social background.

The ruling class of Anselm's world adopted an ideology of hierarchy. Bishop Adalbero of Laon, around 1020, explained how society was a unity of priests, warriors and peasants:

> The community of the faithful is a single body, but the condition of society is threefold in order ... Nobles ... are the warriors and protectors of the churches ... The other class is that of serfs. This luckless breed possesses nothing except at the cost of its own labour ... The serfs provide money, clothes and food, for the rest; no free man could exist without serfs ... the serf never sees an end to his sighs and tears. God's house, which we think of as one, is thus divided into three; some pray, others fight, and yet others work.[27]

I use the word 'ideology' advisedly, for serfs sometimes challenged the situation, and when this happened they were put down with unspeakable ferocity.[28] Social anthropologists call this kind of society an 'honour society', the assumptions of which are nowhere better described than in the great speech which Shakespeare puts into the mouth of Ulysses in *Troilus and Cressida*:

> Degree being vizarded,
> Th'unworthiest shows as fairly in the mask.
> The heavens themselves, the planets, and this centre,
> Observe degree, priority, and place,
> Insisture, course, proportion, season, form,
> Office, and custom, in all line of order ...
> O, when degree is shak'd,
> Which is the ladder of all high designs,
> The enterprise is sick! How could communities,

---

24 I.11.
25 I.20.
26 I.13.
27 Cited by J. Le Goff, *Medieval Civilization*, tr. J. Barrow (Oxford, Blackwell, 1988), p. 255.
28 A rebellion in Normandy in 977 was put down by impaling, tearing out eyes, cutting off hands, burning, and plunging in boiling lead. ibid., p. 301.

Degrees in schools, and brotherhoods in cities,
Peaceful commerce from dividable shores,
The primogenity and due of birth,
Prerogative of age, crowns, sceptres, laurels,
But by degree, stand in authentic place?
Take but degree away, untune that string,
And hark what discord follows![29]

Sin, we have seen, is essentially an infringement of honour, a failure to render someone his or her due, as determined by his or her place in the social order. 'Just as someone who imperils another's safety does not do enough if they merely restore their safety, but must make some compensation for the anguish incurred; so whoever violates another's honour ... must, according to the extent of the injury done, make restoration in some way satisfactory to the person they have dishonoured.'[30] As we have seen, social status determines punishment as much as the character of a crime. The same act, let us say a blow, directed against a peasant, a knight, a nobleman, or the king, is not the same act. A blow exchanged between two peasants might call for nothing but a mutual pardon, but if directed by a peasant against a king would threaten the integrity of the whole social order and demand the death sentence. What, then, of an offence directed against an infinite being, God? Because we owe God our total obedience, even the most trivial offence demands an infinite satisfaction. When Boso suggests that surely repentance would atone for just a *look* contrary to God's will, back comes the famous reply: 'Nondum considerasti quanti ponderis sit peccatum' – 'You have not yet weighed the seriousness of sin.'[31] 'Were there an infinite number of worlds as full of created existence as this, they could not stand, but would fall back into nothing, sooner than one look should be made contrary to the just will of God.'[32] God cannot simply forgive, because this would mean that he was no longer the controller of sin (*ordinator peccatorum*) and that

[29] Act I, sc. 3.
[30] *Cur Deus Homo?* I.II.
[31] I.21.
[32] 2.24; cf. I.21: 'When I consider the action itself, it appears very slight; but when I view it as contrary to the will of God, I know of nothing so grievous, and of no loss that will compare with it.'

disorder would be admitted into his kingdom. Failure to make a distinction between innocent and guilty would be unbecoming to God. It is true that we are enjoined to forgive, but this is because all vengeance belongs to God. God cannot simply will to treat evil as good, because this would deny the righteousness which is his essential nature.

It is at this point that the need of satisfaction makes its appearance. At the beginning of the discussion, as we have seen, Anselm has noted that the intrinsic beauty of God's scheme of redemption does not suffice to convince doubters.[33] They must be shown that the incarnation and death of Christ are strictly speaking *necessary*. This necessity springs from the demands of justice – the basis of retributive theory. 'Necesse est, ut aut ablatus honor solvatur aut poena sequatur': 'It is necessary that either the honour taken away be restored, or that punishment follow.'[34] 'Necesse est, ut omne peccatum satisfactio aut poena sequatur': 'It is necessary that either satisfaction or punishment must follow all sin.'[35] Either humankind will be punished by eternal death, or satisfaction must be paid. Two axioms are involved here: the first, that punishment must follow sin, and the second, that satisfaction may take the place of punishment. In giving reasons for the first it is correct to say that, given the prominence of the theme of wholeness, constituted in society by acts which are fitting, Anselm's argument can be grasped in aesthetic terms.[36] When honour is breached in the social order, satisfaction is demanded, not so much to fulfil the demands of some abstract 'law' as to restore that breach, make things whole again. 'It is not fitting for God to pass over anything in his

---

[33]   1.3, 4.
[34]   1.13.
[35]   1.15.
[36]   Cf. H. Rashdall: 'His notions of justice are the barbaric ideas of an ancient Lombard king or the technicalities of a Lombard lawyer rather than the ideas which would have satisfied such a man as Anselm in ordinary life.' *The Idea of the Atonement in Christian Theology* (London, Macmillan, 1925), p. 355. According to Rashdall Anselm confuses the conception of criminal and civil justice, and identifies moral transgression and personal affront, debt which can be forgiven with penalty due to wrongdoing which cannot be. This is certainly wrong and springs from Rashdall's failure to understand the centrality of the aesthetic theme in Anselm. Ritschl's objections were essentially the same.

kingdom undischarged', says Anselm, because then 'there will be no difference between the guilty and the not guilty; and this is unbecoming to God'.[37] God is not free to do whatsoever he chooses because he must act in accordance with his dignity and choose 'what is best and fitting' (*quod expedit aut quod decet*).[38] Compassion without satisfaction is not possible, for God's justice allows nothing but punishment as the recompense for sin.[39] But this concern for justice is essentially a concern for the integrity of both the social order and the cosmic order which it mirrors.[40] Sin is breach of honour, but honour, in Anselm's theology, is a way of talking of the integrity of God's creation and of his purposes. To dishonour God is to 'disturb the order and beauty of the universe'.[41] The second assumption, that satisfaction can take the place of punishment, is certainly an established part of the legal system of his day, though, as Harnack argues, Anselm might well take it from the system of penance which the church operated.[42] Both understand the possibility of making 'satisfaction' for offences which have been committed. The alternative 'either punishment or satisfaction' was that which eleventh-century law offered to the offender. He might be outlawed, or left to private vengeance, or punished by death or mutilation – or he could make satisfaction.

These two assumptions constitute the hinge of the argument. He now goes on to ask how satisfaction can be made, and integrity be restored, when the offence is against an infinite being. We have nothing with which we can make satisfaction because we already owe God everything. 'The entire will of a rational creature ought to be subject to the will of God ... He who does not render to God this honour which is due to him, robs God of what is his own, and dishonours God; and this is what it is to sin.'[43] Since sin against an infinite being is itself

---

[37] 1.12.
[38] ibid.
[39] 1.24.
[40] 'If there is nothing greater or better than God, there is nothing more just than supreme justice, which maintains God's honour in the arrangement of things, and which is nothing else but God himself', 1.13.
[41] 1.15.
[42] Harnack, *History of Dogma*, vol. VI, p. 56 n. 3.
[43] 1.11.

infinite, only an infinite being could make satisfaction. At the same time it is human beings who have breached God's honour. Hence the need for one who is both God and human, for only a being truly divine and truly human can make restitution. Moreover, human beings have no means by themselves of making satisfaction for the contempt they have brought on God. A true satisfaction would imply restoring what belonged to God by overcoming the devil, so that what was lost by human beings is also gained by them.[44]

The language of satisfaction refers us back to the beauty of the divine nature itself, which is the real heart of Anselm's argument, the 'imaginative construal' which underlies his theology. The language of harmony and order plays a crucial role in the argument. Though the need for satisfaction shows the necessity of the God-Man, Anselm believes at the same time that the scheme of redemption is 'fitting' (*convenienter, oportet*), that the details of our redemption have 'a certain indescribable beauty' (*inerrabilem pulchritudinem*).[45] It is the 'loveliness' (*amabilis*) of Christ's life which has infinite value and outweighs our sin.[46] His transfer of reward to us is the most 'sweet and desirable' thing we could imagine.[47] Sin, by contrast, is 'the violation of the beauty' of creation.[48] The humiliation of God, we can say, was counterpoised to the arrogance of human beings, and thus restored the balance and harmony which had been lost. Again, it is not fitting (*non decet*) that human beings should be raised to angelic status without an atonement: 'truth will not allow this'.[49]

The importance of the aesthetic theme in Anselm is certainly connected with the Platonism which he imbibed from Augustine and, to some extent, probably knew first hand.[50] It is Neoplatonism which theorises the importance of fittingness, order and beauty which the social order must exemplify. This theme also finds expression in the argument about the need to make up the

[44]　1.23.
[45]　1.3.
[46]　2.14.
[47]　2.19.
[48]　1.15.
[49]　1.19.
[50]　See Southern, *Portrait*, p. 134.

number of fallen angels.[51] The purpose of human history, Anselm argues, is that those persons who respond to the redemption wrought in Christ will complete the number of angels, and so bring creation to completion. Once again he tells us, as an axiom, that that rational nature which finds its happiness in the contemplation of God 'was foreseen by him in a certain reasonable and complete number, so that there would be an unfitness in its being either less or greater' (*nec maiorem nec minorem illum esse deceat*).[52]

To emphasise the aesthetic theme in Anselm is not to set it against a moral one, as it would have been after Kant. Rather, morality for Anselm consists in conformity to God's good order. John McIntyre wants to say that Anselm's insight is more religious than legal, more concerned with disobedience to God's will than with dishonour. This, however, is to miss the point that the language of honour is *both* the language of law *and* the language with which Anselm expresses religious insights. The satisfaction argument is launched in a world where these all belong together. It is true that Anselm's argument is not 'legalistic' in the sense that some restatements of it in the nineteenth century were, but it is also true that the presuppositions of the retributive theory of punishment are part and parcel of it. Retributivist theory, a modern writer in jurisprudence notes, needs to appeal to an idea of balance which crime disturbs and which punishment restores.[53] Anselm's argument postulates this metaphysically. It has to, because the earthly is, after all, an analogue of the heavenly.

The third theme of *Cur Deus Homo?* is to some extent independent. In the second book Anselm turns to the question of the 'merit' of Christ's death. He takes it as an axiom that 'satisfaction should be proportionate to guilt' as otherwise sin would remain *inordinatum*, without control, threatening order. However, he has already told us that 'considering the contempt offered' to God,

---

[51]   This is where 1.16 starts, taking up a suggestion of Augustine's (*Civ. Dei* 22.1). In 1.18, however, Anselm inclines to the view that God deliberately created fewer angels so that their places could be taken by human beings. The argument hangs on the necessity for perfect harmony.

[52]   1.16.

[53]   R. A. Duff, *Trials and Punishments* (Cambridge, Cambridge University Press, 1986), p. 204.

the sinner 'ought to restore more than he took away'.[54] Since we
owe God everything, we make no satisfaction unless we restore
something 'greater than the amount of that obligation, which
should restrain us from committing sin'.[55] What Christ in fact
does is infinitely more than this. Death voluntarily suffered is, in
Anselm's view, a unique satisfaction. 'No man except this one
ever gave to God what he was not obliged to lose, or paid a debt
he did not owe.'[56] What such a death expresses is a kind of
superlative work of supererogation, the obedience which is due
from all creatures overflowing to such an extent that it avails for
others. By his voluntary death Christ earns a reward, but he
needs nothing since all things are already his. He chooses then to
bestow the reward on human beings. 'Whom could he more
justly make heirs of the inheritance, which he does not need, and
of the superfluity of his possessions, than his parents and
brethren? What more proper than that, when he beholds so
many of them weighed down by so heavy a debt, and wasting
through poverty ... he should remit the debt incurred by their
sins, and give them what their transgressions had forfeited?[57] It is
in this way that vicariousness 'works', by the transfer of Christ's
merit to sinners. To illustrate this Anselm appeals to a feudal
parable: a king agrees that because such and such an act is well
pleasing to him he will remit the penalties due to him by others
provided they turn up at court on a certain day.[58] This situation,
familiar enough in Anselm's world, is a picture of the church's
role. When we avail ourselves of the sacraments, and put
ourselves in the way of what the church offers, we are in the
position of those who do in fact turn up at court. Anselm further
adds that Christ's voluntary obedience set us a noble example
'that each one should not hesitate to give to God, for himself,
what he must at any rate lose before long'.[59] The introduction of
the theme of merit here seems to represent a real fracture in the
argument, which up to this point has turned on satisfaction. It

[54] I.II.
[55] I.21.
[56] 2.18b.
[57] 2.19.
[58] 2.16.
[59] 2.18b.

was this theme which was to prove the more potent in the next four centuries, but that God takes note of merits in this way seems to strike at the heart of evangelical perceptions about grace.[60]

Anselm's theory, Harnack correctly points out, offers us 'a new construction of the *whole* of dogma from the point of view of sin and redemption', bringing hitherto disparate themes into a powerful synthesis.[61] Still, today, it commands the allegiance of many. Its strength lies in the way it articulates the key questions raised by retributive theory. If we ask why a person ought to be punished, in the wake of wrongdoing, then an essential part of the answer is in terms of seeking to rectify the damage done to the community. What sin or crime does is to deny the values, the bonds of mutual trust and concern, on which the community depends for its existence. It destroys, we can say, the harmony or balance of that society: the analogy with Anselm's understanding of the ordered world is exact. What should be our response? It cannot be to turn a blind eye, for wrongdoing necessarily alters our relations to the offender. To behave as if an offender had done nothing wrong would be to deny the true implications of his or her actions, which have injured the social fabric of the community. Punishment, argues the retributivist, 'is a just and proper response to a past offence, since it restores that fair balance of benefits and burdens in society which crime disturbs; and it respects the criminal's autonomy, since it accords with his own rational will'.[62] This puts in a secularist and socio-logical way what Anselm expresses metaphysically. The Kantian concern for the criminal's autonomy is matched by Anselm's insistence that God cannot simply let his creature go to ruin. At the same time the surd in all retributive thinking remains, namely the idea of commensurability between retribu-tory sufferings and the evil for which the offender is held responsible. In the last analysis, G. H. Mead remarked, writing

---

[60]   The tradition of the theology of merit is not very clear. A theology of the merits of good men is present in first-century Judaism, where it rests on notions of a solidarity which transcends death. It is found in Tertullian, again in *De Poenitate*, but does not seem to play a large part in patristic thinking.

[61]   Harnack, *History of Dogma*, vol. VI, p. 67.

[62]   Duff, *Trials*, p. 205. See also pp. 6off., on which the earlier part of the paragraph draws.

on the psychology of punitive justice, the offender 'suffered until satisfaction had been given to the outraged sentiments of the injured person, or of his kith and kin, or of the community, or of an angry God'.[63] As nineteenth-century critics insisted, this is identical with rationalised vengeance, and it is this which, in Anselm's theory, is given divine sanction.

At the same time the flaws in Anselm's account are obvious. In the first place the attempt to 'prove' the necessity and possibility of redemption without any reference to the gospel story strikes us as perverse. Anselm's thought is profoundly ahistorical. His theory operates at a level of dazzling legal and aesthetic abstraction, far above the hurly-burly of conquest, expropriation and murder in which he lived. That God becomes human is a metaphysical necessity, not a sign of God's commitment to human history, of God's entering the human story. Anselm's theology is constructed, like the retributivist case argued above, for an ideal world. This is why his scheme only works in an ideal world. On his terms humans are by definition 'sinners', because they fail to offer God his due, but this tells us nothing important about sin or the human condition. This was the burden of those nineteenth-century critics, like Moberly, who felt that he conceived sin 'arithmetically'. If a retributivist idea of justice is to undergird our theology, then it needs to arise out of a sensitivity to the complexity and ambiguity of the world in which we live – the ambiguity and complexity which so many of the biblical authors, whom Anselm read daily in his offices, knew so well! The abstraction of the image of satisfaction, the 'necessity' for satisfaction in order to preserve God's righteousness, was part of that move from the compromises of local justice, centred on reconciliation and commutations, towards those notions of strictly equal justice which retributivists insist on. Of course nothing was further from Anselm's mind, yet it is undeniably part of the same cultural current.

Colin Gunton wishes us to believe that Anselm's metaphor establishes the very opposite of oppressive rule. 'It was the duty of the feudal ruler to maintain the order of rights and obligations

---

[63]   G. H. Mead, 'The Psychology of Punitive Justice', *American Journal of Sociology*, 23 (1918), 582.

without which society would collapse. Anselm's God is understood to operate *analogously* for the universe as a whole: as the upholder of universal justice.'[64] But the earthly justice which was the analogue of such 'universal justice' believed that the life of the serf was cheaper than that of the beasts. John of Salisbury knew that this was wrong, fifty years after Anselm's death, and he was certainly not the first to feel this way.[65] Abstractions about the need for justice then, as now, have always underwritten oppression. Pollock and Maitland, neither of whom was in the vanguard of revolution, understood that the legal system of Anselm's day profoundly underscored class division. Anselm's analogy did not, as analogies sometimes do, critique this system, but reinforced it. Even Sir Richard Southern, a defender of Anselm, noting that he is no humanist, observes that *Cur Deus Homo?* bears the marks of a rigorous 'and – if the word can be used without blame – repressive regime'.[66] Moreover, the very notions of satisfaction and expiation were deeply bound up with revenge in medieval culture, as Huizinga argued:

Read the long list of expiatory deeds which the treaty of Arras demanded in 1435 – chapels, monasteries, churches, chapters to be founded, crosses to be erected, masses to be chanted – then one realizes the immensely high rate at which men valued the need of vengeance and of reparations to outraged honour.[67]

In the first chapter I mentioned Nietzsche's brilliant insight that even Kant 'reeks of cruelty'. Exactly the same is true of Anselm's noble and high-minded argument. This was the burden of Abelard's criticism, shortly after Anselm's death, as we shall see. Developing such criticisms, Harnack felt that the worst thing in Anselm's theory was its picture of God 'as the mighty private person, who is incensed at the injury done to his honour and does not forego his wrath till he has received an at least adequately great equivalent'. He saw here a gnostic antagonism between justice and goodness, the notion that God cannot forgive from

---

[64] C. Gunton, *The Actuality of the Atonement* (Edinburgh, T. & T. Clark, 1988), p. 89.
[65] John of Salisbury, *Policraticus*, ed. Webb, vol. I, iv, pp. 390ff.
[66] Southern, *Portrait*, p. 222.
[67] J. Huizinga, *The Waning of the Middle Ages*, tr. F. Hopman (Harmondsworth, Penguin, 1965), p. 20.

love, but needs satisfaction to do so, and 'the blasphemous idea' that the Son's giving of life is a benefit.[68] Even when we have made the utmost allowance for Anselm's conception of cosmic harmony, it is hard to acquit him of these charges. Whilst it is true that this is not a penal theory of the atonement, since Christ voluntarily offers his life, and does not suffer penalty, nevertheless the need for death arises from the demand for justice. Like Shylock, God the Father insists on justice and nothing but justice, but there is no Portia to plead the quality of mercy.

Nor is this the end of the story. In the previous chapter I pointed out the role that concrete remission of debts played in Jesus' teaching. For the Church Fathers it is the devil who – illegitimately – insists on the payment of the debt incurred by humankind. Anselm inverts this. Now it is God who, legitimately, exacts the payment of debt. Franz Hinkelammert points out that this means that God and the devil swap places.[69] In both Old and New Testaments an indebted person could be 'redeemed' by the payment of his or her debt. Jesus, following Deuteronomy, insists on the cancelling of debt as a fundamental aspect of Christian practice. Anselm, however, makes God the one who *insists* on debt. The debt humanity has incurred must be paid with human blood. The God who rejected sacrifice now demands it, for Christ's voluntary offering of himself to death, which is at the heart of Anselm's theory, was inevitably construed in sacrificial terms. From the start sacrifice and satisfaction run together. Law assumes a central function within theology. The God who liberates from law is now, in Anselm, understood as hypostasised, personified law. Rather than *transcending* law God is infinite law, law in himself. What is divinised is the power of law, an intrinsically alienating reality. What remains, as we shall see more fully in the next chapter, but was anticipated by Anselm, is a mysticism of pain which promises redemption to those who pay in blood. In this move a most fundamental inversion of the gospel is achieved, which prepares the way for the validation of criminal

---

[68] Harnack, *History*, vol. VI, p. 76. Harnack's characterisation agrees with Le Goff's placing of Anselm. *Civilization*, pp. 156f.

[69] F. Hinkelammert, *Sacrificios humanos y sociedad occidental: Lucifer y la Bestia* (Costa Rica, DEI, 1991), pp. 55ff. I owe this reference to Adolfo Abascal-Jaen.

law as the instrument of God's justice instead of what it is in the gospel, an alienating construction which is at best a tragic necessity.

The penal consequences of this doctrine were grim indeed. As it entered the cultural bloodstream, was imaged in crucifixions painted over church chancels, recited at each celebration of the eucharist, or hymned, so it created its own structure of affect, one in which earthly punishment was demanded because God himself had demanded the death of his Son. When the social reformer Joseph Gerrald was tried in March 1794, he pointed out that Jesus Christ had himself been a reformer. Lord Braxfield, the presiding judge, turned to his fellow judges and remarked: 'Muckle he made o'that; *he* was hanget.' And many generations of the poor, like Gerrald, paid the price of maintaining the 'justice' of a confessedly hierarchical system.[70]

[70] See E. P. Thompson, *The Making of the English Working Classes* (Harmondsworth, Penguin, 1968), p. 140. Gerrald received a sentence of fourteen years' transportation.

CHAPTER 5

The wounds of Christ

Red my feet with flowing blood,
    Holes in them washed through with that flood.
Mercy on Man's sins, Father on high!
        Through all my wounds to thee I cry!
                                    Anon. (thirteenth century)

The notion of a 'middle age' (*media aetas, medium aevum*) between ancient and modern, characterising the four hundred years between Abelard and Luther, emerged in the fifteenth century, but only became thoroughly familiar after the eighteenth century, with the re-evaluation of medieval art, and the rise of 'Gothic'.[1] Twentieth-century historical scholarship has increasingly challenged the periodisation assumed by Michelet and Burckhardt, tracing the roots of humanism, reform and renaissance as far back as the twelfth and thirteenth centuries.[2] Economic development accelerated from the late eleventh century on. From being uncertain and reversible economic growth became 'rapid, ubiquitous, and for a time apparently limitless'.[3] Land tenure gradually became less important, and money payment more significant. As these centuries wore on the merchant class became ever more important until, by the fifteenth century, the richest merchants bought their way into the elite ranks of the hereditary peerage. Throughout the period social hierarchy remained of great importance, but it was

---

[1] See R. Williams, *Keywords* (London, Fontana, 1976).
[2] See the remarks of J. Huizinga, *The Waning of the Middle Ages*, tr. F. Hopman (Harmondsworth, Penguin, 1965), p. 262.
[3] R. Southern, *Western Society and the Church in the Middle Ages* (Harmondsworth, Penguin, 1970), p. 34.

transformed from within. The basic social distinction shifted from that between noble and non-noble to that between those who were and those who were not entitled to bear arms. At the lower end of the social scale resentment of servile status was reflected in peasant movements, in popular preaching, and in stubborn resistance to some forms of taxation.[4] The church's hegemony in intellectual and administrative life proved short lived, and by the thirteenth century lay officials, often lawyers, were taking leading roles in administration.

Intellectual and cultural changes naturally accompanied these social and economic currents. A profound change in sensibilities seems to have occurred in the eleventh and twelfth centuries, in which devotion to the passion of Christ played its part. 'The civilisation of the twelfth century owes a great deal to the tears which were shed in the eleventh. They were the forerunner of a new world of sentiment, of devotion, and even of action.'[5] In Elias' terms, what we have here is the emergence of new structures of affect. Walter Ullmann sees the notion of the individual emerging in the shift from subject to citizen.[6] 'Courtly love' was born in the songs of the twelfth-century troubadours of Provence, and others have traced the beginnings of individualism to the cultural shift which produced this literature.[7] The romances of Chrétien of Troyes, who wrote in the third quarter of the twelfth century, are 'the secular counterpart to the piety of Cîteaux'.[8] The great allegory of erotic love, the *Roman de la rose*, was begun around 1240 by Guillaume de Lorris. Others point to the growth of a new genre of religious literature concerned with what we would now call self-examination, and the distinction between the self and the other.[9] This was accompanied, as

---

[4]   J. Le Goff, *Medieval Civilization*, tr. J. Barrow (Oxford, Blackwell, 1988), pp. 299ff.; J. A. F. Thomson, *The Transformation of Medieval England* (London, Longman, 1983), p. 34.

[5]   R. W. Southern, *The Making of the Middle Ages* (London, Pimlico, 1993), pp. 51–2.

[6]   W. Ullmann, *The Individual and Society in the Middle Ages* (Baltimore, Johns Hopkins University Press, 1966).

[7]   P. Dronke, *Poetic Individuality in the Middle Ages* (Oxford, Oxford University Press, 1970); R. W. Hanning, *The Individual in Twelfth Century Romance* (New Haven, Yale University Press, 1977).

[8]   Southern, *Making*, p. 232.

[9]   ibid., pp. 218ff.; Colin Morris, *The Discovery of the Individual: 1050–1200* (London, SPCK, 1972).

Caroline Bynum has argued, by a rediscovery of the group. If the inner self was newly found in the twelfth century, this was largely in and through the group. 'In the twelfth century, turning inward to explore motivation went hand in hand with a sense of belonging to a group that not only defined its own life by means of a model but also was itself – as group and as pattern – a means of salvation and of evangelism.'[10] The strident competition between these groups is part of the background to Abelard's condemnation.

The change in sensibility is nowhere as visible as in spirituality. Throughout the period the passion of Christ stood at the heart of the religious life. This was true of the previous century, but the intensity of concentration on the passion grew, and St Bernard and the Cistercians, especially, were responsible for turning the 'thin stream of compassion and tenderness' of the previous century into the 'flood' of the later Middle Ages.[11] The medieval mind, says Huizinga, was saturated with the concepts of Christ and the cross:

In early childhood the image of the cross was implanted on the sensitive heart, so grand and forbidding as to overshadow all other affections by its gloom. When Jean Gerson was a child, his father one day stood with his back against a wall, his arms outspread, saying: 'Thus, child, was your God crucified, who made and saved you' ... Saint Colette, when four years old, every day heard her mother in prayer lament and weep about the Passion, sharing the pain of contumely, blows and torments. This recollection fixed itself ... with such intensity that she felt, all her life through, the most severe oppression of heart every day at the hour of the crucifixion ... The soul is so imbued with the conception of the Passion that the most remote analogy suffices to make the chord of the memory of Christ vibrate.[12]

A late thirteenth-century sermon edifies its hearers with the story of how a woman who could not confess her sin is visited by Christ in her sleep, who tells her to put her hand in his side and to feel his heart. When she woke she found her hand covered with blood, which would not wash off until she went to

[10] C. Bynum, *Jesus as Mother: Studies in the Spirituality of the High Middle Ages* (Berkeley, University of California Press, 1982), pp. 104–5.
[11] Southern, *Making*, p. 222.
[12] Huizinga, *Waning*, p. 184.

confession.[13] Elizabeth of Spalbeck, in the same century, physically imitated the details of the passion of Christ at the canonical hours, beating herself at Matins and lying cruciform at Evensong.[14] The blood of Christ, and the wounds of Christ, are especial objects of devotion. Mechtild of Magdeburg, in the thirteenth century, is centred on the sacred heart, and her piety takes the form of an identification with suffering and pain. Not only Christ but each soul on earth must suffer, in cleansing, preparation and expiation.[15] The spiritual writings of the thirteenth century show 'a sharp decline in the role of the devil and in any sense of cosmic warfare ... a devotion to Christ's humanity that reflects, on the one hand, the fact that Christ is mediator and, on the other hand, a desire to identify with his suffering and model oneself on his example; a flowering of eucharistic piety among all types of women religious, coupled with devotion to Christ's body, blood, wounds and sacred heart'.[16] In the next century the blood of the five wounds of Christ flows through the mouth of Henry Suso into his heart. For Julian of Norwich (born c. 1342) it is the passion which above all discloses that all things were made for love.[17] Suffering is the alchemy which brings good out of evil. A drop of Christ's blood would have sufficed to save the world, says Bernard. Aquinas agrees, in a famous image:

> Pie Pelicane, Jesu domine,
> Me immundum munda tuo sanguine,
> Cuius una stilla salvum facere
> Totum mundum quit ab omni scelere.[18]

This focus on the death of Christ may make it seem strange that no great treatise on the atonement emerged between the mid thirteenth century and Martin Luther. The reason, however, is

---

[13] M. Glasscoe, *English Medieval Mystics: Games of Faith* (London and New York, Longman, 1993), p. 26.

[14] ibid., p. 40.

[15] Bynum, *Jesus as Mother*, p. 231, citing *Offenbarungen der Schwester Mechtild von Magdeburg oder Das fliessende Licht der Gottheit*, ed. Morel (Darmstadt, 1963), Bk 1, chaps. 25, 29–34.

[16] Bynum, *Jesus as Mother*, p. 248.

[17] *Revelations of Divine Love* 8.9.

[18] 'Pious pelican Lord Jesus, cleanse me, impure one, by your blood, of which one drop can save all the world from iniquity.'

not far to seek. The focus of discourse moves more and more to religious experience, to 'mysticism', understood very broadly, and to the eucharist. It was in a discussion of the eucharist that the importance of the redeeming blood of Christ was emphasised. 'In the Mass the redemption of the world, wrought on Good Friday once and for all, was renewed and made fruitful for all who believed. Christ himself, immolated on the altar of the cross, became present on the altar of the parish church, body, soul, and divinity, and his blood flowed once again, to nourish and renew Church and world.'[19] Christ in the sacrament is the 'saving victim'. The story of the passion could be retold in terms of what happens to the Host.[20] The sacraments in turn derived their virtue from the passion of Christ:

This most holy and dere blode of Ihesu cryste shedde for our rdemcyon, bought and gave so grete and plenteous vertue to the sacramentes, that as ofte as any creature shall use and receyve ony of them, so ofte it is to be byleved they are sprencled with the droppes of the same most holy blode.[21]

According to Le Goff it was the centrality of the suffering of Christ which, in the course of the thirteenth and fourteenth centuries, brought the whole human life of Christ into the foreground, and contributed to profound changes in the understanding of the human person.[22] It is this change in sensibility which is the indispensable background to the theology of the period.

FROM ABELARD TO AQUINAS

Abelard (1079–1142), still under twenty when *Cur Deus Homo?* appeared, was the bright star of the next generation of theologians after Anselm. In the ten years after Anselm's death in 1109 he was developing his new and controversial theological method, the *Sic et Non*, in which opposed opinions from Scripture and the Fathers are proposed for resolution. Three years after the end of

---

[19] E. Duffy, *The Stripping of the Altars* (New Haven, Yale University Press, 1992), p. 91.
[20] ibid., p. 106.
[21] John Fisher, *English Works*, quoted in Duffy, *Altars*, p. 108.
[22] Le Goff, *Civilization*, p. 159.

his tragic love affair with Heloise, in 1118, his teaching on the
Trinity was condemned. He returned to Paris some eighteen
years later, but was condemned a second time at the Council of
Sens in 1140. His teaching on the atonement is only one among
many aspects of his theology which was singled out for attack,
though it drew the particular fire of Bernard of Clairvaux, as it
touched the nerve centre of his piety. The ferocity of the attack
on Abelard cannot be explained simply in terms of doctrine. His
attackers represented a long-standing monastic tradition,
grounded in patristic authority, 'meditative, conservative, rich in
psychological and moral experience'. Southern has said of
Anselm that he was 'no humanist', particularly in his relentless
emphasis on contempt for the world.[23] This surely goes also for
Abelard's monastic opponents. Abelard, on the other hand,
represented the new 'humanist' city culture, and appeared to his
opponents as a dangerously free spirit, more interested in *opinio*
than *veritas*, not sufficiently dependent on authority, and too
confident in reason.[24] There is a painful difference of voice in the
letters of Abelard and Heloise, but the experience she witnesses to
with such passion, and which the two of them shared, represents a
dimension not only lacking but feared in the theology of the
period, and found otherwise only in Chrétien of Troyes. Abelard's teaching on the atonement, which we have only in the form
of hints in his Commentary on Romans, in a letter to Heloise,
and in one or two other of his writings, must be understood as
part of his overall challenging of established models.

Abelard has two objections to satisfaction theory, one of which
was to become perennial. 'How cruel and wicked it seems', he
wrote in his Commentary, 'that anyone should demand the blood
of an innocent person as the price for anything, or that it should
in any way please him that an innocent man should be slain – still
less that God should consider the death of his Son so agreeable
that by it he should be reconciled to the whole world!'[25] Abelard

---

[23] Southern, *Portrait*, pp. 447f.

[24] D. E. Luscombe, *The School of Peter Abelard* (Cambridge, Cambridge University Press,
1970), p. 110. Hugh of St Victor attacked Abelard for putting immutable truth above
progressively revealed truth. See Le Goff, *Civilization*, p. 173.

[25] Following the translation in *A Scholastic Miscellany*, ed. E. R. Fairweather (London,
SCM, 1956), pp. 276ff.

here astutely targets the weakness of Anselm's central metaphor. It is true that Anselm was not arguing that God's anger must be appeased, but Abelard implicitly questions the whole notion of satisfaction, the very nerve centre of expiatory atonement. He shifts the question from 'Why did there have to be a God-Man?' to 'Why was it necessary for Christ to die?' His answer to this question is very different from Anselm's.

It appears from Abelard's questioning of the necessity of the incarnation that he may have objected to the notion of satisfaction because it compromised God's freedom, and certainly Bernard of Clairvaux understood him in this way. Abelard appears to imply that if it is *necessary* for God to receive satisfaction before human beings can be reconciled, then there is some necessity over and above God's will.[26] Anselm had insisted on the necessity of *satisfaction*. Abelard changes the emphasis: if satisfaction is *necessary*, where does this necessity come from? The answer, of course, is from God's inner being, which is righteousness, but Abelard either misses this or, more probably, chooses to make God's freedom an absolute value.

What is interesting in Abelard is, of course, not his attack on earlier theories, but his development of an alternative position. 'Through this unique act of grace manifested to us', he writes,

– in that his Son has taken upon himself our nature and preserved therein in teaching us by word and example even unto death – he has more fully bound us to himself by love; with the result that our hearts should be enkindled by such a gift of divine grace, and true charity should not now shrink from enduring anything for him … everyone becomes more righteous – by which we mean a greater lover of the Lord – after the Passion of Christ than before, since a realized gift inspires greater love than one which is only hoped for. Wherefore, our redemption through Christ's suffering is that deeper affection in us which not only frees us from slavery to sin, but also wins for us the true liberty of sons of God, so that we do all things out of love rather than fear.[27]

---

26 R. E. Weingart, *The Logic of Divine Love: A Critical Analysis of the Soteriology of Peter Abelard* (Oxford, Clarendon Press, 1970), p. 92. But we have a letter of Roscelin to Abelard in which he makes precisely this complaint, and for which Abelard rebukes him. Abelard, Letter 15, *PL* 178, col. 362.
27 Fairweather (ed.), *Miscellany*, pp. 283–4.

Abelard puts the question 'Cur Deus Homo?' in his *Epitome of Theology* and answers that humans could only be redeemed 'if the Son of God became man to instruct us'. The incarnation took place, he tells us, to show how greatly God loved us, and to lead us to love God more.[28] Replying to Heloise, in response to a letter telling him that she still dreams of their love, he insists that she turn her attention to the suffering of Christ:

Come, too, my inseparable companion, and join me in thanksgiving, you who were made my partner in both guilt and grace ... Are you not moved to tears or remorse by the only-begotten Son of God, who for you and for all people, in his innocence was seized by impious men ... to die a horrible and accursed form of death? ... Look at him going to be crucified for your sake, carrying his own cross ... It was he who truly loved you, not I ... You say I suffered for you, and perhaps that is true, but it was really through you, and even this, unwillingly ... But he suffered truly for your salvation, on your behalf, of his own free will, and by his suffering he cures all sickness and removes all suffering.[29]

Even in the twelfth century this was construed by Bernard and William of Thierry as exemplarism. How accurate this charge was remains difficult to say. It is true that much of Abelard's talk of grace seems to be a reference to the promise we have in the incarnation. His opponents accused him of neglecting *gratia adjuvans*, presently assisting grace.[30] On the other hand, he insisted over and over again that we are redeemed by grace rather than by our own will, works or merits.[31] 'The grace of God is necessary for everyone', he wrote, 'and ... without it neither a natural faculty nor free will is sufficient for salvation. Grace certainly anticipates us that we may will, then follows us so that we are able, and finally joins with us so that we may persevere.'[32] This

---

28   *Epitome Theologiae Christianae, PL* 178, cols. 1685–1758: 'Et hoc totum factum constat, ut ostenderet quantum dilectionem in homine haberet, ut et hominem magis ad sui dilectionem accendet.'

29   Peter Abelard, *The Letters of Heloise and Abelard*, tr. B. Radice (Harmondsworth, Penguin, 1974), pp. 149–53.

30   William of Thierry accuses him of believing 'Quod libero arbitrio, sine adjuvante gratia, bene possumus et velle et agere'. *PL* 182, col. 532B. In his reply to the charge of Pelagianism in the *Confessio Fidei* Abelard avoids the terminology of different types of grace, though he believes that we both act and persevere through grace.

31   *Exp. in Epist. ad Rom.* 1.1797a, 11.iii.826c, 833a, 11.iv.853c, 11.v.859c, and often. See Weingart, *Logic*, p. 181 n. 2.

32   *Apologia seu Fidei Confessio* 107.

seems to confirm the opinion of one of Abelard's best-known modern interpreters that his concept of grace 'falls within the scope of medieval Augustinianism represented by other major voices in the twelfth century'.[33]

Abelard's implicit rejection of Anselm serves to draw attention to the fact that different accounts of sin generate different atonement theologies. At first sight Abelard's account of sin in his commentary on Romans looks close to Anselm's. Where Anselm defined sin as 'failing to pay God his due', Abelard speaks of it there as 'guilt of the soul and contempt of God ... our perverted will by which we stand before God'.[34] This corresponds with his position in *Sic et Non*: 'Sin is our contempt of the Creator, and to sin is to despise the Creator, that is, never to do for him what we believe should be done by us for him, or not to renounce for him what we believe should be renounced.'[35] In the *Ethics*, which he wrote towards the end of his life, sin is distinguished from evil will and concupiscence. 'Vice is the tendency to sin; sin is the consent to that evil. Only in consent is the soul guilty of sin.'[36] Desiring something evil is not necessarily evil. It is consenting to it which constitutes sin. In the Commentary on Romans Abelard followed the Augustinian line that sin is concupiscence; in the *Ethics* it is not desire but the consent to desire which is sin. Sin always involves guilt and blame, and he anticipates present-day discussions of punishment in saying that only the responsible can be blamed. We commit mortal sin 'with study and deliberation'. Venial sin occurs through forgetfulness. It is intention which is crucial. These views are prime examples of the new emphasis on inner motivation in the twelfth century. The need for atonement, both in Anselm and Abelard, is to be located in human responsibility rather than in the devil's power. To move from a legal metaphor (satisfaction) to the impact the suffering Christ makes on the soul is entirely in accord with the new sensibility, part and parcel of which is a new stress on human responsibility in sinning, and therefore before the law.

---

33 Weingart, *Logic*, p. 177.
34 *Exp. in Epist. ad Rom.* II.v.866b.
35 *Sic et Non* 636ab.
36 Weingart, *Logic*, p. 51, whom this account follows.

When Bernard of Clairvaux (1090–1153) drew up his objections to Abelard's teaching, in his letter to Innocent II, his primary concern was Abelard's denial of the patristic theory of the defeat of the devil, a charge he could have brought more strongly still against Anselm.[37] From the beginning, defenders of Abelard noted that Bernard's attacks were ill researched.[38] Abelard does in fact speak of Christ bearing the penalty of our sins, and liberating us from the slavery of sin.[39] Bernard himself goes on to affirm a rather different idea of satisfaction from that which we find in Anselm: 'It was man who owed the debt, it was man who paid it ... as One bore the sins of all, the satisfaction of One is imputed to all. It is not that one forfeited (*forefecit*), another satisfied; the Head and body is one, viz., Christ. The Head, therefore, satisfied for the members, Christ for his children.'[40]

In addition Bernard defends a principle of vicariousness which he obviously feels Abelard denies. His appeal rests on little more than a rhetoric of equivalence, an appeal to a sort of metaphysical fair play: 'Why should not righteousness come to me from another when guilt came upon me from another? One made me a sinner, the other justifies me from sin; the one by generation, the other by his blood ... if from the one I was infected with concupiscence from my birth, by Christ spiritual grace was infused into me.'

To Abelard's questioning of the necessity of Christ's death Bernard replies:

The necessity was ours, the hard necessity of those sitting in darkness and the shadow of death. The need equally ours, and God's, and the Holy Angels. Ours that he might remove the yoke of our captivity; His own, that he might fulfil the purpose of his will; the Angels', that their number might be filled up. Further, the reason of this deed was the good pleasure of the doer. Who denies that there were ready for the Almighty other and yet other ways to redeem us, to justify us, to set us

---

[37]   *Tractatus de Erroribus* (Letter 190), *PL* 182, cols. 1058C–61B. Over half of this deals with the doctrine of redemption.

[38]   Berengar of Tours, *Apologeticus*, *PL* 178, cols. 1854–70.

[39]   'Redemptio itaque nostra est illa summa in nobis per passionem Christi dilectio, quae non solum a servitute peccati liberat, sed veram nobis filiorum Dei libertatem acquirit.' *Expositio Fidei*, *PL* 178, col. 836B.

[40]   Letter 190. The legal analogy for understanding the atonement is here quite clear: a *forisfactus* was a criminal, *forefactum* a crime, and *forisfactura* the penalty of the crime.

free? But this takes nothing from the efficacy of the one which he chose
out of many.[41]

How exactly Christ's death effects salvation, he is unclear. He
combines a number of different views. In the same sermon we
have a foreshadowing of 'acceptabilist' views of the atonement, so
that 'God the Father did not require the blood of his Son, but
nevertheless he accepted it when offered'; the statement that 'it
was not blood that he thirsted for, but salvation, for salvation was
in the blood'; and at the same time the belief that it was not death
as such that was the cause of salvation, but 'the will of him who
died by his own choice'.[42]

Throughout the twelfth century, Caroline Bynum notes, 'there
was both intense competitiveness (and sometimes virulent invec-
tive) between organized religious groups and a growing sense of
the positive value to be given to "diversity within unity"'.[43] This
competitiveness, as well as the tension between monastic and city
culture, goes far to account for Bernard's virtually pathological
attack on Abelard. Perhaps part of Abelard's problem was that he
did not sufficiently define himself by the group, certainly in the
early stages of his life.[44] For Bernard shared the 'turn to the self'
with Abelard. His Commentaries, especially that on the Song of
Songs, are steeped in erotic imagery, and love of God begins with
love of the self.

When Peter Lombard (c. 1100–60) comes to summarise the
theological situation in his *Sentences*, only ten years after the
condemnation of Abelard, he includes Abelard's position, but
omits the Anselmian notion of satisfaction entirely. He begins
with a lengthy discussion of the merit earned by Christ, which is
the heart of his understanding of redemption.[45] Just as the
discussion of satisfaction in Tertullian was transferred from the
penitent sinner to Christ, so the idea of the merit of the
deserving is now given a primarily Christological reading.

41   Letter 190.
42   Sermon 8.20.
43   Bynum, *Jesus as Mother*, p. 89.
44   See Le Goff, *Civilization*, pp. 279ff.
45   Peter Lombard, *Liber Sententiarum*, Bk III, *Dist.* 18 (Grottaferrata, S. Bonaventura,
      1971).

Christ's suffering 'earns merit' which, since he does not need it, he is able to transfer to us. On our behalf he merits the remission of eternal punishment due to sin, and by bearing our sins on the cross frees the baptised from the penalty of sin. Penance is available for sins committed in this life, and this has its validity in reference to the work of Christ. However, in answer to the question how we are delivered from sin by Christ's death he responds in a straightforwardly Abelardian way: 'Because through his death as the apostle says, "the love of God is commended to us", that is, the commendable and matchless love of God towards us appears in that he gave up his Son to death for sinners. And the pledge of so great love being thus manifest, we are both moved and fired to love God who did so great things for us; and by this we are justified, that is, made just, being delivered from our sins. Hence the death of Christ justifies us when, through it, love is kindled in our hearts.'[46] This thought is not developed, however, and he goes on to restate traditional views of the defeat of the devil, a defeat which was determined by the divine power and justice. Although he speaks of Christ bearing the punishment of our sins, he is careful to note that this did not mean that God's wrath was appeased, since God loved us in all eternity.

Unlike Abelard and Peter, both Hugh and Richard of St Victor teach the need for satisfaction. The abbey of St Victor was near Paris, and Hugh (1096–1141), an Augustinian and Platonist who wrote a commentary on Dionysius the Areopagite's *Celestial Hierarchy*, followed contemporary theology keenly. He takes up the theme of atonement in his *De Sacramentis Christianae Fidei*. According to him human beings have been tricked into subjection by the devil.[47] The devil needs to be 'brought to court', but God will not do this because 'he was still angry at man for his sin'. God then provided the solution by becoming human. Using sacrificial imagery he speaks of Christ appeasing God's wrath. 'Christ, by being born, paid man's debt to the Father, and by dying expiated man's guilt, so that, when he himself bore on man's behalf the death which he did not owe, man because of him might justly

---

[46] ibid., III.19.1.
[47] *De Sacramentis* 1.8.4, *PL* 176, cols. 307D–9C.

escape the death which he owed.'[48] Thus Christ pays our debt and expiates our guilt. God could have redeemed us in many other ways, but it was 'more appropriate to our weakness' that God should become man and 'by taking man's mortality on himself for the sake of man, should transform man for the hope of immortality'.[49] It is the incarnation rather than Christ's death which merits salvation for us. In his death Christ made a vicarious sacrifice by the substitutionary endurance of punishment according to divine justice.[50] The benefits of the passion are appropriated by the sacraments.

Hugh's pupil Richard (d. 1173) likewise teaches the need for satisfaction, partly on the grounds that without it we would have no right to forgiveness and partly because the pride of Adam needed to be balanced by the humility of Christ. Satisfaction is worked out by all three persons of the Trinity. 'The Father punishes, the Son expiates, the Spirit forgives (*ignosceret*) ... the Father demands satisfaction, the Son pays it, and the Spirit interposes between.'[51]

The twelfth century began with Anselm's assault on the patristic teaching about the ransom paid to the devil, but this belief was far too deeply implanted, and too well supported by the monastic tradition in theology, to be easily uprooted. Abelard radicalised it still further. The brevity of his allusions to the atonement is tantalising, especially given the hostility they produced in Bernard, and the notoriety they acquired later. Are his views on redemption purely the product of his own radically questioning intelligence, not prepared to take anything for granted? There is nothing in the *Historia Calamitatum* to suggest,

---

48 *De Sacramentis* 1.8.7.
49 ibid., 1.8.10.
50 ibid., 2.1.5–7.
51 *De Verbo Incarnato*, *PL* 196, cols. 1002–5: 'Divisit itaque Trinitas negotium salutus humanae, ut unam eamdemque hominis culpam Pater puniet, Filius expiavet, Spiritus Sanctus ignosceret ... Pater satisfactionem exigit, Filius exsolvit, Spiritus Sanctus se medium interposuit.' Alexander of Hales (1170–1245) also maintains that redemption is possible only through satisfaction, and satisfaction only through the passion. Objectively (*in rei natura*) Christ's death justifies us by meriting and by satisfying. Subjectively (*secundum esse quod habet in animibus*) it justifies us by love, by faith, by compassion and by leading us to imitation. It urges us to love and therefore 'to make satisfaction for our sins'. *Summa Theologiae* (Florence, Puaracchi, 1924), III.1.i–iv.

what we might otherwise like to believe, that he had learned about the radical power of love from Heloise. The new doctrine of love, beginning in Provence at this time, does not seem to have leavened atonement theology, though a century later, in the *Roman de la rose*, theological images were freely used to describe erotic love. That the inherent power of Abelard's teaching was felt is clear from the place it is given in both Peter Lombard and later in Aquinas. In its own way it lent itself, as we see from the letter to Heloise, to the passion mysticism which increasingly became the heart of Christian piety. In point of fact it is probably the origin of a very different tradition which, as Bernard feared, viewed the historical Jesus as our exemplar in the life of faith.

THE THIRTEENTH CENTURY

The period from the mid twelfth to the mid thirteenth century was one of extraordinary growth and dynamism. The tripartite model of society which Anselm knew began to dissolve under the impact of the rising merchant class, especially in the great Italian trading cities. 'Confrontation between classes, which was a basic feature of life in the countryside, soon reappeared in the towns.'[52] In this conflict the church generally sided with the oppressors. 'Since the Church was active in the world and formed a privileged social group which by the grace of God it had turned into an order, that is to say a caste, it was naturally inclined to lean towards the side where it already found itself.'[53] A pan-European economy expanded, and the humanist movement of the previous century continued to grow. At the same time, whether because of the growth of individualism, or as the shadowside of this growth and change, it also witnessed an intense concentration on suffering. This is the century of Franciscan passion mysticism, of the 'Stabat Mater' and the 'Dies Irae', and of the beginning of the flagellant guilds. A concentration on death was part of this. The popular preaching of the mendicant orders 'had made the eternal admonition to remember death swell into a sombre chorus ringing throughout

52 Le Goff, *Civilization*, p. 304.
53 ibid., p. 308.

the world'.[54] Thomas Aquinas (1225–74), one of a class of itinerant intellectuals working for the most part in either Paris or Italy, represents this mood, the spirituality of suffering, as well as the organising and synthesising trends we find in the study of law.[55]

Aquinas' *Summa Theologiae* represents the intensive theological reflection of another century beyond that of Peter Lombard, a period which includes the assimilation of Aristotle. Aquinas first discusses satisfaction under the head of guilt and punishment. He follows Augustine in defining sin as 'a word, deed or action contrary to eternal law'. Sin consists essentially in the pursuit of some passing good that is inordinately desired and consequently in the extravagant delight of possession. We can therefore say that self-love is the cause of all sin.[56] Sin is essentially located in the will: Aquinas disagrees with Abelard, who finds desire which does not lead to action innocent. On the contrary, there can perfectly well be sin without action.[57] However, a little later, Aquinas recalls Anselm more closely in speaking of sin as disturbance of order.

We live, he says, within three orders: of reason, of government, and the all-embracing order of God's rule (that the 'orders' of reason and government are analogous to divine rule is significant). 'Each one of these orders is upset by sin, since the sinner is in conflict with reason, human law and divine law. He therefore incurs a threefold punishment: one from his own being, the remorse of conscience; the second, from human authority; the third, from God.'[58] For all actual sins a debt of punishment remains. 'A sinful act makes a person punishable in that he violates the order of divine justice. He returns to that order only by some punitive restitution that restores the balance of justice.'

---

54   Huizinga, *Waning*, p. 134.
55   He is anticipated by Bonaventure (1221–74), who tells us that Christ merited salvation for us by his whole life, and still more by his death. When we consider the injury done to God, we see that no man can make satisfaction. Christ atoned for original sin and filled up by his merits what was wanting to our own partial satisfaction. Satisfaction is not *necessary*, but an atonement by the passion is the fittest means to appease the divine wrath, arouse our love and vanquish Satan. He nowhere explicitly defines satisfaction, but he views Christ's death as a work of supererogation.
56   *ST* 1a 2ae 77.5.
57   71.5.
58   1a 2ae 87.1.

Just as we pay damages to a person we have injured, so when we offend against God we submit to something 'not to our liking'. 'The stain (*macula*) of sin cannot be taken away from a person ... unless his will embraces the order of divine justice: either he spontaneously takes on himself some form of penance to atone for a past sin or he patiently bears with one imposed by God. In either case the punishment has the quality of satisfaction.'[59]

Expiation here is understood in a way congenial to Anselm as entailing the restoration of order. Punishment, the undergoing of something intrinsically unpleasant, restores order in the disordered soul. How and why punishment is supposed to do this Aquinas does not explain. In the same way, the logic behind the need for eternal punishment is that if there were no such thing 'there would be something in the universe that escaped divine order'.[60]

In his account of the satisfaction effected by Christ, Aquinas' interest is centred on understanding what role the *sufferings* of Christ play in our redemption. His first question when he turns to this topic is 'utrum necesse fuerit Christum pati pro liberatione hominum' – whether Christ had to suffer to deliver us. He goes on to the question whether Christ endured all pains and whether his passion was greater than all other pain. Unlike many later advocates of the satisfaction theory Aquinas believes that God could have chosen simply to have pardoned sin:

Justice cannot be safeguarded by the judge whose duty it is to punish crimes committed against others, e.g. against a fellow man, or the government, or the head of a government, should he dismiss a crime without punishment. But God has no one above him, for he is himself the supreme and common good of the entire universe. If then he forgives sin, which is a crime in that it is committed against him, he violates no one's rights. The man who waives satisfaction and forgives an offence done to himself acts mercifully, not unjustly.[61]

In his consideration of the incarnation the need to make satisfaction is only the fifth in a list of considerations which made the

---

[59]   1a 2ae 87.6.

[60]   II *Sent.* 42.1.5, cited in vol. XXVII (1969) of the New Blackfriars edition, ed. T. C. O'Brien (60 vols., London, Eyre & Spottiswoode), p. 23.

[61]   3a.46.2.

incarnation 'necessary'. The incarnation is necessary to instruct us, to teach us the dignity of human nature, to do away with human presumption, to combat our pride, and finally 'to rescue man from thraldom'.[62] Later he finds the efficacy of Christ's death to consist in the merit Christ won, the satisfaction he offered, his sacrifice, and his redemption. Although Christ had merits in his own person, his death had superabundant merit. He merits salvation because of what he voluntarily endured. Christ was given grace as head of the church, and if anyone in the state of grace suffers for justice's sake, he merits salvation. Moreover, his suffering also merits salvation. Suffering is not meritorious *per se*, says Aquinas, 'But in so far as a man suffers willingly, it has an inner source and so is meritorious.'[63]

Turning to satisfaction he echoes Anselm in arguing that the passion of Christ was *conveniens*, 'consonant with', both God's mercy and justice. 'With justice, because by his passion Christ made satisfaction for the sin of the human race, and man was freed through the justice of Christ. With mercy, because since man was by himself unable to satisfy for the sin of all human nature ... God gave him his Son to do so ... In so acting God manifested greater mercy than if he had forgiven sins without requiring satisfaction.'[64] The rationale of satisfaction is as follows:

A man effectively atones for an offence when he offers to the one who has been offended something which he accepts as matching or outweighing the former offence. Christ, suffering in a loving and obedient spirit, offered more to God than was demanded in recompense for all the sins of mankind, because first, the love which led him to suffer was a great love; secondly, the life he laid down in atonement was of great dignity, since it was the life of God and man; and thirdly, his suffering was all embracing and his pain so great ... Christ's passion, then, was not only sufficient but superabundant atonement for the sins of mankind.[65]

Christ's satisfaction extends to the members of his mystical body. The love of the suffering Christ more than balances the wickedness

---

[62] 3a.1, 2 *ad* 2.
[63] 3a.48.1.
[64] 3a.46.2.
[65] 3a.48.2.

of those who crucified him, though this does not mean that there will not be a hell where the wicked will suffer.

Christ's death is also described as a sacrifice, which he defines in terms of propitiation. 'Sacrifice, properly speaking, designates what men offer to God in token of the special honour due to him, and in order to appease him.'[66] Christ's flesh is the most perfect sacrifice because it is human, passible, sinless and also 'the flesh of the offerer himself'.[67] The fact that Christ suffered voluntarily meant that God was appeased ('Deus placatus est') in regard to all the offences of the human race.[68]

Finally, Christ's passion also overcomes our slavery to sin and to the devil, and breaks the debt of punishment:

As therefore Christ's passion provided adequate, and more than adequate satisfaction for man's sin and debt, his passion was as it were the price by which we are freed from both obligations. Satisfaction offered for oneself or for another resembles the price whereby one ransoms himself from sin and from punishment; it is written 'redeem your sins with alms' (Dan 4.24). Now Christ offered satisfaction, not by the giving of money or anything like that, but by giving the greatest of all things, namely himself, for us.[69]

Through sin human beings contracted obligations towards both God and the devil. They have offended God and placed themselves in the devil's power. Ransom was not paid to the devil but to God, whose justice demanded the ransom of human beings. The ransom was the blood of Christ, or, to cite Leviticus, his bodily life. Christ's passion delivers us from the debt of punishment, and from this we are delivered at baptism. If we sin after baptism we must experience some penalty or suffering. 'This punishment, which is much less than man's sin deserves, does nevertheless suffice, because Christ's satisfaction works along with it.'[70] Christ's satisfaction brings about its effect in us in so far as we are incorporated into him as members are into the head.

The reference to 'superabundant' atonement introduces the Abelardian theme: because God chose to redeem us through

---

[66] 3a.48.3.
[67] ibid.
[68] 3a.49.4.
[69] 3.48.4.
[70] 3.49.3.

Christ's passion many things pertain to us over and above our liberation from sin and these chiefly consist in our being moved to love God and live a better life by the passion.[71] It follows that Christ's satisfaction does not extend indiscriminately to all people but specifically to all members of the church, because he is the head and they the members. To be a member of the church is to be one who is moved to love God through the passion.[72]

SUFFERING, LAW AND ATONEMENT IN THE MIDDLE AGES

In arguing for the importance of human equality for legal systems H. L. A. Hart draws a picture of a situation which so closely resembles that of the early Middle Ages that it deserves quoting at length. 'If some men were vastly more powerful than others', he writes, 'and so not dependent on their forbearance, the strength of the malefactors might exceed that of the supporters of law and order.'

In these circumstances instead of social life being based on a system of mutual forbearances, with force used only intermittently against a minority of malefactors, the only viable system would be one in which the weak submitted to the strong on the best terms they could make and lived under their 'protection'. This, because of the scarcity of resources, would lead to a number of conflicting power centres, each grouped round its 'strong man'.[73]

This was precisely the situation both rulers and peasants faced during the twelfth and thirteenth centuries, and the development of law was the way of dealing with it. This, perhaps, accounts for the excitement generated by the rediscovery of Roman law in

---

[71] 3a.46.3.

[72] In Aquinas' greatest successor amongst the Schoolmen, Duns Scotus (1264–1308), redemption rests on God's free will. He disputes Anselm's proof of the 'necessity' of a God-Man. God could have saved us through an angel or a mere man had he so chosen. It is simply a given that he chose to save us in this way. *Comm. in Sententiarum, Lib.* III, *Dist.* 20, *Qu.* 1, *Sect.* 10. He likewise denies that sin against an infinite being is itself infinite, since the idea of an infinite evil is incoherent. *Comm. in Sententiarum, Lib.* III, *Dist.* 19, *Qu.* 1, *Sect.* 13. God chooses to save us through recognition of the merit of Christ, and what establishes merit is nothing intrinsic in a deed or deeds but simply the will of the one giving the reward. The value of Christ's death is as high as God chooses to rate it.

[73] H. L. A. Hart, *The Concept of Law* (Oxford, Clarendon Press, 1961), p. 194.

Bologna. 'From every corner of western Europe students flocked to Bologna. It was as if a new gospel had been revealed. Before the end of the century complaints were loud that theology was neglected ... that men would learn law and nothing but law.'[74] England shared this new-found enthusiasm. The first codification of English law, by Glanville, was published just before the death of Henry II, possibly in 1188.[75] Most signally the system of commutations which provided the root metaphor for satisfaction gave place either to fines or the death penalty. In 1115, by the law of Henry I, 'an agreement supersedes the law and an amiable settlement a court judgement'. By the time Chaucer was writing, under Richard II, this was very much in abeyance. The theologians, Abelard prominent amongst them, distinguish between *criminalia*, serious sins committed wilfully and knowingly, and *venialia aut levia*, sins which can be dealt with by confession and penance.[76] This led to the distinction between offences which were *mala in se* and those which were merely *mala prohibita*. The former kind of offence demanded atonement to God as well as others. From the church practice of penance, it has been claimed, came rituals of public shaming, like the stocks and the pillory, with excommunication reserved for the gravest offences.[77] All over Europe, though less in England than elsewhere, local and family-based law gave way to statutory law, 'which emphasized the *res publica* of jurists more than the common good of social philosophers'. This change has justly been described as 'a legal revolution', in which crime came to be defined as categorically different from other wrongs, deserving of special procedures in which punishment was the normal outcome.[78] The state was beginning to arise with its own legal personality, assuming the responsibility, and finally the monopoly, of response to crime. Thomas Aquinas' analysis of the nature of positive law 'in effect

[74] F. Pollock and F. W. Maitland, *The History of English Law before the Time of Edward I* (Cambridge, Cambridge University Press, 1895), vol. I, p. 89.

[75] ibid., p. 144, where the question of whether Glanville was the actual author is also discussed.

[76] Abelard, *Ethics, Petri Abelardi Opera*, ed. V. Cousin (Paris, 1859), vol. II, p. 621.

[77] J. A. Sharpe, *Judicial Punishment in England* (London, Faber, 1990), pp. 22–3.

[78] Howard Zehr, in *Respect in Prison*, Proceedings of a Conference held at Lincoln, July 1991.

writes the first charter for the new class of its servants'.[79] In England Bracton's great work, 'the crown and flower of English medieval jurisprudence', was written between 1250 and 1258. These developments function to distinguish punishment from the arbitrary exercise of power and blood feuds, and are an important part of the 'civilising process'. How are we to understand them in relation to what was going on in theology and piety?

In seeking an answer to this question we need to bear in mind David Garland's remark about the incorrigible complexity and overdetermination of the cultural realm. On the one hand there are profound intellectual changes which we might describe in terms of growing rationalisation, reflected in the growth of statute law. For this development theologians like Aquinas provided the jurisprudential foundations. Justifying the need to obey the sovereign was a key concern in the thirteenth century, when anarchy and lawlessness was a perpetual problem. Unlike his predecessors, Aquinas regards the state as a natural, not a conventional institution, a positive good rather than a bulwark against sin.[80] He roots all truly human behaviour in that natural law which reflects the eternal law, and which legislators seek to express in positive laws. To this extent, in a rather different way from Anselm's, the satisfaction made by Christ is an expression of the eternal law, which lays down that all sin or crime must be punished. The key element is the analogy between the rule of reason, government and God's kingdom. By virtue of this analogy the punishment meted out by the state in the maintenance of law and order is metaphysically justified. The church, said Huizinga, had inculcated gentleness and clemency, and tried, in that way, to soften judicial morals.

On the other hand, in adding to the primitive need of retribution the horror of sin it had, to a certain extent, stimulated the sentiment of justice. And sin, to violent and impulsive spirits, was only too frequently another name for what their enemies did. The barbarous idea of retaliation was reinforced by fanaticism. The chronic insecurity made

[79] *Summa Theologiae*, New Blackfriars edition, vol. xxviii, ed. Thomas Gilby (London, Eyre & Spottiswoode, 1966), p. xxiv.

[80] A. J. and R. W. Carlyle, *History of Medieval Political Theory in the West* (Edinburgh, 1909), vol. v, chap. 2.

the greatest possible severity on the part of the public authorities desirable; crime came to be regarded as a menace to order and society, as well as an insult to the divine majesty. Thus it was natural that the late Middle Ages should become the special period of judicial cruelty. That the criminal deserved his punishment was not doubted for a moment.[81]

Changes in sensibility, Huizinga is saying, had a sort of 'double effect' in which the result was not, as we might expect, the growth of a culture of mercy, but increasing legal savagery. Perhaps, however, if we understood the impact of satisfaction theory and intense concentration on the passion properly we should not be so surprised. Might not such passion mysticism be the obverse of the brutality which characterised the period? Do we not learn, from the paintings of Hieronymus Bosch, that they were two sides of the same coin? In other words, did the structure of affect engendered by these developments not lead, for some centuries, to a more straightforwardly punitive attitude to offenders? To be sure we find in Abelard, and flowing from him right through the Middle Ages, a strong current in another direction, but it takes centuries before it produces significant changes in penal practice. Pieter Spierenberg, in *The Spectacle of Suffering*, relates more humane treatment of offenders to a long-term transformation of sensibilities which is linked with the consolidation of strong states which can effectively impose law and order. His concern is with the seventeenth century, but we find the origins of these develop-ments in the period we have had under review. Changes in sensibility first remarked in twelfth-century France, amongst others in Abelard, are a tiny trickle which becomes a flood only five or six centuries later. It is to that period, beginning with the Reformation, that we now turn.

[81]   Huizinga, *Waning*, p. 22.

CHAPTER 6

Three angry letters in a book

He died so that the penalty owed by us might be discharged, and he might exempt us from it. But since we all, because we are sinners, were offensive to the judgement of God, in order to stand in our stead, he desired to be arraigned before an earthly judge, and to be condemned by his mouth, so that we might be acquitted before the heavenly tribunal of God.

Genevan catechism

No clear date can be assigned to mark the divide between the medieval and the modern world. Many supposedly crucial markers of the new period, such as naturalism in art, can be found in the mid thirteenth century, and not only in Italy.[1] Nevertheless, profound cultural, political and religious changes marking off the fifteenth and sixteenth centuries can scarcely be denied. Such changes were gradual and uneven, more complete in one place or area than in another, but those in the fifteenth and sixteenth centuries who sensed a decisive quickening in the pace of change were not wrong.[2]

Perhaps the single most important change was the growth of the nation state, henceforth the framework for all forms of cultural and political development. Beginning in France, the rulers of Europe slowly gained control over internal enemies and secured their frontiers. In some countries, such as Germany and

[1]   See G. Holmes, *Florence, Rome and the Origins of the Renaissance* (Oxford, Clarendon Press, 1986).

[2]   In the following paragraphs I follow especially S. Ozment, *The Age of Reform, 1250–1550* (New Haven and London, Yale University Press, 1980); H. Grimm, *The Reformation Era* (New York, Macmillan, 1954); R. Pascal, *The Social Basis of the German Reformation* (London, Watts, 1933).

Italy, this happened regionally rather than nationally. This new political configuration was the salvation of Protestantism, which could have been crushed had the Catholic states acted together.[3] The independence from the papacy achieved by Protestant countries was the radicalisation of a movement long in process, in which, in most of the countries of Europe, the Pope's right to appoint senior clerics had been ceded to national monarchies. Marsiglio of Padua's *Defensor Pacis*, which championed secular power, was written in 1324. In sixteenth-century England Thomas Cromwell paid for a printed translation of it, and the staunch Catholic Stephen Gardiner reproduced its arguments for a national church not under papal control. National churches effectively replaced dreams of a universal church, even in Catholic countries. In the seventeenth century, Cardinal Richelieu was prepared to aid the Lutheran Gustavus Adolphus if he saw it to be to the advantage of France.

Fuelling the consolidation of new political realities were profound economic changes of the greatest importance. Merchant capital has its origins in eleventh-century Italy, but the devastating plagues of the fourteenth century had retarded economic development. As trade shifted from the Mediterranean to the Atlantic seaboard, and as towns grew, so investment and industry developed.[4] The expansion of commercial activity has been traced to technical improvements in ship building; new facilities for credit and insurance; and the creation of joint stock companies. The Muscovy Company was founded in 1553, and the most successful of all, the East India Company, in 1600.[5] A money economy grew up, with rulers increasingly dependent on borrowing, and on new taxes. With the money economy came inflation, blamed on the influx of South American gold and silver by Jean Bodin in 1568.[6] The population of Europe grew steadily throughout the fifteenth and sixteenth centuries, and towns and cities attained a

[3]   H. A. L. Fisher, *A History of Europe* (2 vols., London, Longmans, 1935), vol. 1, p. 447.
[4]   The development of sea trade was in part due to the fall of Constantinople in 1453, and the closure of overland trading routes. Advances in seamanship, such as learning to tack and the invention of a reliable compass, were also crucial.
[5]   See H. Kamen, *European Society 1500–1700* (London, Hutchinson, 1984), pp. 77ff.
[6]   For inflation see R. Ehrenberg, *Capital and Finance in the Age of the Renaissance*, tr. H. Lucas (New York, Cape, 1928); Kamen, *European Society*, pp. 52ff.

new importance. The Reformation, it has been claimed, was primarily an urban phenomenon, with the countryside proving resistant to change.[7] In the towns a wealthy merchant class established itself, opposed by an urban proletariat which provided the raw material for radical groups such as the Levellers and Diggers. Merchants, and the landed gentry, slowly began to rise over against the great feudal families, leading to new configurations of political power such as the Parliaments of Elizabeth I.

Changes in sensibility are probably most easily noted through art. The change in perceptions of the human person which began in the twelfth century evidences a decisive shift in the third and fourth decades of the fifteenth century, and is clear for all to see in the portraits of the early decades of the next century, for example those by Holbein. This period saw the advent not only of printed books but of oil painting, wood cuts and copperplate. There was a conscious break with the artistic past, a repudiation of tradition, expressed particularly by Vasari's criticism of Gothic.[8] Religious drama gave over, astonishingly quickly, to the maturity of Shakespeare, and the sonnets of Petrarch to the love poetry of John Donne. Aspects of the old honour society remained, and were to remain in vestigial form into the nineteenth century, but were at the same time parodied by writers like Shakespeare and Cervantes. What took its place is the political absolutism advocated by Machiavelli, on the one hand, and the development of contract theory, already implicit in Roman law and advocated by Marsiglio of Padua, on the other.

With the rise of the nation state the process of transferring judicial power from the local community to officers of the state was hastened. As we have seen, community law had, by and large, been reconciliatory and compensation-based, whereas state law relied more on punitive justice.[9] According to the most famous thesis on penal theory in recent times, the beginning of

---

[7] B. Moeller, *Imperial Cities and the Reformation*, tr. H. Midelfort and M. Edwards (Philadelphia, Fortress, 1972).

[8] See P. Burke, *Culture and Society in Renaissance Italy* (London, Batsford, 1972).

[9] See B. Lenman and G. Parker, 'The State, the Community and Criminal Law in Early Modern Europe', in V. A. C. Gatrell, B. Lenman and G. Parker, *Crime and the Law: The Social History of Crime in Western Europe Since 1500* (London, Europa, 1980), p. 23.

the modern regime of imprisonment was the founding of the Rasphuis in Amsterdam in 1596.[10] Foucault traces a move from spectacles of torture to the penitentiary, and understands it in terms of a shift in the exercise of power. Rusche and Kirchheimer, on the other hand, saw this development as a way of exploiting the labour of prisoners. Instead of the mass hangings of Henry VIII's reign, beggary was dealt with by compelling the poor to work. The growth of the workhouse, therefore, is part of the development of capitalism.[11] Nevertheless, throughout the sixteenth and seventeenth centuries judicial spectacle played a prominent part, and crime and dissent were punished savagely, albeit erratically, by mutilation, burning and hanging. Levels of public safety were low, and violent quarrels common. Society in general tolerated the open infliction of pain, especially on criminals. Judicial spectacles relied for their efficacy on the participation of spectators who might, on occasion, stone a victim in the pillory to death.[12] The rise of vagabondage throughout Europe, whose causes were not understood, was characterised by especially harsh punishments, and by the attempts to coerce people into various forms of 'useful labour'.[13] Religious changes also played their part, as witnessed by the progressive harshening of the criminal code in Tudor England. 'The heightened sensibilities about human propensities to wickedness inherent in protestant theology made the godly rulers of protestant England very sensitive to law and order issues.'[14]

These political, economic and cultural changes coincided with a revision of priorities as to lay and spiritual life. Luther's doctrine of vocation, which held that God could as well be

[10]   M. Foucault, *Discipline and Punish*, tr. A. Sheridan (Harmondsworth, Penguin 1977). The Rasphuis is anticipated by the London Bridewell, opened in 1555.

[11]   G. Rusche and O. Kirchheimer, *Punishment and Social Structure*, tr. M. Finkelstein (henceforth *PSS*) (Columbia, University of Columbia Press, 1938), chap. 2.

[12]   See J. M. Beattie, 'Violence and Society in Early Modern England', in A. Doob and E. Greenspan (eds.), *Perspectives in Criminal Law* (Aurora, Ont., Canada Law Books, 1985). But see also P. Spierenburg, *The Spectacle of Suffering: Executions and the Evolution of Repression* (Cambridge, Cambridge University Press, 1984), who finds the origins of the transformation of public sentiment towards violence in this period.

[13]   See Rusche and Kirchheimer, *PSS*, p. 12; A. L. Beier, *Masterless Men: The Vagrancy Problem in Britain, 1560–1640* (London, Methuen, 1985).

[14]   J. A. Sharpe, *Judicial Punishment in England* (London, Faber, 1990), p. 27.

served in secular as in spiritual life, articulated social and
political realities already well established by 1520. The centre of
religious life shifted dramatically. In the course of the sixteenth
century the monastery, which lay at the heart of Anselm's
religious vision, was in many places dissolved. In place of a
clerical hegemony of learning, and the predominance of Latin,
we have the rise of the vernacular and of secular schools. In
the second half of the fifteenth century, with astonishing speed,
printing spread throughout Europe, so that where, at the
beginning of the century, the repository of human wisdom and
learning was contained in some thousands of handwritten
manuscripts, by its close there were already perhaps six million
books in Europe. It is estimated that half of these were on
religious topics, but after 1530 the proportion of secular titles
grew. The thirst for books sprang from the spread of lay
education, and the increase in the number of universities and
colleges from the beginning of the fourteenth century onwards.
This development was part and parcel of a changed attitude to
learning, in which science and free enquiry took the place of
recourse to authority. The trial of Galileo, in 1633, was a
symbolic marker of tension between the two approaches. With
the advent of printing vernacular bibles could no longer be
prohibited, and the 'Index of Forbidden Books' was only of
limited usefulness.

Religion is by nature conservative, and the reform was no
revolution. Even the Anabaptists preserved much continuity
with the 'heretics' of the medieval church, and especially with
fifteenth-century Hussites. Such a continuity is found in theological doctrine and yet, as we would expect, here too there was
something more than a sea change. The most dramatic of all
reforms in the Western church so far began with someone who
represents almost paradigmatically the bridge between old and
new, Martin Luther – a monk into middle age, and then
married and a family man; trained in Scholasticism, but
leading the way into a new style of theologising around
Scripture; embodying many of the aspects of humanism, but
engaging in bitter polemics with Erasmus about the freedom of
the will.

LUTHER

'Quick, head off, away with it, in order that the earth does not become full of the ungodly.' The voice is distinctly Martin Luther's. Rulers are the ministers of God's wrath, Luther insisted, whose duty it is to use the sword against offenders. They are 'God's hangmen'. Notoriously, at the time of the Peasants' War he advocated the maximum use of force, but usually took a more moderate line. Where punishment is given too wide a scope, he believed, intolerable and terrible injury follows, but injury is also inevitable when it is restricted too narrowly. 'To err in this direction, however, and punish too little is more tolerable, for it is always better to let a scoundrel live than to put a godly man to death. The world has plenty of scoundrels anyway and must continue to have them, but godly men are scarce.'[15] How do such views relate to his theology of atonement?

Preaching in 1543 Luther remarked that 'When I became a doctor, I did not yet know that we cannot make satisfaction for our sins.'[16] This famous remark shows us that before his 'breakthrough' Luther thought of satisfaction, like the Fathers and many of the Schoolmen, as the work of penance we needed to do by way of atonement. His new start was simply a radical rediscovery of what Anselm and Aquinas already knew: that Christ 'makes satisfaction for us'. But how important was the idea of satisfaction for him? His interpreters do not agree. Gustaf Aulen believed that what he called the 'Christus Victor' theory of Christ's defeat of the devil was the heart of Luther's atonement theology and gave the theology of satisfaction a place on the sidelines.[17] Philip Watson agrees and insists that 'Luther leaves us in no doubt that he does not like the term satisfaction.'[18] Notoriously unsystematic as he is, this is nevertheless not a

---

[15] 'Von weltlicher uberkeytt wie weytt man yhr gehorsam schuldig sey', *WA* XI. 245–80, tr. in *LW* XLV.104.

[16] *WA* XLV.86.18: 'Si pecco, ergo oportet me satisfacere. Sic amitto Christum salvatorem et consolatorem et facio ein stockmeister und hencker aus im uber mein arm seele, quasi non satis iudicii in me latum in paradiso. Iterum acquisivimus lucem. Sed ego, cum Doctor fierem, nescivi.'

[17] G. Aulen, *Christus Victor*, tr. A. G. Hebert (London, SPCK, 1932).

[18] P. S. Watson, *Let God be God!* (London, Epworth, 1947), p. 120. Unfortunately he gives us no references to substantiate this assertion.

reading of Luther we can follow. For when he criticises satisfaction theory, it is on the grounds that it does not go far enough:
the term, he says, does not sufficiently honour Christ's sufferings.
Death in itself was not enough, but Christ made satisfaction by
undergoing all the torments of a guilty conscience. It is the fact
that Christ suffers the *punishment* due to sin which is crucial.[19] He
insists that God's righteousness must be satisfied: 'Although God
purely out of grace does not impute our sins to us, still he did not
want to do this unless his law and his righteousness had received a
more than adequate satisfaction. This gracious imputation must
first be purchased and won from his righteousness for us.' Christ
makes satisfaction both by fulfilling the will of God in the law and
suffering the punishment for sin, the wrath of God. Christ stands
under God's wrath and suffers it in his passion, in so doing
'paying God'. Nevertheless, to present Luther as *nothing but* a
protagonist of satisfaction theory does violence to the complexity
of his theology. This is nowhere better stated than in the *locus
classicus* of Luther's atonement theology, his exposition of Gal.
3.13 ('Christ was made a curse for us') in the 1535 commentary.[20]
In the first place what the medieval poets spoke of as the 'blessed
exchange' is the very heart of Luther's understanding. He
expresses it in his incomparably vivid way:

Christ took all our sins upon Himself, and for them He died on the cross
... And all the prophets saw this, that Christ was to become the greatest
thief, murderer, adulterer, robber, desecrator, blasphemer etc. there has
ever been anywhere in the world. He is not acting in His own Person
now. Now he is not the Son of God, born of the Virgin. But he is a
sinner, who has and bears the sin of Paul, the former blasphemer,
persecutor and assaulter; of Peter, who denied Christ; of David, who
was an adulterer and murderer ... In short, He has and bears all the

[19] *WA* xxi.264: Sermon on Easter Tuesday. Crucigers Sommerpostille. 'Und ob man
gleich das Wort Gnugthuung wolt behalten und dahin deuten, das Christus hat fur
unser Sünde gnug gethan, So ist es doch zu schwach und zu wenig von der Gnade
Christi geredt, und das Leiden Christi nicht gnug geehret, welchem man mus hoher
ehre geben, das er nicht allein fur di Sünde gnug gethan, sondern uns auch erloset
von des Tods, Teuffels und der Hellen gewalt und ein ewig Reich der Gnaden und
teglicher vergebung auch der ubrigen sunde, so in uns ist, bestetigt, und also uns
worden (wie S Paulus 1 Cor 2 sagt) ein ewige Erlösung und Heiligung, Wie davon
droben weiter gesagt ist.'
[20] *WA* xl; *LW* xxvi.

sins of all men in his body, – not in the sense that he has committed them but in the sense that he took these sins, committed by us, upon his own body, in order to make satisfaction for them with his own blood.

This 'wonderful exchange' (*mirabilis translaccio*) is, Luther says again and again, the most delightful comfort, 'the most joyous of all doctrines', 'the adorable mysteries of Scripture, the true cabala'. In a swipe at an 'Abelardian' view he maintains that 'the sophists', his Scholastic teachers, deprive people of this comfort 'when they segregate Christ from sins and sinners and set him forth to us as an example to be imitated'. Only exchange will do: exemplarism is worse than useless.

In this way they make Christ not only useless to us but also a judge and a tyrant who is angry because of our sins and who damns sinners ... Whatever sins I, you, and all of us have committed or may commit in the future, they are as much Christ's own as if he had committed them. In short, our sin must be Christ's own sin or we shall perish eternally.[21]

At the same time Abelard's corrective is honoured, for it is only 'to the extent that Christ rules by his grace in the hearts of the faithful' that there is no sin or death or curse.

Bound up with the theology of exchange is, as Aulen rightly pointed out, much language about the defeat of the devil.

Righteousness is eternal, immortal and invincible. Sin, too, is a very powerful and cruel tyrant, dominating and ruling over the whole world, capturing and enslaving all men. In short, sin is a great and powerful god who devours the whole human race, all the learned, holy, powerful, wise and unlearned men. He, I say, attacks Christ and wants to devour him as he has devoured all the rest. But he does not see that he is a person of invincible and eternal righteousness. In this duel, therefore, it is necessary for sin to be conquered and killed, and for righteousness to prevail and live.[22]

But what is it that is overcome? Here and there echoes of the old patristic theme are found: 'when, inside our mask, he was

---

[21] Cf. *WA* XXXI.2.339 on Isa. 43.24: 'Haec est mirabilis translaccio: quod nos facere debemus, et labor et peccatum hoc facit et laborant Christus ... Alius peccavit, aliusperson tulit. Ergo omnes sectare iusticiariae huic doctrinae contrariantur. Non si ipsi suis operibus penam luunt, frustra est Christi satisfacere sua manu. Peccave non satisfacit. Satisfaciens non peccat. Mirabilis est doctrina.'

[22] *LW* XXVI.281.

carrying the sin of the whole world, he was captured, he suffered, he was crucified, he died ... but because he was a divine and eternal person, it was impossible for death to hold him'.[23] Much more profound is Luther's own unique voice: 'the curse, which is divine wrath against the whole world, has the same conflict with the blessing, that is, with the eternal grace and mercy of God in Christ'.[24] This is a radical restatement of earlier patristic theories. Here we come across Luther's daring image of 'God against God', God's *opus proprium* of grace and mercy overcoming his *opus alienum* of judgement and damnation.

Though Luther speaks again and again of God's wrath being overcome, and means it (as opposed to indulging in rhetorical flourish), his doctrine cannot be described as a form of the 'penal theory'. Legal analogies, which are frequent enough, occupy a completely subsidiary position in his theology. The significance of the law, he tells us, is that it establishes guilt by association. 'Thus a magistrate regards someone as a criminal and punishes him if he catches him among thieves, even though he has never committed anything evil or worthy of death. Christ was not only found among sinners: but of his own free will and by the will of the Father he wanted to be an associate of sinners.' Christ 'violated the general law' (of Deuteronomy 27) for us, and 'all other laws as well'.[25]

In the course of the exposition the core of Anselm's argument for the incarnation and crucifixion is turned upside down. It is not that we learn *a priori*, *remoto Christo*, that God's justice and mercy demand an incarnation. We learn, rather, from the effects of redemption, of Christ's godhead. Arianism will not do, because 'to conquer the sin of the world, death, the curse, and the wrath of God in himself – this is the work, not of any creature but of the divine power. Therefore it was necessary that He who was to conquer these in himself should be true God by nature.'[26] As Luther's disciple Melanchthon put it in a famous phrase, 'to know Christ is to know his saving benefits'.

23 ibid., XXVI.284.
24 ibid., XXVI.281.
25 ibid., XXVI.288.
26 ibid., XXVI.282.

Again Anselm's idea of the superabundance of Christ's merit finds drastic restatement. By Christ's death on the cross, says Luther, 'the whole world is purged and expiated from all sins'. God the Father is as it were dazzled by what Christ has done: 'if any remnants of sin were to remain, still for the sake of Christ, the shining Sun, God would not notice them'.[27]

It is altogether misleading, therefore, to speak of Luther's theology of atonement as a variant of the satisfaction theory. The language of satisfaction is rather bent to a new purpose, to speak of the complete exchange made in Christ, whereby he once and for all takes our place. Luther does not shrink from the implications of these assertions. When we look at the church we are not inclined to believe that sins have been done away with once and for all, but, says Luther, 'I deny the conclusion.' 'If I look at Christ, who is the Propitiator and cleanser of the church, then it is completely holy; for he bore the sins of the entire world. Therefore where sins are noticed and felt, there they really are not present.'[28]

To the extent that Luther's account of the atonement can be understood as a response to his own *Anfechtungen*, the 'temptations' to despair which beset him, it can perhaps be understood as signalling another decisive shift in the 'turn to the individual' which we also find at the beginning of the sixteenth century. The drama of his account is, as it were, the theological correlate of the Renaissance portrait. However, we also need to read it together with his political doctrine of the separation of powers. Luther believed, like his predecessors, that the state was under God, for it was the instrument of God's providence, but he sought to avoid the confusion of church and state which he saw in a corrupt papacy. 'God has established two kinds of government among men: the one is spiritual: it has no sword but it has the Word by which men ... may attain everlasting life. The other is Worldly government through the sword which aims to keep peace among men and this he rewards with temporal blessing.'[29] The practical effect of this separation of powers is clear. 'God's

---

[27]   ibid., xxvi.280.
[28]   ibid., xxvi.285.
[29]   *Works of Martin Luther* (Philadelphia, Muhlenberg Press, 1943), 5.39.

kingdom is a kingdom of Grace and mercy, not wrath and severity, but the kingdom of the world is a kingdom of wrath and of severity ... now he who would confuse these two kingdoms ... as our fanatics do, would put wrath into God's kingdom and mercy into the world's kingdom.'[30] It was such a separation which enabled him to view magistrates as 'God's Hangmen'. In his notorious tract against the peasants, during the peasant revolt of 1525, he repeatedly appeals to Romans 13: 'the powers that be are ordained of God'. Such an appeal, which gave the strongest possible theological support to the status quo, was disastrous then and even more disastrous later, when it disabled the German church in its struggle against Hitler.[31] It is at least suggestive that the Ninety-Five Theses and Machiavelli's *Il Principe* both appeared in the same year. Both Luther's (admittedly later) political doctrine and Machiavelli allow for a degree of *realpolitik* which would have been impossible for Anselm's undivided world. The other side of that coin was the possibility of understanding faith as concerned with 'spiritual' issues occupying a separate realm from the secular. That separation of powers which could be cogently advocated by Marsiglio of Padua, against the claims of an overweening papacy, or by Luther, against fanatical theocrats, ended by disabling the possibility of a radical theological critique of secular government or penal practice.

CALVIN

Though Calvin claimed Luther as his teacher, his background was very different. He is a Renaissance new man, where Luther is still a man of the Middle Ages. Despite the fact that his crucial work was done in Geneva, the imaginative construal at the heart of his theology is in terms of the Absolute Monarch, whose power had been theorised by Machiavelli. It is in this way that he fundamentally conceives of God.

'All of us', writes Calvin, 'have that within us which deserves the hatred of God.' 'For seeing no man can descend into himself,

---

[30] ibid., 4.265.
[31] See U. Duchrow, *Global Economy: A Confessional Issue for the Churches?* (Geneva, WCC, 1987), pp. 8ff. Duchrow defends Luther against later Lutheranism.

and seriously consider what he is, without feeling that God is angry and at enmity with him, and therefore anxiously longing for the means of regaining his favour (this cannot be without satisfaction), the certainty here required is of no ordinary description, – sinners, until freed from guilt, being always liable to the wrath and curse of God, who, as he is a just judge, cannot permit his law to be violated with impunity, but is armed for vengeance.'[32]

Formally, Calvin's theology of the atonement is many-sided. In fact its energy and force is to be found in the conviction of guilt, and therefore of certain punishment, expressed so vividly in the previous passage, which Calvin found support for in countless passages of the New Testament. He would himself doubtless have argued that he began with Scripture, and developed his theology from there, but the psychological energy of the depictions of God's wrath suggests sources which are more than intellectual.

He addresses Anselm's question (without, however, mentioning Anselm) in the course of his exposition of Christology. It 'behoved' Christ to become man to perform the office of Mediator. Even without sin a mediator would have been needed to mediate between the divine and the human. This was *a fortiori* necessary given that humankind had sinned.[33] But he immediately goes on: 'Another principal part of our reconciliation with God was, that man, who had lost himself by his disobedience, should by way of remedy, oppose to it obedience, satisfy the justice of God, and pay the penalty of sin.' With Scotus he believed that redemption had no necessity about it but 'flowed from the divine decree'; against him he believes that the incarnation is ordered solely to redemption. It was only on account of sin that Christ became human.[34]

His most original contribution to atonement theology is his exposition of the three offices, which, he rightly observes, 'are spoken of in the Papacy, but frigidly, and with no great benefit, the full meaning comprehended under each title not being

---

[32] *Inst.* II.16.1. I use the translation of H. Beveridge (Grand Rapids, Mich., Eerdmans, 1975).

[33] II.12.2.

[34] II.12.4.

understood'.[35] As prophet Christ is, of course, our teacher, and the gift of the Spirit bestowed on him persists through time, so that 'efficacy of the Spirit' always accompanies the preaching of the gospel. The kingly office refers to Christ's promise of eternal life, for here 'our condition is bitter and wretched'.[36] In words which became the model for countless prison sermons he assures us that the promise of the kingdom 'raises us even to eternal life, so that we can patiently live at present under toil, hunger, cold, contempt, disgrace, and other annoyances'. The exposition really comes alive, however, when he turns to the Priestly office:

Because a deserved curse obstructs the entrance (to heaven), and God in his character of Judge is hostile to us, expiation must necessarily intervene, that as a priest employed to appease the wrath of God, he may reinstate us in his favour.[37]

Calvin is not mealy mouthed about propitiation and appeasement. The only end Scripture assigns to the Son of God, he tells us, is to propitiate the Father by becoming a victim.[38] Scripture tells us that God was our enemy until we were restored to life by Christ's death, and our sins were expiated by sacrifice. This needs to be stressed, for 'Were it not said in clear terms, that Divine wrath, and vengeance, and eternal death, lay upon us, we should be less sensible of our wretchedness without the mercy of God.'[39] Christ took our punishment upon himself, bore the just judgement of God, and by his expiation satisfied and propitiated God. By nature we are the children of hell. This status is changed by the whole course of Christ's obedience, but particularly by his death. Trembling consciences 'find no rest without sacrifice and ablution by which sins are expiated'. For this end only death under the law would do. Had Christ been cut off by assassins or in a riot, no satisfaction would have ensued, 'But when he is placed as a criminal at the bar, where witnesses are brought to give evidence against him, and the mouth of the judge condemns him to die, we see him sustaining the character of an offender and

35 II.15.1.
36 II.15.4.
37 II.15.6.
38 II.12.4.
39 II.16.2.

evil doer ... Our acquittal is in this – that the guilt which made us liable to punishment was transferred to the head of the Son of God (Is 53.12). We must specially remember this substitution in order that we may not be all our lives in trepidation and anxiety, as if the just vengeance, which the Son of God transferred to himself, were still impending over us.'[40] We note here how central the legal metaphor is to Calvin's discourse of redemption.

Calvin's doctrine of Scripture, which does not privilege the New above the Old Testament, facilitates the coalescence of legal and sacrificial themes. The Old Testament language about sacrifice, he argues, sufficiently shows that propitiation and appeasement must be made in this way. 'Mention is always made of blood whenever Scripture explains the mode of redemption.'[41] For Calvin the need for blood to make expiation has the force of a principle. Sacrifice was taken out of its cultic context and reinterpreted within a penal one. 'The offering of a priestly sacrifice is regarded as the equivalent of presenting a satisfaction to an offended judge. The ordering of ceremonial for worship is given an absolute legal validity. And blood shedding as a sacrificial symbol becomes associated with blood-shedding as the direct outcome of capital punishment.'[42] The way is thereby prepared for understanding the procession to Tyburn in terms of expiatory sacrifice.

The differences from Anselm's classical statement of the satisfaction theory are once again clear. Where the restoration of order is central for Anselm, it is the vindication of the law, which stems from the righteousness which is God's own being, which matters for Calvin. For Anselm the background is feudal law and the church system of penance; for Calvin it is the criminal law. Where Anselm conceives sin as failing to render God his due, for Calvin the point is that God has given us the law, which we have defied, thus meriting eternal death. In Anselm Christ pays our debts; in Calvin he bears our punishment. In the foreground is human sin, and the divine wrath it

---

[40] II.16.5.
[41] II.16.6.
[42] F. W. Dillistone, *The Christian Understanding of the Atonement* (London, SCM, 1968), p. 199.

incurs. Only a substitutionary and propitiatory death can possibly meet this.

Wherever Calvinism spread, punitive sentencing followed. Scottish courts burned to death persons condemned for sodomy and bestiality, 'on the authority of Leviticus alone'. Legislation moved freely from the Old Testament to the statute book.[43] In these societies sin and crime were, for more than a century, identical, and furthermore all sins could be regarded as equally damnable in the eyes of God. In seventeenth-century Massachusetts criminals were understood and addressed through the categories of Protestant theology. 'Individual offenders were viewed as sinners whose evil actions bore witness to an individual failure of will but also to the wretchedness of the human condition.' The sinner-offender was 'a kind of Protestant Everyman, a living example of the potential for evil which lies in every heart and against which every soul must be vigilant'.[44]

The perennial power of this theology lies in its acute targeting and insistence on guilt, and its provision of a complete remedy. This avails only for the elect, but the force of Calvinism precisely was, as Weber argued, to prove to oneself that one was of their number. Both Weber and Troeltsch noted the way in which the Calvinist believer finds himself (characteristically, rather than herself), alone with his God. For all the emphasis on revelation Calvin is profoundly rationalist. He represents a religious revolution in which 'The feelings of sin and guilt to which a hostile and uncontrollable environment gave rise were no longer purged communally by ceremonies and scapegoats.' Instead, they were internalised, and this generated the driving moral energy and sense of individual responsibility which alone made it possible to begin to control that environment. 'Puritan self-accusations, the Puritan sense of guilt, were part of the price paid for a more rational and scientific view of the universe.'[45] Although Calvinism

---

[43]   Lenman and Parker, 'State, Community and Criminal Law', p. 37. In 1696 the Scots
      Parliament passed ten statutes condemning blasphemy and swearing and fifteen
      concerning sabbath breaking.

[44]   David Garland, *Punishment and Modern Society* (Oxford, Clarendon Press, 1990), p. 207,
      citing T. Zeman, 'Order, Crime and Punishment: The American Criminological
      Tradition', Ph.D. dissertation, University of California, Santa Cruz, June 1981.

[45]   C. Hill, *Reformation to Industrial Revolution* (Harmondsworth, Penguin, 1969), p. 117.

did bind fellow believers together, the doctrine of atonement, like that of predestination from which which it cannot be separated, is addressed above all to the individual believer rather than to the church of which Christ is head. Christ is our forerunner, and the substitute for each one of us, rather than the representative or inclusive human being we find in Luther.

Troeltsch commented that in Calvin we find the lawyer and practical man, whereas in Luther we have the monk and idealist, and yet, once again, legal analogies are not crucial. They serve only to make vivid the real situation – human beings wretched under the wrath of God. To be a Christian is to seek to escape that wrath through faith in, and obedience to, what we learn in Scripture. It is difficult to resist Edwin Muir's savage comment:

> See there King Calvin with his iron pen,
> And God three angry letters in a book

and not to conclude, with him, that

> There's better gospel in man's natural tongue,
> And truer sight was theirs outside the Law.[46]

In his great history of the doctrine of reconciliation Ritschl commented that the Schoolmen regarded the satisfaction of Christ as a necessity arising from the arbitrary will of a mighty possessor of private rights, whilst the Reformers sought its explanation in the public law of the law-ordered community, of which God and man are constituent parts. In the one case satisfaction is regarded as the arbitrary compensation for a personal injury, and in the other as the necessary punishment of a violation of law. We have seen that this is less than fair as a comment on the Schoolmen, but it accurately focusses a crucial change in the doctrine of satisfaction, which sprang from the theological response to changing political, social, economic and cultural conditions. Ironically it was another lawyer, Faustus Socinus, who mounted the sharpest and most fully worked out challenge to the doctrine of satisfaction that it had ever received.

---

[46] 'The Incarnate One', *Collected Poems* (London, Faber, 1960).

FAUSTUS SOCINUS

Socinus is to seventeenth- and eighteenth-century Protestant Orthodoxy what Arius was to the fourth century. He was a product of the Italian Reformation, a member of an old Sienna family, and like Calvin trained for, and practised, law. His uncle, Laelio Sozzini, to whom Faustus always looked for inspiration, had already published tracts favouring Reformed ideas before his death at the age of thirty seven in 1565.[47] Lecky commented that the Reformation in Italy was virtually confined to a small group of scholars 'who preached its principles to their extreme limits, with an unflinching logic, with a disregard for both tradition and consequences, and above all with a secular spirit that was elsewhere unequalled'.[48] Perhaps his legal background can be seen in a tract on the authority of Scripture which he wrote whilst still in Florence in 1570, which treats the Bible as the legal corpus of the Christian faith. Italy was far too dangerous for someone with his views, and he left for good in 1575, when he was thirty-six years old. He lived in Basle for three years, and there, in 1578, he produced his work on the atonement, *De Jesu Christo Servatore*. About the same time he wrote a catechism which became the basis for the Racovian catechism of 1609, dedicated to James I. Expanded by Crellius, this became the standard statement of Unitarian faith. Like many of those on the 'left wing' of the Reformation, he then went to Poland, where Cracow was already the centre of a strong Reformed movement. Here he spent the rest of his life, and helped to strengthen the Unitarian movement which he found already established. After being nearly killed by a mob riot in 1598 he retired to the country and died in 1604.

From the mid seventeenth century on he was dismissed as a rationalist, an accusation typified by the dismissive comment of Mosheim in 1754: 'The fundamental maxim of the whole Socinian

---

[47] Behind him lay the tract *Beneficia di Christo*, written most probably by a Benedictine, Benedetto of Mantua, and published in 1543. Amongst other things this advocated a clearly exemplarist view of the atonement.

[48] W. E. Lecky, *The History of the Rise and Influence of Rationalism in Europe* (2 vols., New York, Appleton, 1914), vol. II, p. 60.

theology', he wrote, 'is this: Nothing must be admitted as a divine doctrine but what the human mind can fully *understand* and *comprehend*: and whatever the holy Scriptures teach, concerning the nature of God, his counsels and purposes, and the way of salvation, must be filed down and polished by art and reason, till it shall agree with the capacities of our minds.'[49] It is clear that the Christian humanism of the earlier part of the sixteenth century stands in the background for Socinus. Erasmus and other humanists 'tended to regard Christ as an exemplar, a classical hero, a way of living rather than the Saviour on the cross. They saw in the Christian life the struggle of an essentially free and dignified being to control his selfhood and his appetites.'[50] At the same time to dismiss Socinus as nothing but a rationalist is misleading, a fact indicated above all by his closeness to the Anabaptists, with whom he lived for some time, and with whom he was in constant dialogue. If we are to understand his doctrine properly we have to put it in the context of his political thought, as expounded in his short tract *De Verae Sententiae Magistratu Politicu*, published in 1581, in which he takes sides in a continuing Anabaptist debate. One 'Paleologus' had justified the use of force by Christians. Socinus disagrees. There is no exception to the prohibition of killing. Capital punishment is contrary to the principles of Christ, and Christians can neither be executioners nor wage war. Heretics should not be punished by the state. Like many Anabaptists he is politically quietist, and believes that obedience must be given to civil government, and taxes paid. Unlike more radical Anabaptists he believes that a Christian may serve as a magistrate, provided no death penalty is passed, and that it is legitimate to seek redress of injuries through the secular courts.

To what extent do these views bear on his theology of the atonement? It is interesting that in Thomas Munzer, one of the key figures in sixteenth-century Anabaptism, we find a theology of the cross, but no theology of the atonement. In his exegesis of Luke he writes, 'A preacher who is full of grace must preach from

[49] J. Mosheim, *Institutes of Ecclesiastical History*, tr. J. Murdoch (London, 1841), p. 604.
[50] A. G. Dickens, *Reformation and Society in Sixteenth Century Europe* (London, Thames & Hudson, 1966), p. 30.

the desert, that is, from exemplary trials in which he has borne the cross.' 'The true kingdom of David is where Christ rules from the cross and we are crucified with him.' 'All we need to do is to be conformed to his life and passion through the overshadowing of the holy spirit, so bitterly resisted and so coarsely mocked by this fleshly world.'[51] For Munzer punishment is unnecessary.

The remission of sins occurs without any punishment being exacted; it is enough if heart-felt contrition is present as happens in the case of thieves; for the contrition comes from man's own resources ... Punishment is not to be sought after; for man knows himself well enough from his own resources. It is right, therefore, to reject temptations to one's faith which are not of this world, the temptation of hell etc.[52]

If we put Munzer and Socinus together, the question arises whether a *theology of life under the cross* does not take the place of a theology of satisfaction. It is at least suggestive that later in the seventeenth century Ranters, Diggers and Quakers all followed Socinus in rejecting satisfaction theory. Gerald Winstanley taught that humanity must save itself, without relying on a vicarious sacrifice. Even Bunyan, who firmly believed in Calvinistic theories of atonement, did not make them the centre piece of *The Pilgrim's Progress*. 'The subject of Bunyan's allegory is Christian, his experience, his struggles, temptations and decisions, defeats and victories: not the vicarious sacrifice on the cross.'[53]

By temperament a moderate, eirenical in his relations with his enemies, Socinus thought of himself as a defender of truths of the New Testament which had been obscured by needless dogmatism. The satisfaction theory, like the doctrine of the Trinity, he believed to be repugnant both to reason and to Scripture, and the battery of arguments he draws up against it aim to show that it is incoherent.[54] In Scripture we read that God forgives men

51 *The Collected Letters and Writings of Thomas Munzer*, ed. P. Matheson (Edinburgh, T. & T. Clark, 1988), pp. 311, 321, 322.
52 ibid., pp. 380–1.
53 C. Hill, *A Tinker and a Poor Man: John Bunyan and his Church* (New York, W. W. Norton, 1990), p. 210; cf. pp. 82, 193.
54 The summary of Socinus' objections to the satisfaction theory is taken largely from his *Praelectus Theologiae*, chaps. 16–28, in *Opera Omnia* (2 vols., Irenopolis (Amsterdam), 1656), vol. I, pp. 566ff. Also *De Jesu Christo Servatore*, in *Opera Omnia*, vol. II, pp. 121ff., and the Racovian catechism.

freely, but in that case he cannot demand satisfaction, for this would involve a contradiction. Anselm had argued *aut poena aut satisfactio*. Socinus replaces this with *aut venia aut satisfactio*. In his view the two are mutually exclusive. Moreover, the satisfaction theory seems to pit the mercy and justice of God against each other, but this is a fundamental error as God's attributes must be understood together. Here his target is certainly the Swiss Reformers, and he seems not to have appreciated Luther's profound theology of 'God against God'. Further, God's justice is not punitive but *aequitas et rectitudo* – fairness and righteousness. Sin is nothing but an offence to the divine majesty (here Anselm might agree), but if God could not choose to forgive this, he would have less power than human beings. He shares with Calvin a strong insistence on the absolute priority of God's will, so God is free to choose to forgive if he so pleases.

A number of arguments turn on quasi-legal points in a way which is actually quite new, but which became increasingly common from the late sixteenth century on. He argues that although it is possible to pay another's *debts*, it is not possible to bear personal penalties which culminate in death. Vicarious punishment he believes to be both unjust and unscriptural. We can see that the innocent are indeed often punished in the place of the guilty, but this is to be regarded as a tragic error and not a creative and redemptive fact. Further, if an appeal is made to some unstated principle of equivalence, Christ's death might have paid the penalty for one death, but could not pay for all. He cannot be said to have died as the head of humanity, for that character did not yet belong to him during his earthly life. Moreover, the penalty for sin was eternal death, but Christ did not suffer this, but was raised from the dead. Again, Christ cannot both suffer in our place and fulfil the law as our substitute. If he did one, there was no need for the other. Again there is an appeal to an inner contradiction in the doctrine. A similar point is made about satisfaction and imputation. If Christ has indeed made satisfaction then it follows that we are accepted; if Christ's merits must be 'imputed' to us, then there can have been no satisfaction, for this implies that satisfaction has only limited validity.

A further set of arguments turn on the concept of God involved. If Christ was truly the God-Man, then he need not have suffered to such an extent, for the smallest of his sufferings would have weighed in the balance. The theory seems therefore to imply a God who delights in torture. But in any case, to assert suffering of God is incoherent, because God is impassible. The argument of this theory seems to show that we are more indebted to Christ than to God because Christ showed us kindness whereas God, by demanding the full penalty, showed us no kindness at all. Finally it is ethically dangerous, in that it invites indolence or even licentiousness.

Some of these arguments are clearly pettifogging, but others went home, especially those which alleged that the satisfaction theory implied an unworthy view of God. Socinus was not content only with controverting a view he disagreed with, but opposed it with a clear statement of the exemplarist theory, which, confusingly, he insists on speaking of in expiatory terms. 'I think that Jesus Christ is our Saviour', he writes in the first chapter of *De Jesu Christo Servatore*, 'because he proclaimed to us the way of eternal life, confirmed it and clearly showed it forth, both by the example of his life and by his rising again from the dead.' The purpose of the passion was, he tells us, 'that all sinners might be incited and drawn to Christ, seeking salvation in and by him alone who died for them'. Through his patient suffering, but especially through his resurrection, Christ 'inspires us with a certain hope of salvation and incites us to enter on the way of salvation and to persevere in it'.

Ritschl felt that the fundamental flaw of Socinianism was that it reduced the church to the level of a school: ultimately it teaches salvation by instruction. Of course it could be objected, and was objected over and over again, that the problem is a failure to realise 'the seriousness of sin'. That is perhaps true, but even more fundamental, and perhaps what Mosheim is getting at, is that Socinus has absolutely no grasp of the vicariousness of all life. Many of his arguments rest on rejecting the presupposition that it is possible for one person radically to be for others, to take their place in any way. It is this failure of perception which ultimately makes his theology seem thin and superficial. He does not know, as Luther did, that all life is exchange. At the same time his roots in Anabaptism, as well as humanism, mark the beginning of an important strand of theological-political thinking which is liberal, tolerant, critical, and has the potential for radical political statement. In the founding of the North American state it is at least as important as the Calvinism of Jonathan Edwards. Any evaluation of Socinus' contribution to the European theological debate must bear this in mind.

GROTIUS

One of the earliest attacks on Socinus' account of the satisfaction theory was published in 1618 by Hugo Grotius, himself ironically imprisoned the following year for Arminian views, and the following century accounted a Socinian in view of his friendly correspondence with Crellius.

Hugo van de Groot was born in the Netherlands in 1583 into a Protestant family. He went to Leiden University at the age of twelve and became a lawyer by the age of sixteen. Arminius was the Rector of Leiden at the time, and when he died, in 1609, Grotius was incautious enough to write a commemorative ode. This seemed to identify him with the Arminian cause, very much in the minority after the accession of Prince Maurits, who favoured the strictly Calvinist Gomarists. Grotius wrote his *Defensio Fidei Catholicae de Satisfactione Christi* in 1617, when he was already under suspicion of heresy himself, and a year before he received a life sentence for it. Fortunately his spirited wife, Maria, smuggled him out of prison in a clothes basket the following year, and he spent the rest of his life commuting between Sweden and Paris. His *Laws of the Sea* had already been published before his exile, and this, together with his account of the Just War tradition, made him virtually the founding father of international law. It is against this legal background that we have to understand his theological work.

In responding to Socinus Grotius begins by asking whether it is right to think that Christ can be punished in our place.[55] Right

---

[55] H. Grotius, *Defensio Fidei Catholicae de Satisfactione Christi* (Oxford, 1636). An English translation was made by 'WH', published in London, 1692.

punishment belongs to fathers within the household, to kings within the commonwealth, and to God within the universe. As the Congregationalist R. W. Dale aptly commented, to Grotius the divine administration of the universe was but a higher form of that political life with which he was so well acquainted. God therefore certainly has the *right* to punish. But *must* he? God is not, as Socinus seems to think, either an offended party or a creditor, but we know God as our governor, and it is part of the justice of a governor to keep laws, failing which order cannot be preserved. Here the Anselmian theme of order is reintroduced in an almost unrecognisable form. The order that is important is now that of state and society, and God appears as the guarantor of the social status quo. The reason Christ had to be punished was that God would not pass by so many and so great sins without a remarkable example. Christ displays 'great fitness to shew a signal example; which consists both in his great Conjunction with us, and in the unmatched dignity of his person' (chap. 5). We see from both classical and biblical examples that people can be punished for the faults of others. 'God hath power to punish Christ, being Innocent, unto a Temporal Death ... to wit a Lordly power' (chap. 4). This is properly understood as satisfaction. We were to be put justly to death. 'Christ procured us deliverance from this debt by giving something. But to give something that another by that same may be delivered from a debt, is to pay or satisfy' (chap. 6). Such satisfaction had its analogies in the expiatory sacrifices of the Old Testament.

In every commonwealth rightly governed, says Grotius, the king requires punishment by his judges, and if they fail, by himself. 'But because a Lawyer may sometimes relax his own law ... God, the King of the Hebrews, in some cases admitted expiatory sacrifices in the room of the sinner himself, and by these, and no other ways, would he free the sinner from the punishment of death' (chap. 10). This exercise of prerogative is, however, tantamount to that free exercise of divine will which we find in Scotus, Calvin and Socinus. As many of his critics pointed out, Grotius found himself in the same boat as his adversary. Socinus thinks that we are delivered as much by the resurrection as by Christ's death but 'we are delivered by the punishment of

Christ, which he paid for our sins' (chap. 8). But how is this consistent with divine grace? This, we see, is '*above* the law, because we are not punished; *for* the law because punishment is not omitted; and therefore is remission given, that we may in time to come live to the Divine Law' (chap. 5). The purpose of satisfaction is, then, that we should live according to the law. Socinus is wrong to think that there is any contradiction between satisfaction and remission, because the one necessarily precedes the other.

Although Grotius' tract remained a standard source of anti-Socinian arguments for the next one hundred and fifty years, it has to be said that he scarcely meets Socinus' arguments point by point, and the case he makes for the satisfaction theory is less than compelling. Satisfaction has to be made because otherwise the legal basis of the state would be threatened: this is what it comes down to, and this provides the background for much of the later debate in the eighteenth century. In effect Grotius replaces retributivist with consequentialist justifications of punishment. As Ritschl commented, Grotius replaces penal satisfaction for past sins with a penal example for the prevention of future sins.[56] Law must be maintained, and punishment is needed for this. We are liable for this but we find someone from within the community to bear it for us, and thus preserve justice. The authority of law is maintained by making the forgiveness of sins conditional on the sufferings of Christ. It is a very far cry indeed from the doctrine of Anselm.

FROM HOOKER TO STILLINGFLEET

The English debate of the seventeenth century does little more than develop the theses of Calvin and of Grotius. It is of some interest, however, in that England was the only state which, in the seventeenth century, underwent a genuine bourgeois revolution which rewrote the terms of political power. Grotius' vision of civil law was, as it were, enfleshed in the English state, which moved

---

[56] J. Ritschl, *History of the Doctrine of Justification and Reconciliation*, tr. J. S. Black (Edinburgh, Edmonton and Douglas, 1872), p. 309.

towards the acceptance of a social contract. The theology of the
atonement follows this development.

According to the thirty-first of the Church of England's Articles
'The Offering of Christ once made is that perfect redemption,
propitiation, and satisfaction for the sins of the whole world, both
original and actual; and there is none other satisfaction for sin but
that alone.' A full-blooded Anselmian theology is here presupposed, but it is perhaps characteristic of Anglicanism that in the
first major statement of Anglican theology, Hooker's *Ecclesiastical
Polity*, it plays an entirely minor part. Hooker effectively goes back
to Tertullian and understands satisfaction in terms of penance.[57]
Repentance denotes the operation of grace in us, satisfaction the
effect which it has. Our repentance, 'the satisfactory or propitiatory sacrifice of a broken and contrite heart', thus satisfies God,
changing his wrath and indignation to his mercy. There is,
therefore, as far as Hooker is concerned, a sort of hierarchy of
satisfaction: the satisfaction made by Christ, on which the satisfaction of our own penance depends.

John Davenant, Lady Margaret Professor of Divinity at Cambridge, and later Bishop of Salisbury, vigorously contested this
view, without mentioning Hooker, in his lectures to his Cambridge students. He deals with satisfaction in the eighth of his
'Determinations or Resolutions of Certain Theological Questions,
publicly discussed in the University of Cambridge'. For him it is
not *aut poena aut satisfactio* as it was for Anselm; rather 'satisfaction'
is a way of talking about punishment. It is allowed by all, he
writes, that remission of sins cannot be obtained except by the
intervention of a full and exact satisfaction. Christ offered to God
that expiatory sacrifice by which alone the guilt, as well as the
punishment, of all our sins is expiated and expunged, so that the
duty of satisfying God for the injury offered to him does not rest
on the penitent in any part. As often as we act or suffer well and
holily we endeavour to satisfy the call of duty, and to approve
ourselves to God by fulfilling his will; but we do not dream that
by these works we are expiating the vengeance due to our sins, or
making up for the injury done the Divine Majesty, by exhibiting

---

[57] *Ecclesiastical Polity*, in *Works* (2 vols., Oxford, Clarendon Press, 1865), vol. II, Bk VI,
       chap. 5.

to him, in this endeavour of ours, a worthy satisfaction. Justice never inflicts the vengeance of punishment, except with regard to the debt of guilt. When, then, the satisfaction of Christ abolished the guilt on which the debt of punishment is founded, he took away the object of divine justice and consequently the necessity of human satisfaction. To this it must be added that, according to the laws of justice, no satisfaction can redeem the punishment due to sin, except by an express ordinance of God for accepting such satisfaction in the room of a ransom. Christ's satisfaction has this privilege by the eternal decree of God.

In mid century the voluminous writings of John Owen centred on the atonement, but chiefly turned on the question whether the number of saved was limited (Owen believed it was). In Owen's writings commercial metaphors for the atonement – the debt owed and paid off – have priority over arguments about law and order. Satisfaction is 'a full compensation of the creditor from the debtor ... If I owe a man a hundred pounds, I am his debtor, by virtue of the bond wherein I am bound, until such things be done as recompense him, and moveth him to cancel the bond, which is called satisfaction.'[58] On the cross Christ pays the same quantitative penalty as is owed by the elect. Christ was 'sued by his Father's justice unto an execution, in answer whereunto he underwent all that was due to sin'.[59] Whilst this is an obvious response to the growth of mercantile capitalism, it did not become a dominant theological idiom. Instead both Richard Baxter, in his controversy with Owen, and Stillingfleet prefer to understand the atonement through political analogies.

Edward Stillingfleet, who, despite his roots in Presbyterianism, became Bishop of Worcester in 1689, is a splendidly eirenical figure of broad sympathies, the friend of John Locke and owner of one of the best private libraries in England. He felt the need to to counter Socinian views in *Two Discourses concerning the Doctrine of Christ's Satisfaction*.[60] He maintains, with Grotius, that universal justice in God is that whereby he not only punishes sinners but

---

[58] J. Owen, *The Death of Death*, in *Works*, ed .Goold (23 vols., London and Edinburgh, Johnstone and Hunter, 1852), vol. x, Bk IV, chap. 5.
[59] ibid., Bk III, chap. 9.
[60] In vol. III of his *Collected Works* (London 1710).

takes care of preserving the honour of his laws. With Calvin, and against Grotius, however, he goes on to argue that justice is part of what it is to be God and that therefore God must exercise punitive justice and accept satisfaction. He makes the by now familiar distinction between debts and punishments. 'The reason of debts is dominion and property, and the obligation of them depends upon voluntary contracts between parties; but the reason of punishments is Justice and Government and depends not upon mere contracts, but the relation the person stands in to that Authority to which he is accountable for his actions.'[61] He rejects the nominalist view that the reason for punishment lies simply in God's will, and finds it rather in God's opposition to sin. True to Anselm he argues that God cannot pardon sin without satisfaction, for 'if it be not only necessary that the laws be compensated but the dishonour too; then so much greater as the dishonour is, so much higher as the person is, so much more beneficial to the world as his honours are, so much more necessary is it that in order to pardon there must be a satisfaction made to him for the affronts he hath received from man'.[62] We have to understand God and humankind as being bound together in one community. God is the Governor, and we the governed, and 'whatever tends to the vindication of the right of God's honour and sovereignty, tends to the good of the whole'.[63] God's end in punishing is the advancing of his honour, 'not by the meer miseries of his creatures, but that men, by beholding his severity against sin, should break off the practice of it'.[64] God accepts the punishments we ourselves undergo 'as a full satisfaction to his honour, if they be such as tend to break men off from sin, and assert God's right, and vindicate his honour in the world'.[65]

Where, then, does Christ's satisfaction come in? This is understood on the analogy of the exercise of royal prerogative. God, being justly provoked to punish human sin, was nevertheless pleased to accept the sufferings of his Son, 'as a sufficient sacrifice

[61] ibid., p. 247.
[62] ibid., p. 251.
[63] ibid., p. 259.
[64] ibid.
[65] ibid., p. 260.

of Atonement for the sins of the world, on consideration of which he was pleased to offer those terms of pardon, which upon mens' performance of the conditions required on their part shall be sufficient to discharge them from that obligation to punishment which they were under by their sins'.[66] The death of Christ is to be understood as 'properly penal, being such a kind of death, which none but Malefactors by the Law were to suffer; by the undergoing of which punishment in our stead he redeemed us from that curse which we were liable to by the violation of the Law of God'.[67]

As can be seen, Stillingfleet steers his own course, and is not a slave to theological fashion. His statement of the satisfaction theory is closer to Anselm than that of most of the Reformers. And yet, if we ask where the heart of his argument really lies, it seems to be very much in that Lockian defence of private property which emerges at this time, in the need for the laws to be affirmed. Locke defined political power as the 'right of making Laws with Penalties of Death, and consequently all less Penalties, for the Regulating and Preserving of Property'.[68] Stillingfleet underwrites this theologically. In place of Anselm's cosmic order is the social order, for which in any case the former was always a figure. The doctrine of satisfaction provides the moral and metaphysical ground for the continuance of a law-governed society. The problem with this is that the church has no power to develop an internal critique in the situation where the laws are wicked. It is the religious arm of the state, its theologians paid ideologues.

CRIME AND ATONEMENT IN THE SIXTEENTH AND SEVENTEENTH CENTURIES

In the world of penal practice we have noticed three changes over these two centuries. The first is the consolidation of that movement, stretching back to the twelfth century, whereby power was finally vested in the state rather than in the local community.

---

[66] ibid., p. 276.
[67] ibid., p. 279.
[68] Locke, *Two Treatises of Government*, Bk 2, chap. 1.

Second, as argued by Pieter Spierenberg, there is some evidence for a change in sensibilities which was to issue, in the next century, in the rejection of 'cruel and unusual punishments'. The fall, in the second half of the seventeenth century, in the number of mutilations is evidence for this, though the replacement of various forms of corporal punishment and execution by transportation may well have more to do with labour needs in the colonies than humanitarian sentiment, as Rusche and Kirchheimer argued. Third, and not unrelated to the second, is that shift of power to surveillance and institutionalisation which is the heart of Foucault's thesis.

The theological response to this changing world is very varied. More important than Luther's Two Kingdoms doctrine is the growth of Erastianism, in both Protestant and Catholic countries, whereby clergy become chaplains to the apparatus of the state, including, of course, gaols. Calvinism and Socinianism pull in opposite directions, in their bearing on penal practice as elsewhere. Calvinism, I have argued, presupposes retributive theory both in its doctrine of atonement and in the penal practice it sanctions. On the other hand, because all are sinners, and sin and crime are understood together, there is the possibility of identifying with those in prison, even if it is recognised that their punishment is just. Few states were governed with this ideology in the background, and in those that were, such as New England or Scotland, broad church or sceptical movements quickly emerged to challenge its assumptions. Calvinist concerns were very significantly rerouted by Grotius and Stillingfleet, for whom the purpose of religion is bound up with justifying the law-governed, and property-owning, community.

Socinianism, both in its roots in humanism and in Anabaptism, is opposed to the death penalty and wary of magistracy. As a 'vector' of tolerance (to use E. P. Thompson's term) it prepares the way both for Quakerism and for the Deist humanism of the following century, which championed Montesquieu and Beccaria against those who believed in judicial severity. Consistently with Quaker principles William Penn attempted to reduce capital punishment to a minimum and spoke of 'the wickedness of exterminating, where it was possible to reform'. In the nineteenth century in Massachusetts Calvinists and Unitarians were opposed on the issue of abolition of the death penalty.[69] The theological lines drawn in the debate of the sixteenth and seventeenth centuries prepared the ground for the intense penal debate of the following two centuries.

[69] See Edwin Powers, *Crime and Punishment in Early Massachusetts 1620–1692* (Boston, Mass., Beacon Press, 1966); H. Potter, *Hanging in Judgement* (London, SCM, 1993), pp. 32, 61.

CHAPTER 7

The moral government of the universe

Could it really be that all the talk about justice, goodness, law, religion, God and so on, was nothing but so many words to conceal the grossest self-interest and cruelty?

Tolstoy, *Resurrection*

Ah! Little think the Gay . . .
Whom Pleasure, Power and Affluence Surround
How many Pine in Want, and Dungeon Glooms.

James Thomson

The attempt to place the atonement theology of the eighteenth century in its context is made the more difficult because the century is the contemporary focus of the *Streit der Historiker*. Historians overtly committed to right- and left-wing ideologies interpret the same evidence very differently. Legal history has shared in the difficulty.[1]

The rise in population has been described as 'The outstanding feature of the social history of the eighteenth century'.[2] In fact, this growth occurred only from mid century on, and the population actually fell both in the late 1720s and in 1741.[3] Mid century the population of England stood, as it had at the beginning, at approximately $5\frac{1}{2}$ million, three-quarters of whom lived and

---

[1] Jonathan Clark challenges the 'orthodoxy' of E. P. Thompson, Christopher Hill, Lawrence Stone and others from the standpoint of the 1980s, when it is possible to see once again that England's commercial and industrial achievement rested on 'virtues of loyalty, diligence, discipline, subordination and obedience in the work-place, whether factory, mine or office', and after the break-up of the consensus stemming from Attlee. J. C. D. Clark, *English Society 1688–1832* (henceforth, *ES*) (Cambridge, Cambridge University Press, 1985), pp. 41, 73.

[2] T. S. Ashton, *The Industrial Revolution* (London, Oxford University Press, 1948), p. 2.

[3] See P. Langford, *A Polite and Commercial People* (Oxford, Oxford University Press, 1989), p. 146.

worked in the country. This had risen to 9 million at the time of the first census in 1801.[4]

In 1700 London, the biggest city in Europe, with a population of more than five hundred thousand, was the only really great city in Britain. Norwich was the second city, with a population of nearly thirty thousand, followed by Bristol with twenty thousand and York, Exeter and Newcastle upon Tyne with something over eleven thousand each. Of the seven hundred or so other towns and cities in the country most had populations of between three and six thousand. By the middle of the eighteenth century there were fourteen towns with populations of thirty thousand or more. In the next fifty years, but especially in the last thirty years of the eighteenth century, the old pattern was changed irrevocably. What was said of Birmingham was true of many of the new industrial cities, that 'a traveller who visits this city once in six months supposes himself well acquainted with her, but he may chance to find a street of houses in the autumn where he last saw his horse at grass in the spring'.[5]

Popular perception at the time believed that crime was increasing, and the provisions of the Waltham Black Act of 1722 have something of an air of panic. Recent studies suggest that crime levels were fairly stable until pushed up by the rise in the population.[6] Certainly the machinery of justice was quite unprepared for any significant rise in crime. The system of assizes, courts and gaols had grown up in response to the needs of a much smaller population, where most crime was local. When John Howard published his first report on prisons in 1777 the gaols and prisons he looked at dated mostly from the sixteenth century or before. Some of them were dungeons in the worst sense.[7]

The range of penalties was limited. Whipping, branding, putting in the stocks, fining and transportation were available as

---

[4]   By 1831 it had reached 14 million, and by 1901 37 million.

[5]   For a more conservative estimate of the change see Clark, *ES*, pp. 69ff.

[6]   J. M. Beattie, *Crime and the Courts in England 1660–1800* (Oxford, Oxford University Press, 1986).

[7]   Howard notes that in the dungeon in Knaresborough, underground, and without any light, the rats were so large that they killed a dog a prisoner took with him for protection, and seriously disfigured the prisoner's face.

secondary punishments, whilst hanging was the punishment for serious offences.[8] The period witnesses a huge increase in capital offences. From the accession of Edward III to the death of Henry VII only six capital statutes were executed. A further thirty were added before 1660. From this date until 1810 187 capital statutes were added, the great majority after 1722.[9] Since these statutes allowed the death penalty to be inflicted for many variations of the same offence, it is calculated that the scope of the death penalty was three or four times as extensive as the number of statutes. It was applied for an enormous variety of offences including marking the edges of a current coin, cutting hop binds on any hops, destroying the heads of fish ponds, picking pockets to the value of more than 12 pence and being in the company of gypsies.

No one under seven could be hanged, but children very little older were. Three of those hanged after the Gordon Riots in 1780 were under fifteen, and fourteen others under eighteen; in 1814 a boy of fourteen was hanged for stealing, and in 1831 John Bell, aged thirteen, was hanged for murder. Two years later a nine-year-old boy was sentenced to death for pushing a stick through a cracked window and stealing printer's colours to the value of twopence, though he was finally reprieved. Women convicted of petty treason were burned to death. The sixteen-year-old Mary Troke was burned at Winchester in March 1738 for poisoning her mistress. This punishment applied also to coinage offences. In 1777 a fourteen-year-old girl was sentenced to be burned for hiding some farthings at her master's request. She was saved by the accidental intervention of Lord Weymouth who happened to be passing. Women were burned for coining in 1721, 1779, 1786 and finally 1789. Huge crowds turned up for these events, in one case preventing the hangman from the usual practice of strangling the woman before she was burned.

The great majority of new capital offences in the eighteenth

---

[8] Transportation had been introduced in the last years of the Republic, was put on the statute book in 1679, and was extended in 1717.

[9] L. Radzinowicz, *A History of English Criminal Law and its Administration from 1750*, vol. 1 (London, Stevens, 1948), p. 4. Much of the information in the next two paragraphs is drawn from this volume.

century were for crimes related to property, and many sprang
from the Waltham Black Act, which was enacted in 1722 for a
three-year period and repeatedly renewed until 1758, when it was
made permanent.[10] Under this Act nearly three hundred and fifty
types of case, many of them involving being accessory to the fact,
were liable to the death penalty. Its provisions were repealed only
in 1823.

The Black Act, and its implications, has been the subject of
intense scrutiny in recent decades. The thesis of Douglas Hay,
that it was a product of implicit class conspiracy, has been
vigorously challenged.[11] It may be that an account of this system
and its execution which is stated purely in class terms is insufficiently nuanced. On the other hand, neither will it do to accept
the ideology of its eighteenth-century defenders of 'one equal
justice before the law'. The class element is clear in the way the
Black Act protects the property rights of the gentry at the expense
of ancient common rights. The need to defend the rising
commercial classes is also evidenced by the fact that two-thirds of
those convicted for forgery were executed. Blackstone noted that
housebreaking was made a capital offence because of 'improvements in trade and opulence'.[12]

It is true that juries often refused to convict, that the Crown
often commuted death sentences, and that judges often exercised
a 'merciful' interpretation of the statutes. As the century wore on,
and particularly in the first decade of the nineteenth century, the
proportion of those capitally convicted who were actually executed certainly fell. Nevertheless the comment of Sir James
Stephen, writing in the *Cornhill Magazine* in 1863, can scarcely be
gainsaid. Stephen, who was no liberal, spoke of 'this barbarous
system, which ... was adapted to the altered circumstances of
society by some of the clumsiest, most reckless, and most cruel

10 For example, of those executed in London and Middlesex between 1800 and 1804 five
    were for murder, eleven for burglary, three for horse stealing, eleven for robbery, and
    fifteen for forgery.
11 See the discussion in E. P. Thompson, *Whigs and Hunters* (Harmondsworth, Penguin,
    1975); *Albion's Fatal Tree*, ed. D. Hay et al. (Harmondsworth, Penguin, 1975); the best-
    known critique is J. H. Langbein's 'Albion's Fatal Flaws', *Past and Present*, 88 (February
    1983), 96ff.
12 Cited in M. Ignatieff, *A Just Measure of Pain: The Penitentiary in the Industrial Revolution
    1750–1850* (henceforth *JMP*) (Harmondsworth, Penguin, 1989), p. 18.

legislation that ever disgraced a civilised country'. He then added, 'If this blood thirsty and irrational code had been consistently carried out, it would have produced a reign of terror quite as cruel as the French Revolution, and not half so excusable.'[13]

As it was, it was quite bad enough. According to tables Howard provided in his 1777 report, 60 per cent of capital offenders who came before the courts in London between 1749 and 1771 were executed.[14] The proportion fell after 1790. Simply noting the figures of executions takes no account of those who died in gaol from a mixture of starvation, dysentery, smallpox and 'gaol fever' (typhus), which killed far more than those actually executed. Howard estimated that a quarter of the prison population died of disease.

The clergy were implicated in the penal process both as magistrates and as chaplains or 'Ordinarys' of the prisons, whose attendance at executions was required, and where they were supposed to preach repentance and obtain conversion. On the whole, Ignatieff notes, 'The parson's sermons were set pieces on social obligation, delivered at the gallows and subsequently hawked in the streets with an account of the offender's life and descent into crime.'[15] It is hardly surprising that hostility to the Ordinary, and irreligion, was commonplace.[16] Moreover, we find, in the eighteenth century, the same kind of appeal to an alternative theological tradition which we find in the peasant revolts of the Middle Ages and the radical movements of the mid seventeenth century. One of the ballads of Dick Turpin runs:

> He said, The Scriptures I fulfill'd
> Though I this Life did lead,
> For when the Naked I beheld,

13 *Cornhill Magazine*, 7 (January 1863), 189–202, quoted in Radzinowicz, *History*, p. 24.
14 The number was 678 of 1,121. Five hundred and eighty-four of these capital offences were against property. On the Norfolk Circuit between 1750 and 1772, 117 were executed and 834 were transported, whilst on the Midland Circuit 116 were executed and 1,057 transported. Fifty of these executions were for murder or petty treason. The rest were for robbery, housebreaking, forgery, or returning from transportation. The figures for the whole country would be very high, as Radzinowicz points out: *History*, p. 148.
15 Ignatieff, *JMP*, p. 21.
16 P. Linebaugh, *The London Hanged: Crime and Civil Society in the Eighteenth Century* (Harmondsworth, Penguin, 1991), p. 149.

I clothed them with speed:
Sometimes in Cloth and Winter-frieze,
Sometimes in Russet-gray;
The Poor I fed, the Rich likewise
I empty sent away.[17]

Someone at least had reflected on the text of the Magnificat!

Despite the notorious executions in the eighteenth century of Lord Ferrers and Dr Dodds, it is clear that the vast majority of those who were executed were poor.[18] Jonathan Clark seeks to argue that traditions of deference still characterised the eighteenth century, and were only destroyed in the first decades of the next century. Whilst acknowledging that we still know little about the 'inarticulate millions', he goes on to characterise the 'really poor' as 'those who thought they found dignity and meaning in their relations to things they did not create – their religion, their country, their rulers'.[19] In his view the Anglican church commanded the assent of the vast majority of the populace until well into the century, when this assent was undermined by the growing impact of Dissent. The church and king mob which sacked Priestley's house, and burned Dissenting chapels in Birmingham in 1791, is, for him, evidence that labouring people were loyal to the *ancien régime* and the Anglican church. E. P. Thompson's account of the incident, as might be expected, is very different. He agrees that it was 'an episode in which the "country gentlemen" called out the urban mob to draw the dissenting teeth

---

17 *Folksongs of the Upper Thames* (1950), pp. 253–4, 275–7, cited by Linebaugh, *London Hanged*, p. 203.

18 Langbein argues against Hay that the jurors were not members of the ruling elite, but concedes the point that most of those executed were likely to be poor. He cites a case of highway robbery committed to feed a starving family where the judge, Dudley Ryder, gave the convicted man a complete discharge. We have to set against this, however, cases such as those of Wilkes, where other kinds of social necessities could lead to death for crimes which involved no bodily harm. Crowds at executions seem to have shown their awareness of the barbarity of the legal system by showing respect and compassion for the likes of Wilkes. When a real criminal, like Jonathan Wild, was hanged, he was cursed and pelted with mud and stones. *Celebrated Trials* (1825), vol. IV, p. 359.

19 Clark, *ES*, p. 42. There are still no adequate studies of the extent of deference in the eighteenth century. Clark's picture, culled straight from Hannah More, overlooks the profound anti-clericalism implicit in the caricatures of Smollett, for example, and the hatred of the rural community for 'tithe consuming clergy'. See E. P. Thompson, *The Making of the English Working Classes* (Harmondsworth, Penguin, 1968), pp. 170, 257–8.

of the aggressive and successful Birmingham bourgeoisie'. There were not only ideological issues at stake. One of those attacked was a commissioner for a court which enforced small debts. It was also, therefore, 'an explosion of latent class hatred and personal lawlessness triggered-off by the fortuitous coming together of old religious animosities and new social and political grievances'.[20]

When the 'inarticulate millions' do come into view, both before and after this period, it is often with a very different aspect from the loyal labourer in his cottage, with his Prayer Book and copy of the *Whole Duty of Man* painted by Clark. The complaint that people did not know the Lord's Prayer, and hardly knew who Christ was, was common in the sixteenth and seventeenth centuries.[21] The same complaint was made by prison chaplains in the nineteenth century.[22] Two girls from Merthyr Tydfil Iron-works had never heard of a saviour. The Chaplain of Preston Gaol, John Clay, examined twenty-five prisoners at random. None knew what month Christmas fell in, sixteen did not know which year it was, seventeen did not know the queen's name and, interestingly, more had heard of Dick Turpin and Jack Sheppard than knew the name of the Duke of Wellington.[23] The eight-eenth-century sailor 'rarely thinks, seldom reads, and never prays ... Speak to him about the call of God, he tells you he hears enough of the boatswain's call.'[24] The Poaching ballads of the late eighteenth century often express profound bitterness about the landlord class, and often about the clergy.[25] The poet John

---

[20]   Thompson, *Making*, p. 80, citing R. B. Rose, from whom these quotations come, 'The Priestley Riots of 1791', *Past and Present*, no. 18 (November 1960), 68–88. On the fickleness of the English mob see further Thompson, pp. 21, 66ff., 77, 184. Their loyalties could be enlisted on very different sides of the political fence.

[21]   See K. Thomas, *Religion and the Decline of Magic* (Harmondsworth, Penguin, 1973), pp. 195–7.

[22]   L. Radzinowicz and R. Hood, *The Emergence of Penal Policy* (Oxford, Oxford University Press, 1986), p. 55.

[23]   Cited in P. Priestley, *Victorian Prison Lives* (London, Methuen, 1985), p. 107.

[24]   Joshua Marsden, *Sketches of the Early Life of a Sailor* (possibly 1812), cited in Thompson, *Making*, p. 62.

[25]   See the Muggletonian song from 1763 cited by E. P. Thompson, *Witness against the Beast: William Blake and the Moral Law* (Cambridge, Cambridge University Press, 1993), p. 75:

> You who by long prayers do prey on the poor
> The bread and the substance of widows
> devour;

Clare was a 9-shilling-a-week labourer, living in his parents'
cottage. He began his poem 'The Parish' with the lines:

> The parish hind, oppression's humble slave,
> Whose only hope of freedom is the grave.

Taxed with being unduly bitter, he replied that the poem was
written 'under the pressure of very heavy distress ... a state of
anxiety and oppression almost amounting to slavery when the
prosperity of one class was founded on the adversity and distress
of another'.[26] It is true that most of these reports come from the
nineteenth century, when, according to Clark, the deferential
consensus was breaking down, but it is not at all clear that the
condition of the very poor was better in the eighteenth century.
The rookeries which Mayhew described so vividly were there
when Defoe was writing, and we catch echoes of those whose
main knowledge is of the great criminals in *Moll Flanders* and in
John Gay.

From the moment Beccaria published his famous essay, in
1762, the issue of crime and punishment was on the European
agenda, and Howard was lionised in his lifetime, and had to take
urgent steps to see that a statue was not erected in his honour.[27]
In one way or another the church was deeply involved in the
debate, if only through the sermons required before every assize.
In 1785 the Reverend Martin Madan, an energetic pamphleteer
on behalf of both polygamy and the Thirty-Nine Articles,
published his *Thoughts on Executive Justice with Respect to our Criminal
Laws*, arguing that prevention is 'the great end of all legal
severity', and that therefore the law should be enforced with its
full rigour. A kind of vicarious principle ran behind this: 'The

> Of external righteousness make a fair show,
> While nothing but praise and gain's in your
> view;
> Ye vipers, ye serpents, ye seed of the
> devil,
> How can you escape the last great day of
> evil?

[26] Cited in H. Hopkins, *The Long Affray* (London, Macmillan, 1986), p. 21.

[27] For a distinctly sceptical view of Beccaria and other eighteenth-century prison
reformers see G. Rusche and O. Kirchheimer, *Punishment and Social Structure* (henceforth *PSS*) (Columbia, 1938), pp. 75ff.

terror of the example is the only thing proposed, and one man is sacrificed to the preservation of thousands.' His particular worry was that the capital statutes were not enforced, and he reproached the judges for putting their human feelings before their judicial role. According to Romilly, Madan's pamphlet had an effect, as there was at once a dramatic increase of executions in London.[28]

The Archdeacon of Carlisle and moral philosopher William Paley devoted one section of his *Principles of Moral and Political Philosophy* to issues of crime and punishment. He too considered the object of punishment to be deterrence. Only God was in a position to make the punishment fit the crime:

A Being whose knowledge penetrates every concealment, from the operation of whose will no art or flight can escape, and in whose hands punishment is sure; such a Being may conduct the moral government of his creation in the best and wisest manner, by pronouncing a law that every crime shall finally receive a punishment proportioned to the guilt which it contains ... But when the care of the public safety is entrusted to men, whose authority over their fellow creatures is limited by defects of power and knowledge ... a new rule of proceeding results from the very imperfection of their faculties. In their hands, the uncertainty of punishment must be compensated by severity. The ease with which crimes are committed or concealed must be counteracted by additional penalties and increased terrors.[29]

He argued that punishment should be graded not according to the crime but according to the difficulty of detection and the danger to the community. Sheep stealing or horse stealing therefore demand the death penalty because only the severest penalties could protect this kind of property. He took a very low view of the chances of malefactors reforming. 'The end of punishment is twofold, *amendment* and *example*. In the first of these, the *reformation* of criminals, little has ever been effected, and little, I fear, is practicable.'[30] He believed that the state of the law as it then was, was more or less ideal: the death sentence applying to a great many misdemeanours, but not consistently put into effect. 'By this

[28] On one occasion twenty people were executed at once.
[29] W. Paley, *The Principles of Moral and Political Philosophy* (2 vols., London, 1785), vol. II, p. 280.
[30] ibid., p. 309.

expedient few actually suffer death, whilst the dread and danger of it hang over the crimes of many.'[31] Hanging, however, was an exact analogy of divine justice: 'By the satisfaction of justice, I mean the retribution of so much pain for so much guilt; which is the dispensation we expect at the hand of God, and which we are accustomed to consider as the order of things that perfect justice dictates and requires.'[32] The nineteenth-century prison chaplain John Clay remarked tartly that 'Christianity was almost wholly excluded' from Paley's philosophy and theology.[33]

In arguing that deterrence was the principal object of criminal justice Madan and Paley were going against the current of penal reform set in motion by Montesquieu in France, Beccaria in Italy, and William Eden in Britain. Eden was opposed to capital punishment, except for the severest crimes, and equally to imprisonment. According to him, 'the idea of shame should follow the finger of the law'. Unlike Paley, prison reformers such as John Howard, James Nield, Samuel Romilly, and later Elizabeth Fry, all of whom were inspired by Christian conviction, believed that prisoners might be changed and 'redeemed'. In his account of Swiss prisons Howard noted that the principal object was to make the prisoners better people. 'This indeed should be the leading view in every House of Correction. As *rational* and *immortal* Beings, we owe this to them; nor can any criminality of theirs justify *our* neglect in these particulars.'[34] The comparison of the sinful soul to a prisoner, and of redemption to reform and release, was a commonplace which looked back to St Paul, and it was one of the most powerful rhetorics in the development of the penitentiary.

I have concentrated thus far on capital punishment, but historians of punishment have focussed their attention on the rise of the prison as a way of dealing with crime. Prior to the mid eighteenth century, imprisonment was not the normal mode of punishment, and prisons were largely used to hold people awaiting trial. In the space of thirty years, between 1780 and 1810, imprisonment became the normal form of punishment. Whereas

---

[31] ibid., p. 295.
[32] ibid., p. 286.
[33] W. L. Clay, *The Prison Chaplain* (London, Macmillan, 1861), p. 354.
[34] J. Howard, *The State of the Prisons* (London, 1777), Appendix, p. 89.

in the 1780s about half of those sentenced to death were actually hanged, by 1808 the figure was not much over 10 per cent.[35] People like Howard and Bentham urged a new model of prison on the authorities, and in the course of the debate, as Ignatieff notes, two clear rhetorics emerged. On the one hand were rationalists like Bentham and Montesquieu who sought to prevent crime by improving manners and who thought of it as a form of insanity which doctors could cure. On the other side were many clergy and theologians who thought in terms of sin and guilt which needed to be atoned for in 'penitentiaries' which took some, at least, of their disciplinary ideas from monasticism.[36] The idea of the separate and silent system, which prevailed in British prisons for a hundred years from the end of the eighteenth century on, was that absolute solitude would lead the prisoner to reflect on his sins, repent, and amend. The clergyman John Brewster, one of many who took a keen interest in penal issues, spoke of there being 'cords of love as well as fetters of iron', which bound people by remorse. The prison chaplain was, in Ignatieff's phrase, 'the technician of guilt'. We can see this clearly enough in the pamphlets produced by Thomas Bowen, Chaplain of Bridewell Hospital: *Thoughts on the Necessity of Moral Discipline in Prisons* and *A Companion for the Prisoner*.[37] One of the hymns proposed was 'When Rising from my Bed of Death', the verses of which included:

> Then see the sorrows of my heart,
> Ere yet it be too late;
> And hear my Saviour's dying groans,
> To give those sorrows weight.

The prisoner is bidden to concentrate on the passion:

> See, streaming from the fatal tree,
> His all-atoning blood!

---

[35] Ignatieff, *JMP*, p. 170.
[36] ibid., pp. 65ff.
[37] Earlier works for prisoners included an Office for Prisoners by Jeremy Taylor, produced in 1658. Kettlewell published one, and Archbishop Tenison, who died in 1715, was much concerned by it. Howard proposed a recommended list of texts for prison sermons, which included 'The Prisoner of Hope', Zech. 9.12; 'The Use of Solitude in Prisons', Psalm 102; Ps. 19.20; 'On the Influence of Evil Companions', 1 Cor. 15.33; and 'The Penitent Thief', Luke 23.32ff.

Is this the Infinite? – 'Tis He!
My SAVIOUR, and my GOD!

For me these pangs his soul assail,
For me the death is borne!
My sin gave sharpness to the nail,
And pointed every thorn.

Let sin no more my soul enslave
Break, Lord, the tyrant's chain;
Oh save me, who thou com'st to save,
Nor bleed or die in vain!

In hymns like these, as in many of the hymns of early Methodism, the connection between crime, punishment and the passion of Christ is spelled out in the clearest possible way:

Long my imprisoned spirit lay
Fast bound in sin and nature's night;
Thine eye diffused a quickening ray,
I woke, the dungeon flamed with light;
My chains fell off, my heart was free;
I rose, went forth, and followed thee.

(C. Wesley, 'And Can it Be')

The hymns witnessed, as E. P. Thompson noted, to the 'transforming power of the cross' in a rhetoric which sublimated latent class conflict.[38] For this period they are amongst the most potent examples of those structures of affect through which theology influences attitudes towards offenders. Against utilitarians like Bentham, who saw in prisons the opportunity to exploit cheap labour, Christians like G. O. Paul insisted that 'the great purpose' of imprisonment was 'reformation by seclusion'.[39] In this they were but extending their own religious experience to the prisoner. The biographies of people like Howard and Elizabeth Fry make very clear the role of a sensibility structured by the cross in understanding the function and purpose of imprisonment. The regime Howard proposed for prisoners was not so very different from his own. Nurtured in Protestant asceticism, convicted of sin and seeking assurance of grace daily, he believed that this was a

---

[38] See Thompson, *Making*, chap. 11 and pp. 916ff. for a discussion of criticisms of the theory.
[39] Cited in Ignatieff, *JMP*, p. 112.

universal human destiny, and that he could help the unfortunate best by inducing such experiences. 'Philanthropic activism provided a vital emotional release for men and women whose passions were . . . completely yoked to religious ideals.'[40]

To do them justice, we have to note that according to John Clay's son, his father and other prison chaplains were well aware of the ambivalence of the idea of prison as a 'moral hospital'. 'In the actual state of English crime, the idea of a moral hospital is perfectly defensible; but viewed in the abstract, it is at variance with the whole tenor of Christianity.'[41]

The nineteenth-century Rector of Lincoln College, Oxford, Mark Pattison, in his youth a disciple of Newman, complained that 'the reasonableness of Christianity' was 'the solitary thesis of Christian theology in England for the greater part of a century'.[42] Coleridge had earlier been equally dismissive of the 'Socinian moonshine' of the eighteenth century, though he had been comprehensively taken in by it as a young man. The nineteenth century was notoriously unable to do justice to its predecessor, and the reality was far more complex and interesting than such remarks indicate.

The Anglican Reformation produced no Confessionalism like that on the Continent. There were no seminaries to produce schools of theologians. In the ancient universities a theological debate was carried on, mostly around the issues of Deism, the relations of church and state, and the claims of Dissent for toleration. Providence was the great theme of eighteenth-century theology, and could be used in the crudest way, by someone like Hannah More, for example, to keep the poor in their place.[43]

---

[40]   ibid., p. 152.

[41]   Clay, *The Prison Chaplain*, p. 361.

[42]   M. Pattison, *Essays and Reviews* (London, J. Parker, 1860), p. 258.

[43]   See H. More, *Works* (11 vols., London, 1830). From thousands of doggerel verses, just one sample:
That some *must* be poorer, this truth I will sing
Is the law of my Maker and not of my King.
And the *true Rights of Man*, and the life of his cause,
Is not equal POSSESSIONS, but equal, just LAWS.
Clark believes that belief in providence was a casualty of Deism (*ES*, p. 280). This is incorrect. In Scholastic terminology, the Deists maintained belief in 'general' providence but dispensed with 'special' providence. The rhetoric of providence was retained by Deists.

Compared to this the doctrines of the atonement, of justification, or of the Trinity were but side-shows.[44] A number of important tracts, pamphlets and monographs nevertheless kept up the debate on satisfaction theory.

John Bampton's will, which was published in 1751, included a bequest to endow eight annual lectures for the exposition and defence of the Christian faith in St Mary's, Oxford. The first series was given in 1780, and the atonement was taken up, in a more or less orthodox way, in both 1794 and 1795. The Dissenting Academies, which trained both Butler and Priestley, were the real powerhouse of theological education. They were 'the greatest schools of their day. During a period when the grammar schools slept and the Universities were sterile they were thoroughly alive and active.'[45] As the century moved on they came, however, to adopt more and more the views of the Enlightenment. Outside the universities and the academies the eighteenth century remained, like the seventeenth, the age of the pamphlet, and much of the most interesting theological work was done by clergy working alone, or, like William Law, working as private tutors, taking on all comers in a soap-box war. The theological passions of the seventeenth century, to which Latitudinarianism represents a reaction, by no means disappear. They are to be found in the continuing Calvinist tradition, especially in Scotland; in Methodism; in William Law; and, as E. P. Thompson has impressively demonstrated, in an antinomian tradition of radical Dissent which was beaten but unbowed. Over against these the tone of Orthodoxy, represented supremely by Joseph Butler, is of a broad-minded high seriousness, much inclined to reverent agnosticism. Alongside these we have Joseph Priestley, the doughty champion of Socinian views.

Jonathan Clark argues for the interrelationship of Dissent, and especially Socinianism, with political radicalism. We have seen that sixteenth-century Socinianism had roots both in Erasmian humanism and in Anabaptism, and that Socinus himself disallowed

---

[44] Pace Langford, *People*, p. 237, who finds justification the centre of eighteenth-century theology, and Clark, who refers to the defence of the doctrine of the Trinity.

[45] Cited without ascription by B. Willey in *The Eighteenth Century Background* (Harmondsworth, Penguin, 1940), p. 185.

capital punishment. For him, this went with a disavowal of satisfaction theory. When we turn to the eighteenth century we find a lively debate about satisfaction theory, with non-jurors and Socinians seeing eye to eye, but almost no theological comment on either prisons or the Bloody Code. The reason for this is not far to seek: all sides were agreed that the metaphor by which God's rule must be understood was the divine magistracy.

THE DIVINE MAGISTRACY

The eighteenth century was the period of the magistrate. Through the century more and more responsibility was laid on their shoulders, and large numbers of country clergy were admitted to their ranks. The corruption of many JPs was a byword, and could be satirised by Smollett, but in London the long tenure of John and Henry Fielding showed that good magistrates could make an enormous difference.[46] In a charge to the Grand Jury in 1749 Henry Fielding reminded them of the famous words of Matthew Hale, Lord Chief Justice at the end of the previous century: 'Christianity is Parcel of the Laws of England: Therefore to reproach the Christian Religion is to speak in Subversion of the Law.'[47] Small wonder that this analogy appealed by way of understanding God's work in Christ. I shall offer four examples of the use of this analogy: two from Anglicans, one from a Dissenter, and one from Priestley himself.

My first Anglican is John Balguy, the son of a schoolmaster at Sheffield Grammar School, who was ordained after studies at Cambridge and served in a family of northern gentry before becoming vicar of two small parishes in Durham. He was a disciple and admirer of the rationalist theologian Samuel Clarke. His *Essay on Redemption*, published in 1741, is one of the most substantial pamphlets on the atonement in the first half of the century.[48] In 1730 he published an essay, *Divine Rectitude*, in which

---

[46] See Langford, *People*, pp. 302ff.
[47] *Charges to the Grand Jury 1698–1803*, ed. G. Lamoire (London, Royal Historical Society, 1992).
[48] The argument of this essay was followed closely by R. Holmes, Professor of Poetry, and Fellow of New College, in his *Four Tracts* (1788).

he argued that justice and fairness was the first spring of action in the Deity. This means, amongst other things, that Christ cannot be said to have been punished in our place, for to punish an innocent person is completely unjust. He holds that vicarious punishment is an utter impossibility, and that the substitutionary passages in the New Testament must be understood as a concession to the thought of the first century. At the same time Christ's sufferings are the real and meritorious cause of our redemption. Redemption means deliverance or release from the power and punishment of sin by the meritorious sufferings of Jesus Christ. Our redemption is not penal but 'premial', a word he appears to have coined himself from the Latin verb *praemiare*, 'to stipulate for a reward'. Christ deserved a reward for his obedience and piety and so pardon was granted to penitents through Christ.

He offers us a parable. There is a province whose inhabitants rebel. The king sends his son to deal with them, but they treat him badly. In this situation he sets an example of the profoundest submission and most practical obedience. In the mean time through his care, counsel and conduct some of the rebels become sensible of their folly and guilt and grow ashamed of what they have done. They separate from the rest and apply to the king, acknowledging their fault and suing for pardon. He appears and is well pleased with their return to their duty, but on several accounts judges it improper to grant them entire forgiveness and absolute indemnity. Hereupon they have recourse to the prince and desire his intercession. He mediates with his father on their behalf and earnestly entreats him to restore them to his royal favour. In honour of so obedient and deserving a son and as a recompense for his faithful services and high merit his request is fully granted. On his account and for his sake they not only obtain impunity but are favoured and encouraged in the same manner as if they had never offended. Such treatment, says Balguy, 'conforms to the wisdom of government and the rule of truth'.[49] Like Stillingfleet, to whom he is indebted, he sees God and humankind as bound together in one community. God has pleased in his infinite wisdom to interweave public and private

[49] J. Balguy, *An Essay on Redemption* (London, 1741), p. 89.

good and to unite and incorporate the interests of mankind, 'thereby knitting the several members of the great communities to each other by strong ties and powerful ligaments'.[50] Our repentance could not procure us that entire pardon or that immense degree of favour which are now set before us. 'What remained then to save us and bless us, effectively and fully, but a Mediator of transcendent merit and boundless benevolence.'[51]

We could scarcely find an atonement theology which so admirably expresses the *contrat sociale*, the Whig Orthodoxy of the first half of the century. The key point, he felt, was that any theory must 'afford an equal testimony of [God's] abhorrence of sin and discountenance of sinners: equally support the authority of his laws and vindicate the majesty of his government'.[52] This is the theology of the best kind of eighteenth-century magistrate. Were the parable pressed, were justice to follow the divine example, then the radical challenge of the New Testament to the eighteenth-century status quo could hardly have been clearer. What appears to have been in Balguy's mind, however, is rather the prerogative of pardon, a prerogative taken with immense seriousness, for example by George III later in the century. Law and order come first, but mercy must be exercised. For someone like Paley such a practice was as near as possible to judicial perfection.

Douglas Hay has maintained that 'the criminal law was critically important in maintaining bonds of obedience and deference, in legitimizing the status quo, in constantly recreating the structure of authority which arose from property and in turn protected its interests'. Hay notes that in its rituals, judgements, and channelling of emotion, criminal law 'echoed many of the most powerful psychic components of religion'.[53] The inverse also applies: this religion underwrites the criminal law, and its symbolic celebration of property and social class.

As our second Anglican representative we have to take Balguy's

---

[50] ibid., p. 90.
[51] ibid., p. 99.
[52] ibid., p. 104.
[53] D. Hay, 'Property, Authority and Criminal Law', in Hay et al., *Albion's Fatal Tree*, pp. 25, 33.

contemporary, Joseph Butler (1692–1752), the most considerable Anglican theologian of the century.[54] He learned his theology in the Dissenting Academy, and it was youthful disagreements with his teachers which led to his removal to Oxford. From there, after studying law, he entered the Church of England ministry, becoming Bishop of Durham in 1750. Like Balguy he was of broadly Whig sympathies, being first appointed to the Bench at the recommendation of Queen Caroline. His *Analogy of Religion Natural and Revealed*, published in 1736, when he was forty-four, was to eighteenth-century Anglicanism what Hooker had been to the seventeenth century.

Butler set out to show that it is no more difficult to believe in a religion of revelation than in a religion of nature and that if you believe in the latter you must consistently believe in the former. Deists appealed to the clear light of nature, which they opposed to the obscurities of revelation. Butler showed that 'nature' was profoundly obscure and mysterious. As religion is marked only by an analogous obscurity, there is no reason to discount it. The facts of nature give us grounds for inferring the probable truth of revealed religion. The political implications of this doctrine, as manifest in the account of redemption, are revealing.

When he turns to the question of redemption, his fundamental axiom is that the world is under the proper moral government of God, so that the consequences of vice must be misery in some future state. What happens when creatures who are moral agents presumptuously introduce that confusion and misery into the kingdom of God which mankind have, in fact, introduced; blaspheme the Sovereign Lord of all, condemn his authority, and are injurious to the degree they are to their fellow creatures? It is unclear how the natural consequences of this could be prevented consistently with the eternal rule of right, or with what is, in fact, the moral constitution of nature. However, we have to hope that the universal government is not so severely strict, but that there is

---

[54] At the end of the century we find the first Norrissian Professor of Divinity at Cambridge, John Hey, equally appealing to the analogy of magistracy. In his *Lectures in Divinity*, published in 1796, he modestly tells his readers that they must not expect to find anything wholly *original* in them. If the lecturer compiles with judgement what will be most useful to his particular hearers, and sometimes advances a step or two beyond his predecessors, he does all that ought to be expected of him.

room for pardon, or for having those penal consequences prevented. Yet, there seems no probability that anything we could do would alone and of itself prevent their following or being inflicted. 'Consider then: people ruin their fortunes by extravagance; they bring diseases upon themselves by excess; they incur the penalties of civil laws; and surely civil government is natural; will sorrow for these follies past, and behaving well for the future, alone and of itself prevent the natural consequences of them? ... it is clearly contrary to all our notions of government.'[55]

Something more is needed, and this was recognised by the sacrificial system. The general prevalence of propitiatory sacrifice in the heathen world shows that repentance is insufficient to expiate guilt. So from what we can tell, the general laws of God's government must lead to our punishment. Here revelation comes in. Christ interposed in such a manner as to prevent that punishment from actually following which, according to the general laws of divine government, must have followed the sins of the world. Christ is therefore a propitiatory sacrifice.

How and in what particular way it had this efficacy, there are not wanting persons who have endeavoured to explain; but I do not find the Scripture has explained it ... Some have endeavoured to explain the efficacy of what Christ has done and suffered for us, beyond what the Scripture has authorized: others, probably because they could not explain it, have been for taking it away, and confining his office as Redeemer of the world to his instruction, example and government of the Church. Whereas the doctrine of the gospel appears to be, not only that he taught the efficacy of repentance, but rendered it of the efficacy of which it is, by what he did and suffered for us.[56]

We can see in daily life that the innocent suffer for the guilty. 'Vicarious punishment is a providential appointment of every day's experience.'[57] Also, the tendency of the doctrine to vindicate the authority of God's laws and deter his creatures from sin is plainly unanswerable. The usual objection to satisfaction theory, that the innocent cannot be punished for the guilty, is 'not an objection against Christianity' but 'an objection to the

---

[55]　J. Butler, *The Analogy of Religion* (London, Bell, 1902), p. 245.

[56]　ibid., p. 252.

[57]　ibid., p. 255.

constitution of nature'.[58] We cannot object to the need for a mediator, because all living creatures are brought into the world and their life preserved by the instrumentality of others. Though the category of sacrifice is not the primary one under which we grasp Christ's work, it remains a necessary part of the datum because it is part of how things are.[59]

Politically, Whigs were opposed to the ideology of passive resistance, but their commitment to the status quo amounted to something very similar. In his sermon to the House of Lords in 1741 Butler insisted that 'Civil liberty, the liberty of a community, is a severe and restrained thing; implies in the notion of it, authority, settled subordinations, subjection, and obedience; and is altogether as much hurt by too little of this kind, as by too much of it.'[60] Butler's grasp of the vicariousness of human life, of the fact that 'vicarious punishment is part of every day's experience', is at the same time profound and chilling. It is profound in that it does most certainly represent a reality which lies at the heart of the gospel. As an account of what was actually happening in the mid eighteenth century, especially in the courts, it is chilling. Coleridge maintained, in his Socinian days, that Butler's idea of satisfaction is not blasphemy only because it is nonsense.[61] The usual Socinian objections to satisfaction theory may have been in mind here, but possibly Coleridge may have seen the extent to which, in Butler, love seems to be an exercise in calculation. His well-known sermons 'On Resentment' and 'On Forgiveness' consider crime from the standpoint of what Rashdall described as 'a cool and calculating utilitarian analysis'. And he comments, 'There must be something more in forgiveness than the mere limitation of vengeance by the demands of public welfare.'[62] This kind of theology would be incapable of prophetic protest.

---

[58] ibid.

[59] Christ is first our Mediator as revealer of the will of God; second, he founded a church to be to mankind a standing memorial of religion and invitation to it. Sacrifice is only a third and subsidiary function.

[60] In *Works* (2 vols., Oxford, Clarendon Press, 1820), vol. II, p. 347.

[61] S. Coleridge, *Lectures on Religion* (1795), in *Collected Works* (London, Routledge & Kegan Paul, 1971), Lecture v.

[62] H. Rashdall, *The Theory of Good and Evil* (Oxford, Oxford University Press, 1907), vol. I, p. 310.

Our first Dissenter is John Taylor 'of Norwich', as he is always known, who wrote a much-cited essay on the atonement, *The Scripture Doctrine of Atonement Examined*, published in 1751. Like Butler he was a product of the Academy, studying at Whitehaven and later teaching at Warrington. His *Hebrew Concordance* marked a real advance in study of the Hebrew text, whilst his earlier essay on original sin did much to undermine Calvinism in the Congregational Church. Like so many others he undertakes a close examination of all the biblical texts on sin and atonement, which he sets out in two columns, with the text on one side and an analysis of its effect and means on the other. His ideas are so interesting as an account of the interrelation of atonement and attitudes to crime that I shall quote him at some length. The conclusion of his study is that Christ's sacrifice is not literal, but one of obedience. The notion of Christ's dying in our stead, paying an equivalent, or suffering a vicarious punishment, will not bear the test of Scripture or reason:

Not Law and Justice but Wisdom and Goodness are the Rules and the *only* Rules, of pardoning Mercy. And all the world allows that several just considerations may possibly occur to *satisfy* the Lawgiver, or to render it expedient and proper for him to relax the penalty of the Law and to extend his Favour and Mercy to offenders ... As therefore the Scripture never speaks (nor, in any consistency can speak) of Christ's satisfying the Divine law or Justice, so it is evident, there is no necessity for it: for all the ends of Redemption may be obtained without it, by satisfying the Wisdom of the Lawgiver.

Law and justice can never admit of one man's dying in the stead of another; or of his suffering the punishment which in law and justice is due to the offender only.

God must be considered in a publick capacity, as a Magistrate, as the Governor of the Universe; and sin as the only Disorder, Mischief and Misery among his subjects, which alone can corrupt and ruin them; and which therefore above all things he must be concerned to prevent and reform. Now in this view are we sure that a single absolute Pardon, even of the Penitent, is agreeable to rectoral goodness, and the ends of government, which are good order and happiness of the rational creation? The punishing and pardoning of crimes are very important concerns to every government. And as the one ought not to exceed the bounds of justice and equity, so the other ought to be granted with caution and prudence. Easy, indiscreet pardons may give encouragement to transgress; and forgiveness lightly obtained may give a light opinion of wickedness; not only to the offender himself, but to all his Fellow subjects. It is therefore evident that the Governor who consults the *publick* good ought to guard, qualify and circumstance his pardons in such a manner as not to propagate, but, if possible, to extirpate a Spirit of Disorder and Rebellion, and to spread a loyal, well affected Temper throughout the whole community.

In language reminiscent of Abelard, Taylor argues

That the death of Christ hath a natural and strong Tendency, as a moral mean, to affect the Mind in this Manner, I am fully satisfied, when I consider; that a person of so transcendent Eminence and Excellency, who was in the Form of God ... laying aside the form of God, actually came down from Heaven, sank into the low condition of a man, and took upon him the humble form of a servant, for this end, that he might instruct us in the will of God, and under all our trials and temptations, exhibit in his own person and actions, the most perfect example of all holiness, obedience and goodness ... How forcibly, far beyond any abstract reasonings, do these considerations urge us to love our God and Saviour; to devote our all to his Honour; to prize and cultivate our Nature, as our most inestimable Possession; as above all things to be ambitious, diligent and jealous in practicing the Instructions and following the Example of our best friend, who shed his precious blood to do us the greatest service and to make us virtuous and happy.

The Jewish sacrifices were 'symbolical instructions in Holiness', and so is Jesus' death, but in a more perfect manner. Thus we can say that Christ's death makes atonement, or is a reason for God forgiving our sins, but we speak metaphorically. Thus, in a way perfectly rational and Scriptural, we obtain all the blessings of redemption.

As for Balguy, Taylor's central metaphor for God is of the Magistrate disposed to pardon. Neither of these men could have condoned, on theological grounds, the ferocity of the penal law of their day, though we have no protest from their pens against it. In general the church was silent, until the issue of prison reform was put on the agenda by Howard. Significantly, Taylor's essay drew a lengthy response from John Wesley, who condemned it as 'worse than Deism'. Taylor's views on forgiveness were contemp-

tuously cast side. God has the perfect right to destroy his
creatures, if he so chooses, as he is their 'Lord and Proprietor'.[63]
We have only one assize sermon from Wesley, a tremendous
piece which must have lasted well over an hour, in which all
present, both magistrates and prisoners, are dangled over the pit
of eternal condemnation, but which ends with all being committed to the mercy of God, 'especially those who are going to
meet their maker this day'.

I turn finally to the avowedly Socinian Joseph Priestley, the
discoverer of oxygen ('dephlogisticated air'), nitric acid and
nitrous oxide, amongst other things. Although he was made a
Fellow of the Royal Society for his *History of Electricity*, and wrote
on metaphysics, politics, history and grammar, his main interest
was always in theology. Naturally he was interested in the
question of prisons, and defended Howard's idea of penitentiary
education on the grounds that criminals had forfeited their right
to freedom of conscience.[64] He was a materialist who defended
revelation, and who combined materialism with faith by believing
in the general resurrection at the last day. Three years after his
house, books and priceless collection of scientific instruments were
destroyed, in 1791, he sailed to America, where he died in 1804.
He uses the metaphor of the divine magistracy in a very different
way from Taylor and Balguy, arguing not from analogy but from
*dis*analogy.

In his *Memoirs* he writes, 'By reading with care Dr Lardner's
Letter on the Logos, I became what is called a Socinian soon after my
settlement at Leeds (1767 aet 34); and after giving the closest
attention to the subject I have seen more and more reason to be
satisfied with that opinion to this day and likewise to be more
impressed with the idea of its importance.' In an open letter to
Dr Linn in 1803 he wrote, 'In the days of my ignorance I
maintained the doctrine that you now hold [i.e. the satisfaction
theory] ... but the first thing I did after I became a minister, and
had leisure, was to collect and write out every text in the Old or
New Testament that bore any relation to this subject; and the

---

[63]   J. Wesley, *The Doctrine of Original Sin. According to Scripture, Reason and Experience* (Bristol,
       1757).
[64]   Ignatieff, *JMP*, p. 117.

result was the clearest conviction which has remained to this day, that the doctrine of atonement, in every sense of the word, is as contrary to Scripture as to reason.' His major essay on the topic, published in 1761, bore the lengthy title *The Scripture Doctrine of Remission which sheweth that the Death of Christ is no proper Sacrifice nor Satisfaction for Sin: but that pardon is dispensed solely on account of repentance, or a personal reformation of the sinner.*

Priestley argues, as Socinus had done, that we must recognise the figurative use of words. 'But such is the nature both of our ideas and words, and such the power of association, that what was at first evidently compounded or figurative, by frequent use ceases to be conceived so.' It is clear from the Old Testament that men expected pardon only from their integrity. In the New Testament 'our Lord's discourses are chiefly in a moral strain'. Jesus never hints at the necessity of any satisfaction being made to the justice of God for them. It is urged, in favour of the doctrine of the atonement, that the scheme is necessary in God's moral government. But we must bear in mind that divine justice is not that blind principle which, upon any provocation, craves satisfaction indiscriminately of all that comes within reach.

God's justice can be no other than a modification of goodness, a benevolence that is the sole governing principle; the object and end of which is the supreme happiness of his creatures and subjects. This happiness being of a moral nature, must be chiefly promoted by such a constitution of the moral government we are under as shall afford the most effectual motives to induce men to regulate their lives well.

Magistrates cannot simply pardon the penitent, because they do not know men's hearts – but God can (a sentiment with which Blackstone agrees). 'Thus the principles of just government are so far from illustrating and vindicating the necessity of any satisfaction for sin, besides the repentance and the reformation of the offender that, when brought to this test, its absurdity proves the most glaring, and our minds become more strongly disposed to reject it.'

Clark wishes to argue that radical Dissent, by which he means principally Socinianism, had defined its position after 1772 in terms so extreme, in relation to society's ruling orthodoxy, 'that radicalism itself could easily be equated with the destruction of civilisation'.[65] Ideologists of the status quo, such as Burke, believed that Anglicanism and the Hanoverian Establishment sank or swam together. The Socinian form of Dissent represented a radical challenge to that view. Like Socinus himself, however, Priestley was no foe to magistrates, though he believed that their authority should not extend to religious opinion.[66] As far as the implementation of the law goes, as we have seen, he is at one with the century's greatest jurist, William Blackstone. He fully supported the principles of 'just government', and for most of his life held a basically Whig view of the need to maintain a balance of power between king, Commons and House of Lords.[67] As the Government in England became more repressive, after the French Revolution, he began to argue that the only source of power should be the will of the people as represented in a reformed House of Commons, and, later still, an element of genuine millenarianism appears in his writing, but in both of these opinions he is but representative of a widespread mood in these years.[68] These views would certainly not have portended 'the destruction of civilisation' to many in the immediate aftermath of the French Revolution, even to Fox, Romilly, or the great Whig lawyer Erskine. They characterise, rather, the extreme reaction of Pitt's Government and the vindictive judge Lord Braxfield.[69] Romilly noted gloomily the way in which reaction put an end to the chances of prison reform. Moreover,

---

[65] Clark, *ES*, p. 346.

[66] See, for example, his 1789 sermon, *The Conduct to be observed by Dissenters in order to procure the Repeal of the Corporation and Test Acts*; also, his *Essay on the First Principles of Government*, *Works*, vol. XXII, which Clark quotes very selectively, p. 33.

[67] 'The English government is a mixture of regal, aristocratical and democratical power.' *Essay*, p. 53.

[68] *Letters to Edmund Burke occasioned by his Reflections on the Revolution in France*; *A Political Dialogue on the General Principles of Government* (both 1791). For the millenarianism, see *The Present State of Europe Compared with Antient Prophecies* (1794). In general Clark seems to use the category 'millenarian' very loosely, to describe any radical political thinking. He argues that Socinianism was proscribed because it was loathed, especially because it challenged Arminian Anglicanism's offer of salvation to every individual. This it precisely did not – rather the reverse, to the extent that there were many who assented to the Church of England's Calvinist articles. For the millenarianism of the early 1790s, and for radical opinions identical to Priestley's, see Thompson, *Making*, pp. 52ff., 127.

[69] See A. Briggs, *The Age of Improvement 1783–1867* (London, Longman, 1979), pp. 129ff.

'The rational Christianity of the Unitarians ... seemed too cold, too distant, too polite, and too much associated with the comfortable values of a prospering class to appeal to the city or village poor.'[70] The links which were certainly there between Dissent and radicalism lay elsewhere.

Coleridge, notoriously, reacted strongly against Socinianism, and returned to Orthodoxy. 'I owe, under God, my return to the faith, to my having gone much further than the Unitarians and so having come round to the other side.'[71] He made the astute remark that if you push Priestley, you end up in atheism.[72] On the other hand we must not underestimate the constructive work done by people like Elizabeth Gaskell's husband, in the next century, especially in the matter of penal reform, where Unitarians consistently took a more humane stance than the orthodox. The contrast between Calvinist and Unitarian on these issues is clearly illustrated by a response to Priestley published in 1793 by Andrew Fuller, in his *Calvinistic and Socinian systems examined and compared as to their moral tendency*.

Those who embrace the Calvinistic system believe that every degree of revolt from God is rebellion against the general good and that if suffered to operate according to its tendency it would destroy the well-being of the universe by excluding God and righteousness and peace from the whole system. Seeing that it aims destruction at the infinite good and tends to universal anarchy and mischief, it is in this respect an infinite evil.

Those, on the other hand, who embrace the Socinian system entertain diminutive notes of the evil of sin. Socinian writers, when speaking of the sins of men, describe them in the language of pollution, language tending to convey an idea of purity, but not of blame. There is a kind of vindictive justice in God, as Jonathan Edwards allows. 'No considerate citizen, who values the public mind, could blame a magistrate for putting the penal laws of his country so far in execution as should be necessary for the honour of good government, the support of good government and the determent of wicked men.' It is on this analogy that we

[70] Thompson, *Making*, p. 31.
[71] *Table Talk*, 23 June 1834.
[72] Clark is right about the progression from Socinianism to utilitarianism: *ES*, p. 345.

must understand God's relation to us. The implications of these views for penal theory scarcely need spelling out.

RADICAL LOVE

The most interesting opponent of satisfaction theory in the century was not Priestley but the high Tory non-juror William Law (1686–1761), who could never be brushed aside as a heretic in the way Priestley could. Law is just one of the better-known examples which serve to illustrate the inaccuracy of Pattison's view of the eighteenth century.[73] The high seriousness of mid-seventeenth-century Christianity was alive and well in Law, as it was in many Anglican clergy of the century.[74] He became a Fellow of Emmanuel in 1711, but as a non-juror, who believed passionately in the Divine Right of Kings, he resigned his Fellowship in 1716 when George I acceded to the throne. This put an end to any chances of promotion he might have had. In 1723, after some years when we know him only as the author of polemical tracts, Law became tutor to Edward Gibbon, the father of the historian. In 1726 he published his *Practical Treatise upon Christian Perfection*, and three years later achieved fame with *A Serious Call to a Devout and Holy Life*, which became the most famous devotional book of the century, going through many editions. Both of these books had a great impact on the Wesleys,

---

[73] We have a rule of life he drew up for himself, possibly on going to Cambridge at the age of nineteen in 1705. There are eighteen precepts, which include:

1. To fix it deep in my mind, that I have but one business upon my hands, to seek for eternal happiness, by doing the will of God.

3. To think nothing great or desirable, because the world thinks it so; but to form all my judgements of things from the infallible Word of God, and direct my life according to it.

5. To remember frequently, and impress it upon my mind deeply, that no condition in this life is for enjoyment, but for trial; and that every power, ability, or advantage we have, are all so many talents to be accounted for, to the Judge of all the world.

16. To pray, privately, thrice a day, besides my morning and evening prayers.

17. To keep from public houses as much as I can, without offence.

18. To spend some time in giving an account of the day, previous to evening prayer: how have I spent this day? what sin have I committed? what temptations have I withstood? have I performed all my duties?

[74] On energetic and devout clergy in the eighteenth century see Langford, *People*, pp. 244–6, and Clark, *passim*. But see also the warning of E. P. Thompson, *Customs in Common* (Harmondsworth, Penguin, 1993), pp. 49ff.

who thought highly enough of Law to walk from Oxford to Putney to meet him. In 1740 he retired to Kings Cliffe with Gibbon's aunt and a widowed lady and set up a small religious community, possibly modelled on Little Gidding.

From his time in Cambridge onwards, Law had relished the writings of mystics such as Tauler and Suso, but in 1735 came across the Lutheran mystic Jacob Boehme, who thereafter had a decisive influence on his thought. Boehme's thought on the atonement finds expression in Law's later work *The Spirit of Love*, published in 1754, and in a letter written three years later, 'In Answer to a Scruple'.[75] He condemns the satisfaction theory on five major grounds. First, in his view, it completely fails to do justice to Scripture. The idea that Christ's death is something chiefly done with regard to God to alter or atone for an infinite wrath is 'in the grossest Ignorance of God, of the Reason and Ground, and Effects of Christ's Death, and in full Contradiction to the Express Letter of Scripture'.[76] There we are told that God is love and that the only thing which needed satisfaction was the infinity of his love, which 'could not be satisfied, with anything less than Man's full deliverance from all the evil of his fallen State'.[77] Christ's teaching on forgiveness, and the parable of the king and the indebted servants, completely overturn all notions of satisfaction. In the parable the king requires no payment. 'Can there therefore be a greater Folly, than to appeal to this, and the like Scriptures, to make God a Creditor, whose vindictive Wrath against his Debtor will not be appeased, till full Payment is made to it?'[78] The petition to 'Forgive us our trespasses' in the Lord's Prayer 'Teaches the same frank forgiveness as the foregoing parable, and is utterly inconsistent with the Doctrine of an infinite Satisfaction, necessary to be made'.[79]

Second, not only does Scripture deny the idea that God demands an infinite satisfaction, but 'the Light of Nature abhors it'. The implications of positing wrath in God are, in Law's view,

---

[75]   W. Law, *Works* (9 vols., London, 1762), vol. v (*The Spirit of Love*) and vol. ix.
[76]   ibid., vol. ix, p. 139.
[77]   ibid.
[78]   ibid., p. 143.
[79]   ibid.

atheism. 'If you want to believe in the wrath of God you must be a Spinozist.'[80]

For if Wrath is in the Supreme God, then Nature is in God, and if so, then God is Nature, and nothing else; for Nature cannot be above itself. Therefore if Nature is in the most high God then the lowest Working of Nature is the true Supreme God ... This is the atheistical Absurdity that necessarily follows from the supposing a Wrath in God.[81]

In various ways the theology of satisfaction distorts our understanding of God. Anticipating J. S. Mill, Law argues that to posit wrath in God is to make God less moral than human beings:

If you have Wrath in the God you must have a God in whom is Selfishness, Envy and Pride, with all the Properties of fallen Nature. In a Word, a vindictive Wrath in God, that will not forgive, till a Satisfaction equal to the Offence, is made to it, sets the Goodness of God in a lower State than that which has been found in Thousands of Mankind.

Again, it completely misunderstands the nature of God's righteousness. 'What a paltry Logic to say, God is Righteousness and Justice, as well as Love, and therefore his Love cannot help, or forgive the Sinner, till his Justice, or righteous Wrath has Satisfaction?'[82]

Every Word here, is in full ignorance of the Things spoken of. For what is Love in God, but his Will to all Goodness? What is Righteousness in God, but his unchangeable Love of his own Goodness, his Impossibility of loving anything else but it, his Impossibility of suffering anything that is Unrighteous, to have any Communion with him?[83]

People who argue like this are 'Dividers of the Divine Nature'. God is a perfect unity, and we cannot divide the attributes.

God did not and could not love or like or desire the sufferings and death of Christ, for what they were in themselves, or as sufferings of the highest kind. On the contrary, the higher and greater such sufferings were, the less pleasing would they have been to God. They were prized only because everything that Christ was and did and suffered was that which gave him full

---

[80]   ibid., p. 140.
[81]   ibid.
[82]   ibid., p. 144.
[83]   ibid.

power to be a Common Father of Life to all who died in Adam. Suffering and dying was necessary as a way of giving up and parting from fallen nature. Christ, as suffering and dying, was nothing else but Christ conquering and overcoming all the false good, and the hellish evil, of the fallen state of man.

Finally, if Christ died to atone, or extinguish God's wrath, then it must be said that Christ made an atonement for God and not for man; that he died for the good and benefit of God, and not of man; and that that which is called our redemption ought rather to be called the redemption of God, as saving and delivering him, and not man, from his own wrath.

When the New Testament says that Christ is given 'for us', it means that Christ is given *into* us. He is in no other sense our full perfect and sufficient atonement than as his nature and spirit are born and formed in us which so purge us from our sins, that we are thereby in him. As Adam is truly our defilement and impurity, by his birth in us, so Christ is our atonement and purification by our being born again of him, and having thereby quickened and revived in us that first divine life which was extinguished in Adam. In a restatement of Irenaeus' recapitulation theory Law argues that Christ stands in the same fullness of relation to all humankind as Adam did. Christ could not be our Redeemer until he had stood out his trial and overcome all that by which Adam was overcome. Everything which had overcome Adam was overcome by Christ; and Christ's victory did, in the nature of the thing, as certainly and fully open an entrance for him and all his seed into paradise as Adam's Fall cast him and all his seed into the prison and captivity of this earthly bestial world. Nothing supernatural came to pass in either case but paradise lost and paradise regained according to the nature of things, or the real efficacy of cause to produce its effects.

The political metaphor of the divine magistracy could scarcely have received a more crushing rejection than it does in Law, for all his non-juring principles. If we ask why it was not accepted by other theologians, we have only to look at Wesley's response to *The Spirit of Love*. Law and the Wesleys had already fallen out in 1738, over the mystics, and especially their account of the atonement and justification, but the publication of these books

prompted an angry response from John Wesley in an open letter
in 1756. He attacks Boehme's speculative philosophy, but especially maintains that to deny the wrath of God strikes at the
credibility of the Bible. Wrath and justice, Wesley maintains, are
almost synonymous terms. He cites forty-two Scriptural passages
to show that there is a vindictive or punitive justice in God.
How can Law speak of the folly of the debtor and creditor
scheme of the atonement? Christ himself taught it, as we see
from the parable of the king settling accounts (Matt. 18.23f.).
Christ is not our Redeemer because he brings new birth but
because he made a sacrifice for our sins. To deny everlasting
punishment is to deny revelation, from which we learn that the
bodies and souls of the wicked will both be punished in hell with
unimaginable torments. Whilst Wesley frequently preached 'free
pardon' to 'convicted felons', this note was found on a young
man who had previously worked for him, and who was to be
hanged for robbery: 'He fell a sacrifice to the justice of a long
offended God. O consider this, ye that now forget God, and
know not the day of your visitation!'[84] The criminal justice
system, and retributivism, could scarcely find more complete
religious sanction. In accounting for Law's failure to go with this
current E. P. Thompson notes that, although Law was completely unsympathetic to political radicalism, 'there is a kind of
spiritualised antinomian pressure' to be found in him.[85] That
there are two sides to Law follows exactly from the ambivalence
of the Protestant emphasis on justification by faith alone. This
could, as it does with Wesley, feed in to a preoccupation with
the religious experience of the individual. On the other hand, it
could mount a radical challenge to the authority of ruling
ideology, which included theological Orthodoxy. 'It displaced
the authority of institutions and of received worldly wisdom with
that of the individual's inner light – faith, conscience, personal
understanding of the scriptures or (for Blake) "the Poetic
Genius" – and allowed to the individual a stubborn scepticism
in the face of the established culture, a fortitude in the face of its
seductions or persecutions sufficient to support Christians in the

84   *Journals*, 11 January 1742 (1913 edition), vol. II, p. 521.
85   Thompson, *Witness*, p. 37; cf. p. 47.

face of the State or of polite learning.'[86] This fortitude might produce a radical quietism, as it does in Law, but it could also produce a much more active faith – as it does in Blake.

The one person in the century who saw the direct connection between such a theology of atonement and the criminal law of the day was William Blake. In an unjustly neglected book Margaret Bottrall argued that the decisive influence on Blake was not Boehme directly, but Boehme mediated by Law.[87] In addition to such literary influences E. P. Thompson has maintained that Blake's theological milieu is the network of Dissenting congregations, largely peopled by artisans and craftsmen like himself, which were spread all over London.[88]

Since Northrop Frye's great rehabilitation of Blake many studies have offered interpretations of his work. David Erdman drew attention to his passionate and consistent opposition to war.[89] He can be read convincingly in psychological terms.[90] No one, however, has sufficiently explored Blake's preoccupation with Tyburn tree. When Blake moved to South Molton Street he saw the Tyburn victims carted to the gallows up Tyburn Road (now Oxford Street) at every assize. He had good enough reason to know about Tyburn in any case, for his father had tried to apprentice him to the printer Ryland, who was hanged in 1783 for forging bills of exchange. In 1804 he came near enough ending up there himself as he was framed on a charge of sedition. Blake spells out the connection again and again throughout *Jerusalem*. Albion sits in his secret seat:

> Cold snows drifted around him: ice cover'd his loins
> around.
> He sat by Tyburn's brook, and underneath his heel shot
> up
> A deadly Tree: he named it Moral Virtue and the Law

[86] ibid., p. 5.
[87] M. Bottrall, *The Divine Image: A Study of Blake's Interpretation of Christianity* (Rome, 1950).
[88] Thompson, *Witness*, chaps. 1 and 2.
[89] D. Erdman, *Blake: Prophet Against Empire* (Princeton, Princeton University Press, 1954).
[90] M. Paley, *The Continuing City* (Oxford, Oxford University Press, 1983).

Of God who dwells in Chaos hidden from human sight.
The Tree spread over him its cold shadows, (Albion
groan'd)
They bent down, they felt the earth, and again
enrooting
Shot into many a Tree, an endless labyrinth of woe.

From willing sacrifice of Self, to sacrifice
of (miscall'd) Enemies
For Atonement. Albion began to erect twelve Altars
Of rough unhewn rocks, before the Potter's Furnace.
He nam'd them Justice and Truth. And Albion's Sons
Must have become the first Victims, being the first
transgressors,
But they fled to the mountains to seek ransom,
building A Strong
Fortification against the Divine Humanity and Mercy,
In Shame & Jealousy to annihilate Jerusalem.

Then the Divine Vision like a silent Sun appear'd
above
Albion's dark rocks, setting behind the Gardens of
Kensington
On Tyburn's River in clouds of blood, where was mild
Zion Hill's
Most ancient promontory.[91]

Tyburn is a symbol for the wicked slaughter of human beings in
the name of law and religion, justified by the penal theology of
the atonement. In those who die there, sacrificial victims more
appropriate to Druid worship than to the religion of Christ, 'the
Lamb is slain in his children'.[92] Both the theory of law and the
theology have to change. 'All Penal Laws commit transgressions
and are cruelty and murder.'[93] They are based on the assumption that the 'general' interest must be preserved, both by law
and religion. 'Prisons are built with stones of Law, Brothels with
bricks of Religion.'[94] Although Christ stood at the centre of
Blake's religious vision, Blake believed that the church, which

[91] *Jerusalem*, 28.9; cf. 12; 27.
[92] ibid., 24.2.
[93] Annotations to Watson, in G. Keynes, *The Writings of William Blake* (3 vols., London,
       Nonesuch Press, 1925), vol. II, p. 166.
[94] *The Marriage of Heaven and Hell*, Keynes, vol. I, p. 185, Plate 8.

sanctified the slaughter of Tyburn's victims, betrayed him: 'The Modern Church Crucifies Christ with the Head Downwards.'[95] And, in the spirit of William Law: 'Where are those who worship Satan under the Name of God? Where are they? Listen! Every Religion that Preaches Vengeance for Sin is the Religion of the Enemy and Avenger and not of the Forgiver of Sin and their God is Satan.'[96] According to Blake's friend Crabbe Robinson, Blake 'spoke of the Atonement. Said, "It is a horrible doctrine. If another man pay your debt, I do not forgive it."' Thus Los says to Albion in *Jerusalem*:

> Must the Wise die for an Atonement? does Mercy endure
> Atonement?
>   No! It is Moral Severity and destroys Mercy in its
> Victim.[97]

Blake understood that salvation involves death and sacrifice, but he redefined these.

> Albion reply'd: 'Cannot Man exist without Mysterious
>   Offering of Self for Another? is this Friendship and
> Brotherhood?
>   I see thee in the likeness and similitude of Los my
> Friend.'
>
> Jesus said: 'Wouldest thou love one who never died
>   For thee, or ever die for one who had not died for
> thee?
>   And if God dieth not for Man, Man could not exist;
> for Man is Love
>   As God is Love; every kindness to another is a
> little Death
>   In the Divine Image, nor can Man exist but by
> Brotherhood.'[98]

Christ's death is the perpetual example of that self-sacrifice by which alone human beings can live. What threatens human life, 'Satan', is 'the Great Selfhood', man's self-righteous pride: 'In Hell all is Self Righteousness; there is no such thing there

[95] *The Last Judgement*, Keynes, vol. III, p. 160.
[96] *Jerusalem* 52.
[97] 39.25, 6; cf. 61.17, 8; 46.28.
[98] 96.20–8.

as Forgiveness of Sin; he who does Forgive Sin is Crucified as an Abettor of Criminals, & he who performs Works of Mercy in Any Shape whatever is punish'd &, if possible, destroy'd, not thro' envy or Hatred or Malice, but thro' Self-Righteousness that thinks it does God service, which God is Satan.'[99] Forgiveness is the heart of Christianity, something the bishops have not understood: 'The Bishops never saw the Everlasting Gospel any more than Tom Paine ... The Gospel is Forgiveness of Sins and has no Moral Precepts; those belong to Plato, & Seneca & Nero.'[100] Accusation of sins is essential: 'Severity of judgement is a great virtue.'[101] But forgiveness has to follow. 'A society's index of civilization is not in a high proportion of murderers who get hanged, but in a low proportion of murders; and while it takes less time to hang a murderer than to organize society so as to reduce the motives for murder, there is no imaginative progress in the former. Progress comes only from the "forgiveness of sins" which among other things is the transference of the will from the Selfhood to the imagination.'[102] What the cross does, according to Blake, is to demystify the pretensions of law, morality and religion. It exposes them as ideology. What must take its place is praxis: 'Are not Religion and Politics the Same Thing? Brotherhood is Religion.'[103] For Blake true religion was the exercise of imagination. False religion is characterised by teaching an unknown God, and by insisting on submission, acceptance and obedience. Such state religion 'is the source of all cruelty'.[104] He understood the ideological function of religion better than Marx:

God is only an Allegory of Kings & Nothing Else ... God is The Ghost of the Priest and King, who Exist, whereas God exists not except from their effluvia.[105]

---

[99] *A Vision of the Last Judgement*, Keynes, vol. III, p. 160. Cf. *Jerusalem* 33.
[100] Notes on Bishop Watson, Keynes, vol. II, p. 169.
[101] Marg to Lavater, Keynes, vol. I, p. 105.
[102] N. Frye, *Fearful Symmetry* (Princeton, Princeton University Press, 1947), pp. 297–8.
[103] *Jerusalem* 57, Keynes, vol. III, p. 251.
[104] Keynes, vol. II, p. 166.
[105] ibid., vol. III, pp. 387–8.

This God, whom Blake refers to as 'Old Nobodaddy', loves offerings of human blood. At the French Revolution

> old Nobodaddy aloft
> Farted & belch'd & coughed,
> And said, 'I love hanging & drawing and quartering
> Every bit as well as war & slaughtering
> Damn praying & singing,
> Unless they will bring in
> The blood of ten thousand by fighting or swinging.'[106]

Praying and singing did in fact, as Blake well knew, go together with the slaughter of the innocent, either in wars or on the gallows.

There are doubtless many reasons for the alienation of the working class from the established church in the nineteenth century. Certainly contributory to that is the role the church played in relation to the Bloody Code, the bishops voting down Romilly's reform, Wilberforce applauding the sentencing of the Unitarian minister T. F. Palmer to seven years' transportation for encouraging 'low weavers and mechanics' to read Tom Paine, and parson magistrates enforcing the poor law. At the heart of the church's theology lay a reading of the crucifixion which developed sensibilities which underwrote rather than challenged what even James Stephen called a 'barbarous' penal code. It was almost without exception Dissenters and Unitarians who challenged this theology, the only exception being William Law. He showed how a return to the gospel sources could produce a quite different theology of redemption even alongside a political theology of the most conservative kind. Since Blake was by and large not read, the extent of the church's betrayal of its gospel, of what Aloysius Pieris has called 'God's solidarity pact with the poor', was not grasped. Blake was a prophet who made articulate the perceptions of millions who later showed what they felt by their practice, by their contemptuous abandonment of the church of the status quo. As the pace of industrial change increased, as the eighteenth century passed into the

---

[106] 'Let the brothels of Paris be opened', ibid., vol. I, p. 349

nineteenth, the penal rhetoric of the theologians became shriller yet. It was not until the end of the next century that theologians – some, but not all – began to reflect the implications of the century's debate on criminal justice in their work. The full implications of Blake's work, on the other hand, have not been recognised to this day.

CHAPTER 8

The age of atonement

Thanks be to those who plann'd these silent cells,
Where Sorrow's true-born child, Repentance, dwells;
Where Justice, sway'd by Mercy, doth employ
Her iron rod, to chasten, not destroy;
The slave of vice to virtue deigns restore,
And bids him, once enfranchised, sin no more.

George Holford, MP

This too I know – and wise it were
If each should know the same –
That every prison that men build
Is built with bricks of shame,
And bound with bars lest Christ should see
How men their brothers maim.

Oscar Wilde, 'The Ballad of Reading Gaol'

The period from the end of the eighteenth century to the mid nineteenth century has been referred to variously as an age of revolution, of reform, and of improvement, but more recently, and perhaps more aptly, as an age of atonement.[1] The language of atonement pervaded politics and literature, as well as religion, in a way which it never did in the eighteenth century. As the

---

[1] Boyd Hilton, *The Age of Atonement, The Influence of Evangelicalism on Social and Economic Thought 1785–1865* (henceforth *AA*) (Oxford, Oxford University Press, 1988). Cf. E. J. Hobsbawm, *The Age of Revolution* (London, Sphere, 1977), E. L. Woodward, *The Age of Reform 1815–1870* (Oxford, Clarendon Press, 1962) and Asa Briggs, *The Age of Improvement 1783–1867* (London, Longman, 1979). Hilton's characterisation is correct, but I differ from him on a number of points. In the first place his book is much more concerned with providence than with atonement. Second, he suggests that the shock of the French Revolution was the principal cause of this. My own view would be that it should be tied much more closely to the industrial revolution. Third, he finds the climax of the 'age of atonement' in the earlier part of the century, where theological literature would point much more to the Victorian period proper.

debate on the abolition of slavery went on, it was seen in the first instance as an act of atonement for national sins. Whilst some evangelicals regarded the Irish famine of 1845 as God's judgement on 'an indolent and un self-reliant people', Gladstone wrote to his wife that unless England atoned for its neglect of the Irish it must expect 'a fearful retribution'.[2] A National Fast day was proclaimed for this and other occasions of war and famine. The eighteenth century had also had its days of National Fasting, but the importance of religious guilt as a social and political factor is unquestionably higher in this period.

If we ask why, then we can point to the seismic shock of the industrial revolution, rapidly rising populations, the emergence, for the first time in history, of really great cities, and also the emergence of a middle class which was, sometimes to the point of anguish, aware of being parasitic on the labouring poor. In the first thirty years of the century Manchester, Glasgow, Birmingham, Leeds and Liverpool virtually doubled their populations, and by mid century a third of the population lived in large towns.[3] The slums of the great cities, which form the dark background of Dickens' novels, were both threatening and fascinating to the upper classes. In the first forty years of the century this growth generated a soaring crime rate which could not be dealt with by the old penal apparatus and which led to the construction of the great Victorian prisons. The view of what Mary Carpenter was later to call 'the dangerous classes' was clearly signalled by the title of Edward Gibbon Wakefield's *Householders in Danger from the Populace,* published in 1831. Twenty years later Thomas Plint in a report *Crime in England* spoke of the criminal classes as an alien force '*in* the community, but neither *of* it, nor *from* it ... completely isolated ... in blood, in sympathies, in its domestic and social organisations'.[4] Even the sympathetic Mayhew spoke of a criminal class which was 'a distinct race of individuals, as distinct as the Malay is from the

---

[2]   Hilton, *AA*, pp. 209, 113.
[3]   A. F. Weber, *The Growth of Cities in the Nineteenth Century* (New York, Columbia University Press, 1899).
[4]   Cited in L. Radzinowicz and R. Hood, *The Emergence of Penal Policy* (Oxford, Oxford University Press, 1990), pp. 74ff.

Caucasian tribe'.[5] The pimps who maintained the flourishing trade in prostitution were described as consisting largely of Negroes and Jews, 'reduced below the level of the brutes' and 'slick low living degenerates'.[6] Notorious scares like the garrotting panic of 1862, when a number of well-to-do people, including an MP, were robbed in broad daylight, fuelled these fears. From the publication of *The Origin of Species* onwards eugenics began to make its mark, influencing even Sidney and Beatrice Webb and the reforming Home Secretary, Winston Churchill.[7] The historian Harriet Martineau believed that persistent offenders should be subject to 'perpetual sequestration', and forbidden to breed, whilst Sir James Fitzjames Stephen and F. H. Bradley believed that they should be eliminated.[8]

The underclass who lived in the filthy and cramped streets, which Dickens could not characterise in a lurid enough light, constituted, as it were, the repressed part of the Victorian consciousness, as these reactions indicate. Middle-class people, the novel-reading public, felt both guilty and helpless before these social changes. William Wilberforce and Elizabeth Fry were lionised because they seemed to show the middle class successfully redeeming these aliens.

The reformative ideal had deep appeal for an anxious middle class because it implied that the punisher and the punished could be brought back together in a shared moral universe. As a hopeful allegory for class relations in general, it proved capable of surviving the repeated frustrations of reality because it spoke to a heartfelt middle class desire for a social order based on deferential reconciliation.[9]

Precisely such a deferential reconciliation is the theme of Mrs Gaskell's *North and South*. Guilt and doubt remained constitutive of the Victorian agenda. It was not just that evangelicals like George Eliot's Bulstrode needed atonement because of things in their individual biographies. It was an age which sought atonement. As

5   *London Labour and the London Poor* (4 vols., London, Griffin, Bohn & Co., 1861–2), vol. IV. Actually written by John Binny.
6   Radzinowicz and Hood, *Emergence*, p. 701.
7   ibid., pp. 27ff., 770ff.
8   ibid., p. 239.
9   M. Ignatieff, *A Just Measure of Pain: The Penitentiary in the Industrial Revolution 1750–1850* (henceforth *JMP*) (Harmondsworth, Penguin, 1989), p. 213.

I hear the long low melancholy roar on Dover Beach, where do I find salvation? The answer was only very partially articulated in the sermons, tracts and treatises which poured out on the theme of atonement, as the authors of *Essays and Reviews* knew very well. It was given in poetry and in art; in his own way Marx sought it and articulated it; but perhaps most characteristically men and women found an answer in that creation of a world of moral discourse which is, in part at least, what the great novel is. It is noteworthy that, in the mid-Victorian novel, not only is atonement a central theme, but in almost all cases it is young women who are presented as the redemptive agents in society. This reaction to centuries of male-dominated redemption-discourse also opened the way for a creative re-envisaging of how redemption might be accomplished.[10]

The nineteenth century witnessed incessant controversy over penal practice.[11] Parliamentary committees reviewed it frequently, and new Acts were passed in 1823, 1835, 1865, 1877 and 1898. A notorious scandal at Birmingham Gaol in 1851 shook middle-class consciences. The Deputy Governor was preferred above a Governor considered by the Prison Committee to be too lenient. With their connivance he tortured people to death by the use of the straitjacket and dousings with water. When the scandal broke Charles Reade rushed into print with a fictionalised version of the events, *It's Never Too Late to Mend*. The more liberal regime of Joshua Jebb, Surveyor General from 1848 to 1864, was nevertheless followed, from 1877 onwards, by nearly twenty years of extreme rigour, and frequent cruelty, under Sir Edmund Du Cane. The following of the separate and silent system, whereby prisoners were forbidden all contact with others, led to frequent

---

[10] For example, consider the dialogue of Rose Maylie and Bill Sikes' girlfriend Nancy, in *Oliver Twist*, in which Rose insists that 'It is never too late for penitence and atonement'; in *Bleak House* it is Esther who bears the guilt of her illegitimate birth, and loses her beauty looking after the dying crossing sweeper, Jo; in Mrs Gaskell's *North and South* Margaret is the mediator between management and men, the instrument of reconciling love; Jane redeems Rochester in *Jane Eyre*, helping him through repentance to new life; whilst George Eliot's Dorothea Brooke is 'a new Theresa' who has 'an incalculably diffusive' effect for good on all those around her, and is part of the struggle of the divine power against evil.

[11] Sidney and Beatrice Webb, *History of English Prisons under Local Government* (London, Longmans, 1922), *passim*.

insanity and suicide. Though advocates of severity were plentiful, pressure for reform grew through the 1880s under the pressure of a series of other complaints and scandals. Penal issues were so prominent that theologians could not but be far more conscious of them than their predecessors in the previous century, and the three most important essays on the atonement in the century all made prison analogies central. From the great mass of literature I shall select only those which best represent certain types of theological response to varieties of penal practice.

PAYING THE PRICE

It was in 1811 that Samuel Romilly made his great speech in the House of Commons which really began the process of penal reform. He managed to convince the Commons that the number of capital offences should be reduced, but, with the help of seven bishops, including one archbishop, the bill was thrown out by the Lords. When he died in 1818 nothing had yet been accomplished. In 1823 Robert Peel got through an Act which adopted Howard's four principles of sufficient, secure and sanitary accommodation; making the gaoler a salaried member of local government; the subjection of all criminals to a reformatory regime; and the inspection of every part of the prison by visiting justices. Here and there prisons had followed Howard's suggestion of allowing prisoners to earn their keep. As crime rose after the end of the Napoleonic War, and demobbed soldiers flooded on to the labour market, a cry went up against prisons which were too comfortable. Prisoners must be made to pay the price! This turn to a harsher regime was mirrored throughout Europe.[12] The noted clerical wit Sidney Smith used the *Edinburgh Review* to advocate the view that the purpose of prisons was deterrence through the terror of punishment. The treadwheel, which was habitually injurious to the health of prisoners and deliberately degrading, was introduced into prisons at this period. Smith argued:

---

[12] G. Rusche and O. Kirchheimer, *Punishment and Social Structure* (Columbia, 1938), pp. 96ff.

I would banish all the looms of Preston Gaol, and substitute nothing but the tread wheel or capstan, or some species of labour where the labourer could not see the results of his toil – where it is as monotonous, irksome and dull as possible – pulling and pushing, instead of reading and writing – no share in the profits – not a single shilling. There should be no tea and sugar, no assemblage of female felons round the washing tub – nothing but beating hemp and pulling oakum and pounding bricks – no work but what was tedious, unusual and unfeminine ... Man, woman, boy and girl, should all leave the jail ... taught, by sad experience, to consider it as the greatest misfortune of their lives to return to it.[13]

The same logic lay behind the atonement theologies of this period. Strongly Calvinist defences of the atonement appeared in 1828, from John Pye Smith, resident tutor at Homerton College; in 1824 and 1830 from Ralph Wardlaw, the friend of Thomas Chalmers; and in 1845 from the hyper-Calvinist J. A. Haldane.[14] It is, however, Thomas Jenkyn, writing in 1831, who is most explicit about the penal analogy.[15]

The universe, he argues, must be viewed as a public commonwealth. Of this commonwealth God is the public head and chief

---

[13]   S. Smith, 'The State of Prisons', *The Edinburgh Review*, 35 (1821), 286–302. 'Prisons', ibid., 36 (1822), 353–74.

[14]   In *Four Discourses on the Sacrifice and Priesthood of Jesus Christ*, lectures delivered in 1813 and published in 1828. Pye Smith is in debate especially with Stillingfleet and Grotius. Calvinist views of the atonement found credence in very Establishment circles, for example in Edmund Nares' Bampton Lectures for 1805, *A View of the Evidences of Christianity at the Close of the Pretended Age of Reason*. He argues that there is no choice but to regard Christ's death as a sacrifice. 'Those who regard the Bible as a revelation from God have only to search and enquire whether such doctrines are to be found *there*.' Ralph Wardlaw was the Professor of Systematic Theology at the Glasgow Theological Academy. His arguments are developed in *A Concise View of the Leading Doctrines Connected with the Socinian Controversy* (1824), written with John Dwight, the President of Yale; and in *On the Assurance of Faith and on the Extent of Atonement and Universal Pardon* (1830).

These views were far too liberal for J. A. Haldane, who, in a book deservedly unread, castigated Wardlaw for teaching that the atonement was only display and accused him of being worse than a Socinian: *The Doctrine of the Atonement (With Strictures on the Recent Publications of Drs Wardlaw and Jenkyns)* (1845). The pages of the Bodleian copy were uncut in 1992.

Thomas Chalmers argued from principles of government to the atonement. He opposed poor relief because he believed it was morally vicious to put humanity before justice. In the same way Unitarians abolish the distinction between justice and benevolence and thus 'set aside the doctrine of the Atonement'. Hilton, *AA*, p. 84.

[15]   T. Jenkyn, *The Atonement in Relation to God and the Universe* (London, Hamilton, Adams & Co., 1833).

member. In administering its offices he does everything in his
official capacity and public character as the Governor of it. All
the measures proposed and executed in it are for the public good
of the whole commonwealth. In its government every wrong and
every sin is treated, not as a private offence, but as a public
injury, to be publicly answered, whether in punishment or
pardon. God deals with us on the principle of public justice, that
justice which a government exercises to preserve the public good
and the public honour of the whole community. Sin is a public
injury to God and the universe. It is not in the nature of mercy,
nor does it become its character, to forgive such a public wrong
without an expression of its abhorrence of the crime. Such a
mercy would be weak indifference, a foolish and blind passion.
Everyone sees that a family governed on such a principle would
soon become the pest of the commonwealth. The ends of
government in the punishment of offenders are, first, to show the
goodness and benevolence of the law; second, to demonstrate the
impartial justice of the governor; and third, to exhibit the evil
consequences of breaking the law and to impress offenders with
the hopelessness of escaping the punishment due to crime. In
human governments the chief magistrate has a power of suspending penalties, provided he does not exercise such a prerogative to the detriment of the public good. A father will not be
afraid of relaxing the bonds of good discipline in forgiving a child
when a mother, in tears and anguish, expresses abhorrence of the
child's offence but also begs for forgiveness.

The sin of man is a public injury to the divine commonwealth,
and for such a public injury the law has provided a public
punishment. Such punishment can only be suspended if there is
an atonement, which Jenkyn defines as any expedient that will
justify a government in suspending the literal execution of the
penalty threatened, which answers the purpose of government as
effectively as the infliction of the penalty on the offender himself
or herself would. Such a means supplies the government just, safe
and honourable grounds for offering and dispensing pardon to
the offender. It is not an expedient contrary to law, but above
law, as it preserves the 'spirit and truth' of the constitution.

In this way Christ is an atonement. He acts as our substitute, and makes a voluntary engagement to undergo for the ends of divine government degradation, trouble, reproach and sufferings, so that the penalty threatened by the law may *not* be executed on offenders. The death of Christ serves all the ends of the law, as if the sinner himself or herself had been punished. It deters men from breaking the law and answers the end of punishment. The history of salvation shows that the atonement *is* of greater value than the original penalty, because it contains in its arrangement a greater number of motives to deter from sin and to attach the subjects to the government. In fact we can say that the world was created a theatre for the atonement and that the machinery of providence was constituted to introduce its operations.

The love of God, then, is not love expressed by a weak and an unreasonable fondness, or love exercised by arbitrary power; it is rectoral love, expressed, indeed, freely and gratuitously, but also judiciously and safely. To understand it properly we must see that the influence of the Holy Spirit forms an indispensable link in the chain of these means. Without this all the other links are of no effect.

Boyd Hilton argues that shortly after mid century a reaction against forensic views of the atonement set in. Certainly, alternative views of the atonement appeared at about this time, but Arthur Lyttleton, writing in *Lux Mundi*, in 1889, still framed his account of the atonement in terms of law and propitiation. 'The death of Christ', he wrote, 'is the expiation for those past sins which have laid the burden of guilt upon the human soul, and it is also the propitiation of the wrath of God.'[16] Moreover the classic Calvinist statement of the atonement in the nineteenth century is to be found in the Congregational Union Lectures for 1875, given by R. W. Dale. Dale offers the theological underpinning of the Du Cane regime, and echoes the views of the most famous legal theorist of the time, James Fitzjames Stephen, whose *Liberty, Equality, Fraternity* had gone through two editions in the previous two years. In the debates on capital punishment going on at this time Stephen argued consistently for retention. Crimes

[16] A. Lyttleton, 'The Atonement', in *Lux Mundi*, ed. C. Gore (London, John Murray, 1889), p. 285; see also pp. 277, 288. He does then go on, citing Mcleod Campbell, to speak of forgiveness.

must be punished, Stephen maintained, to gratify the feelings of hatred, revenge and resentment which criminal behaviour excites in all healthily constituted minds.[17] He believed that flogging, now much more widespread in prison under Du Cane, ought to be made more severe because 'At present it is little, if at all, more serious than a birching at a public school'(!).[18] Christianity had two sides, a gentle and a 'terrific' one, and there was nothing un-Christian about capital punishment:

There is as much moral cowardice in shrinking from the execution of a murderer as in hesitating to blow out the brains of a foreign invader. A mind which feels this shrinking and calls it a Christian feeling must have a strangely partial and one-sided view of Christianity ... The Sermon on the Mount stands in front of a background on which is the worm that never dies and the fire that is not quenched ... Will Mr Bright tell us that Quakers alone have been Christians? Have not all the constitutions and most of the legislation of modern Europe grown up under the auspices of Christianity, and have they no stern side?[19]

Du Cane believed that prisons must be made as unpleasant as possible since they exist to deter 'the enormous number of *possible* criminals'. In this Dale agreed with him, and he took up the theme in his ninth lecture on the atonement. Is punishment to be regarded as a reformatory process, a process intended to promote the moral benefit of the sufferer, he asks? If it were that and nothing more, and if the justice of punishment consisted in its fitness to produce a favourable moral impression on the sinner, God would be free to inflict or remit the penalties of the law without regard to any other consideration than the moral disposition of the person by whom the precepts of the law had been violated. Such a view was implied by the prison reformers. Their intentions were good but the theory behind the change was false and pernicious. From the principle that in punishing crime it is both the duty and interest of the state to attempt to reform the criminal, it was inferred that the object of punishment is the criminal's reformation. This inference, although no man was

[17] J. F. Stephen, *Liberty, Equality, Fraternity*, 2nd edn (London, Smith, Elder & Co., 1874), p. 152.
[18] J. F. Stephen, *A History of the Criminal Law of England* (London, Macmillan, 1883), pp. 91–2.
[19] 'Capital Punishment', *Fraser's Magazine*, 69 (June 1864), 70.

irrational enough to take it to its logical conclusion, seriously affected the spirit and temper with which a considerable number of persons regarded the administration of the criminal law. It made the gaol a philanthropic institution, and the treadmill an instrument of national education, invented for the benefit of an exceptionally unfortunate and backward class of scholars. This theory was utterly rotten. Society has no right to send a man to gaol, to feed him on bread and water, and to make him pick hemp or work the treadmill merely because society thinks that a discipline of this kind will do him good. It is the fact that the criminal deserves to suffer which constitutes the ultimate foundation of criminal law. Here he agreed with Archbishop Whateley, who argued in the Lords that we cannot admit that the reformation of the convict is an essential part of punishment; it may be joined incidentally, but cannot belong necessarily to the penal system.

Between human legislation and divine, between the imperfect processes by which the state punishes the violation of its imperfect laws and the processes of eternal justice, the analogy is very incomplete. But when we consider sin as a transgression of the eternal law of righteousness, this principle that the transgression deserves punishment reappears. The conscience affirms it vehemently. The fear of punishment is often the earliest form in which a sinful man acknowledges the authority of the law which he has broken. Nor is the punishment regarded either by the conscience or by the terror-stricken heart as a painful process to effect further reformation; it is the suffering which has been deserved by past sin. To make it anything other than this is to destroy its essential character. The only conception of punishment which satisfies our strongest and most definite moral convictions, and which corresponds to the place it occupies both in the organisation of society and in the moral order of the universe, is that which represents it as pain and loss inflicted for the violation of a law. God cannot be separated even in idea from the law which has been violated, and which affirms the principle that sin deserves to be punished. Is it necessary, or is it not, that this principle should be asserted, and asserted by God himself? If it is not asserted then the eternal law of righteousness can no longer be perfectly identified with the will of God. Dale then offers us a new version of Anselm's dilemma: must God then inflict the penalties sin has deserved? We cannot deny that God can be hostile to men on account of sin, for this is to emasculate and degrade our conception of him. He is not a mere 'good-natured' God (the view Benjamin Warfield caricatured as 'benevolencism'). His righteousness as well as his love is infinite. He offers us a very nineteenth-century parable. We are to imagine an impenitent seducer. What ought God's relation to be to such a man as that? Ought God to be at peace with him? If he were, there would be no justice in the universe.

My hope and strength and consolation in the presence of such a crime as this comes from the certainty that wherever that man goes, under whatever disguises he may live, whatever his wealth may be, whatever his rank, he is pursued by One who is the relentless enemy of his sin – and who will be *his* relentless enemy if he will not renounce his sin.[20]

The eternal law of righteousness declares that sin deserves to be punished, and the will of God is identified both by the conscience and by the religious intuitions of man with this law. To separate the ideal law – or any part of it – from the Living and Divine Person is to bring darkness and chaos on the moral and spiritual universe. Some divine act is required which shall have all the moral worth and significance of the act by which the penalties of sin would have been inflicted on the sinner. Christ is the one by whom the sentence should be executed. 'It belonged to Him to assert, by his own act, that suffering is the just result of sin. He asserts it, not by inflicting suffering on the sinner, but by enduring suffering Himself.'[21]

Dale summed up his position in three propositions. First, the Lord Jesus Christ, the Moral Ruler of the human race, instead of inflicting the penalties, has submitted to them. He has died, 'the Just for the unjust' and has been 'made a curse for us'.[22] Next, sin makes it impossible for the original relation of Christ to the Father to continue to be the ideal of the human race to God. In the presence of God fictions can have no place. If, therefore, we

[20] R. W. Dale, *The Atonement* (London, Hodder & Stoughton, 1875), p. 344.
[21] ibid., p. 397.
[22] ibid.

were still to be related to God through Christ, it would seem to
be necessary that there should be included in his actual relation
to the Father an expression of the truth of that relation into which
we had come through sin. That expression is found in his death.
Third, the destruction of evil within us is the effect and fulfilment
in ourselves of the mystery of Christ's death, as the development
of our positive holiness is the manifestation of the power of his
life.

On this theology Moberly commented tartly that it provokes
the query, 'May I, if my child is shamefully wicked, "forgive"
him, provided that, as an adequate expression of "hostility", I cut
off my own finger first?'[23] At the heart of their disagreement lay
different views of punishment. For Dale punishment was essentially retribution, and forgiveness was simply remission, or non-
infliction, of penalties. As far as Moberly was concerned no
rational explanation of atonement was possible while these meanings for the two words were assumed. Dale's work spoke for
many, perhaps the majority, of churchgoers. In 1875 it caught the
public mood. Throughout the century, however, there were those
who advocated more liberal approaches, and it is to these we now
turn.

LIFE FOR OTHERS

One of the most important and original works on the atonement
in the nineteenth century was John Mcleod Campbell's *The Nature
of the Atonement and its Relation to the Remission of Sins and Eternal Life*,
published in 1856. We can take, as part of the setting for this
essay, the publication five years earlier of Mary Carpenter's
*Reformatory Schools for the Perishing and Dangerous Classes and for the
Prevention of Juvenile Delinquency*. Her work was part of a movement
which sought to reclaim young offenders which went back to the
mid eighteenth century, and which was particularly inspired by
the work at Le Mettray in France.

Mary Carpenter was the daughter of a Unitarian minister. She
sought to practise the tolerance and compassion of this creed, and

23 R. C. Moberly, *Atonement and Personality* (London, John Murray, 1909), p. 393.

above all to imitate men like John Howard. From a 'Visiting Society' of Ladies emerged a ragged school, in Bristol, and from her experience there, and her study of poverty and juvenile recidivism, her book emerged. She called a conference in Birmingham in 1851, the very year that the scandal in Birmingham Gaol broke. Two further books on reformatory schools and juvenile delinquents followed in 1853. Though no radical she had an acute sense of the class bias in British justice, insisting that children of middle-class parents got away with offences which incurred imprisonment or hard labour for the poor, and that 'if the criminal class of the lower part of the population were not placed in the circumstances in which they are ... now, they would become very different'.[24] She believed passionately that a sense of responsibility was acquired through socialisation, and that therefore no child should be held culpable by the law until aged sixteen. Hence, children should not be punished, because this made them vindictive, hardened and antagonistic, but chastened and corrected. It was through her efforts that, in her lifetime, a network of ragged schools, industrial schools and reformatories was set up.

John Mcleod Campbell was, like Chalmers and Wardlaw, a Scots Presbyterian. In 1831 the General Assembly of the Church of Scotland convicted him of heresy after an all-night debate which finished only at 6 a.m., and deposed him from ministry. He was convicted of believing in the universal efficacy of the atonement. Thereafter he found unpaid employment as the minister of a small independent congregation in Blackfriars Street, Glasgow. *The Nature of the Atonement* was his apologia, the mature statement of his views, written out of his own experience of pain, poverty and forgiveness.[25] Campbell would have had little enough sympathy with Mary Carpenter's theology, as he had rejected Socinianism. But intellectual currents run deep, and just as we find in Dale the theological apologist for Du Cane, so we find in Campbell the apologist for the work of Mary Carpenter.

Jenkyn had cited an English judge who said to a criminal before him: 'You are condemned to be transported, not because

---

[24] Cited in Radzinowicz and Hood, *Emergence*, p. 166.
[25] J. Mcleod Campbell, *The Nature of the Atonement* (London, James Clarke, 1959).

you have stolen those goods, but that goods may not be stolen.'[26] This is quoted in illustration of the position that 'the death of Christ is an honourable ground for remitting punishment' because 'His sufferings answer the same ends as the punishment of the sinner.' Campbell responded that he recognised no harmony between this sentiment of the English judge and the voice of an awakened conscience on the subject of sin. The full revelation of God is *not* that divine love has been content to suffer *for* our sin but that the suffering of Christ is the suffering of divine *love caused by* our sins. Campbell could not accept penal substitution. To understand Christ's death he turned for an analogy to an unlikely text in the Book of Numbers (25.10–13). In that story the priest Phinehas turns God's anger away from Israel. He found Phinehas' zeal for God, his sympathy for God's judgement on sin, to be the essence of the atonement. The sufferings of Christ are not penal, but the expression of the divine mind regarding our sins, a manifestation by the Son of what our sins are to the Father's heart. As the representative human being Christ makes 'a perfect Amen in humanity to the judgement of God on the sin of man'.[27] The atonement is 'the living manifestation of perfect sympathy in the Father's condemnation of sin'.[28] In Christ human righteousness, in the shape of a true and righteous confession of sin, met divine righteousness condemning human sin. By this confession the righteousness of God was satisfied, and demanded no more than this righteousness found in Christ. To repent and confess sin is to expiate it. What such a confession does is to make us understand the divine wrath against sin, which must be acknowledged and then repented. We must realise that there is a crucial distinction between the legal and the filial, and it is the latter which is the sphere of the gospel. The atonement is from start to finish a work of the fatherliness of God. The stern teaching of Calvinism must be rejected. 'Pardon for sin in any other sense than the revealing, and the opening to us of the path of life ... is inconceivable.'[29] When the New Testament speaks of

26   Jenkyn, pp. 175–6.
27   Campbell, *Nature*, p. 136.
28   ibid., p. 132.
29   ibid., p. 211.

the blood of Christ, it has in mind not primarily Christ's physical death, but its spiritual power. Christ's bearing our sin, confessing our guilt on our behalf, awakes faith in us, teaches us that our well-being must consist in communion with God, and that our salvation lies in joining in that worship of God which is in spirit and in truth. Atonement is the development of this life which was in Christ.

In place of vicarious punishment, with the retributive views it implies, Campbell had put vicarious penitence. This enabled a realisation of true sonship to God which led to a new awareness of fellow humanity. Called to share Christ's self-sacrifice, we are called to poverty and a life of service for others. Campbell's atonement theology advocated the life Mary Carpenter embraced.

Campbell's work was only properly taken up, and its potential exploited, by the greatest work of Anglican Victorian theology, R. C. Moberly's *Atonement and Personality*. The background to this book was, without doubt, the Gladstone Report of 1895, and the end of the Du Cane regime in that year. Du Cane's regime of repression produced repeated riots and violence, which were savagely crushed. Information on gaols dried up, and annual reports became routine and full of stock phrases. His fall was precipitated by attacks in the press in 1893. The following year a commission was set up, chaired by Herbert Gladstone. The report, which followed within a year, turned its back on deterrence and recommended that prisons should aim at reform:

We think that the system should be made more elastic, more capable of being adopted to the special cases of individual prisoners; that prison discipline should be more effectually designed to maintain, stimulate, or awaken the higher susceptibilities of prisoners, to develop their moral instincts, to train them in orderly and industrial habits, and whenever possible to turn them out of prison better men and women, both physically and morally, than when they came in.[30]

Three days after the report was published Du Cane resigned. A new Prison Act was adopted in 1898. *Atonement and Personality* is, without question, the theological response to these events.

[30] Parliamentary Papers, 56 (1895), pp. 12–13.

The book falls into three parts. In the first Moberly frankly examines the major themes both of atonement and of prison reform, namely punishment, penitence and forgiveness. He at once distances himself from the retributivist mainstream. Punishment does not exist to make a point about the law, whether moral, civil or divine. Unless punishment is conceived as a moral means to a moral end, we cannot acquit it of a certain degree of rationalised hatred. The only form of punishment which is moral is that which is designed to produce penitence. Punishment, taken up into the suffering personality as penitence, represents a real transformation of the situation. It diminishes my guilt – not in virtue of the bearing of pain itself, but in virtue of the change of attitude effected.

Punishment, then, is designed to lead to penitence. This is a condition of the personality, an emotion of love. The sin of the past remains with us as present guilt and present power. Real deliverance from sin must mean a real removal from the conscience of guilt, which makes present and future holiness possible. For this to be possible guilt must be forgiven, but forgiveness is only possible when a person is forgivable. Forgiveness is not equivalent to refusing to punish, or treating someone as if they are innocent when they are not. We cannot *impose* forgiveness on a person, but neither can we wait censoriously until we judge that sufficient signs of penitence have been evidenced. Love is forgiveness when it outruns the capacity of deserving. At the heart of his understanding of redemption, and constituting the second part of his book, is the perception that divine love acts pre-emptively in Christ, making penitence, and therefore forgiveness, possible.

The second stage of Moberly's argument is to turn to Christology. The basic intuition behind his atonement theology is that 'a friend who will bear is the best practical hope of the sinner's reformation'. Such an idea is impossible in a forensic atmosphere, and so we need to turn to the realm of the personal. We see, for example, how a mother may often step in between the wrath of a father and his erring child. Here is a mediation, but to the extent that there is no real identity, it breaks down. Christ, however, according to Christian teaching, is both wholly God and wholly human. The essence of his humanity is his complete and perfect obedience to the Father. In him the two things which can restore the relationship between human beings and God, perfect holiness and perfect contrition, are a reality. In attempting to explain how this helps us he introduces a parable suggested by Campbell, and relevant to the Victorian penal debate.[31] Imagine a parent – pure, holy, tender, loving-hearted – whose beloved child is branded with irretrievable disgrace. Although he says 'parent', it is actually a mother he has in mind. We have to recall here the prison reminiscences of 'Half-Timer', who claimed that 'there is magic in the word *mother*, for I have seen young lads whose life has been given up to deeds of ill, rain tears of sorrow or something at the mention of the word'.[32] The mother's anguish is more intense to the extent that it is without the confusing presence of sin. The purer she is, the deeper her shame. Her power of penitence depends both on the extent of her self-identification with holiness and on her identification with her child. *She* repents where her son is unable to. By seeing her shame he is for the first time moved to remorse. Genuine remorse makes forgiveness possible: the road to redemption is opened.

This parable is Moberly's fundamental analogy for the work of Christ. He has taken Campbell's insight, put it into the context of the penitentiary, and made it fundamentally more cogent. What Christ does is to repent in our place, and it is that repentance which teaches us the heinousness of sin. That vicarious penitence, in other words, is, in language which had come into fashion during the nineteenth century, the *objective fact* which made *subjective* repentance, and therefore redemption, possible. The objective becomes subjective in belief, contemplation and love.

Thus far Moberly has simply reworked Campbell. His basic criticism of his predecessor was that Campbell had insufficiently emphasised the move from new sonship to God to new brotherhood with all men. Here, then, he makes his decisive move, and I believe that it is not too fanciful to see Christian ministrations in

---

[31] See Campbell, *Nature*, p. 140. Campbell does not develop the idea.
[32] *Prison Reminiscences* by 'Half-Timer' (London, Eliot Stock, 1917).

gaol behind it. No theology of the atonement can speak simply about Calvary, and what happened there. An exposition of atonement which leaves out Pentecost leaves it unintelligible. It is only through Pentecost that the meaning of human personality is ever actually realised at all. A fault with most expositions of the atonement is that they talk of persons as if they are complete and ready made. But persons are always in process. To the extent that we are able to make wholly our own what is wholly our truest self, to the extent that our reason is guided by spiritual insights, and to the extent that we ever learn to love, we are responding to the Spirit of God shaping our personality. The church and the sacraments exist as 'channels' of the Spirit. The sacraments are the means of the divine education. Human personality achieves its central focus through the education of the sacramental life. The atonement is then a process of education, both life long, for each individual, and as long as human history. And the realisation of the atonement is 'Christ in us', and ourselves realised in Christ.

The new Act of 1898 was centred on reform, and despite more than a century of negative experiences, end-of-the-century legislators still looked to the church for moral education. For a moderate High Churchman like Moberly it would be obvious that any real moral education would happen 'where the gospel was preached and the sacraments rightly administered', and where the church as a living body was created. In terms of the relation between penal theory and atonement the move is momentous. For a thousand years the prisoner was the paradigm of the sinner, and his sentence a warning of wrath to come. Moberly has turned this round. The prisoner is still the paradigm of the sinner, but *as an instance of the possibility of redemption.* Prison, or other forms of punishment, is no longer a metaphor for judgement, but for the reformative process. Alas, no matter how cogent Moberly's views, they do not represent prison experience. 'The evidence is quite overwhelming', say Hood and Radzinowicz, 'that the chaplains played a very minor role indeed in the life of the prison.'

For all practical purposes, they were completely subordinate to the governors. A number of prisoners, known as 'foxes', tried to take advantage of them in the hope that a show of religious zeal would improve their lot ... Of all the convict chaplains there was hardly one who stood out as a spiritual leader. They seemed to be more like tired functionaries, expected to discharge difficult duties in a hostile environment.[33]

SEEKING RECONCILIATION

For those who hope to find in the witness of the church some signs of the work of the Holy Spirit an examination of the role of the church in the penal debates of the nineteenth century is depressing indeed. From start to finish the bishops proved staunch supporters of flogging and hanging. When the Duke of Argyll echoed Luther in calling society a minister of divine justice in imposing capital punishment, Samuel Wilberforce, the Bishop of Oxford, cried, 'Hear, hear!' In a debate on flogging in 1883 the Bishop of Rochester, in an extraordinarily unpleasant intervention, said that offenders should be 'scoured to the bone'. In the prisons chaplains were not simply functionaries, but often did their best to extract confessions of guilt, and in attending executions gave divine sanction to legal violence. By and large religious opposition came from Quakers and Unitarians, not wedded to the verbal inspiration of Scripture and a literal insistence on the command of Gen. 9.6: 'Whosoever sheds man's blood, by man shall that man's blood be shed.' Apart from Campbell and Moberly, however, and a very small group of clerical reformers, there also grew up, from the time of F. D. Maurice onwards, an important liberal school within theology. Maurice had attacked satisfaction theory in 1853, in a book dedicated to Tennyson.[34] It was not absolutely clear what he put in its place: he seemed to be commending himself to Unitarians through the doctrine of the incarnation! The American Congregationalist Horace Bushnell espoused a frank advocacy of exemplarist theory, but on the grounds of the recognition of the vicariousness of all life, in books published in

[33] Radzinowicz and Hood, *Emergence*, pp. 541–2. Books and tracts on offer in Maidstone Gaol in mid century included Josephus, Bishop Watson's *Apology*, and Leslie's *Short Method with Deists* and *Short and Ready Method with the Jews*.

[34] F. D. Maurice, *Theological Essays* (London, Macmillan, 1853).

1866 and 1874. The doyen of English liberalism, however, was Hastings Rashdall. He is today best known for his 1915 Bampton Lectures, *The Idea of the Atonement in Christian Theology*, often vilified for displaying a rationalist optimism in the midst of the horrors of the Great War. His views on the atonement, however, took shape in the course of his great study *The Theory of Good and Evil*, published in 1907, in which he directly engaged with the debate about punishment of the last two decades of the nineteenth century.

Rashdall believed that any doctrine which regarded the death of Christ as expiatory implied the retributive theory of punishment.[35] This theory he regarded as 'at bottom a survival of primitive modes of thought'. Punishment undoubtedly originated in the instinct of revenge. With the progress of morality it was recognised that this instinct should be controlled by a rational principle, but there still lingered the notion that, when authorised and entitled to punish for real wrongdoing, the just ruler ought still to punish, as primitive man in his anger had punished, as though vengeance or punishment were an end in itself.[36] The demand of the wronged individual for vengeance was transferred to an impersonal but objective 'justice'. From the time of Socrates and Plato, however, thoughtful men began to feel that it could not be rational to inflict evil except as a means to good. On this view of punishment, the notion that suffering or death could do away the guilt of sin, except in so far as it produces repentance or change of character, becomes impossible.[37] The idea of expressing moral guilt in terms of the cat or birch, gallows or pillory, hard labour or penal servitude, seemed to Rashdall to be essentially and intrinsically unmeaning. 'There is absolutely no commensurability between the two things.'[38] The retributive theory, he says, must be recognised to have three elements of truth. First, it rests on the psychological truth that punishment originates in the instinct of

[35] *The Idea of the Atonement in Christian Theology* (London, Macmillan, 1925), p. 207.
[36] I follow now the exposition in *The Theory of Good and Evil* (Oxford, Oxford University Press, 1907), pp. 284ff.
[37] Rashdall, *The Idea of the Atonement in Christian Theology* (London, Macmillan, 1925), p. 422.
[38] *Theory*, p. 289.

vengeance. In its origins the criminal law was a substitute for private vengeance. Second, it is true that punishment can be reformatory. We must recognise, however, that 'when a man is induced to abstain from crime by the possibility of a better life being brought home to him through the ministrations of a prison Chaplain, through education, through a book from the Prison library, or the efforts of a Discharged Prisoners' Aid Society, he is not reformed *by punishment* at all. No doubt there are reformatory agencies much more powerful than punishment; and without the co-operation of such agencies it is rarely that punishment makes the criminal into a better man.' Third, it is true that the state has a spiritual end, and must seek to advance that end.[39]

Over against these elements of truth, the retributive view of punishment is vicious because it justifies the infliction of evil upon a living soul, even though it will do neither him or her nor anyone else any good whatever. Only punishment inflicted for an educative purpose is moral. Retributivists argue that to punish in order to reform is to manipulate a person, and so to fail to respect moral autonomy, but it is the retributive theory which shows a disrespect for human personality by proposing to sacrifice human life and human well-being to a lifeless fetish styled the Moral Law, which apparently, though unconscious, has a sense of dignity and demands the immolation of victims to avenge its injured *amour propre*. The Kantian appeals of the hangers and floggers amount to the mixture 'of a little truculent Theology borrowed from primitive Judaism with a good deal of pure paganism'.[40]

Retributive theory, Rashdall claimed, cannot give any consistent account of the duty of forgiveness and its relations to the duty of punishment. He agreed with Carlyle (and hence also with Durkheim, whom he read) that punishment was a necessary expression of society's moral outrage – but not rigidly and universally. Sometimes forgiveness is required, and forgiveness involves remission of penalty. Butler had attempted to consider punishment and forgiveness together, by distinguishing the pun-

---

[39] ibid., pp. 291ff.
[40] ibid., p. 305.

ishing official from the forgiving human being. 'He forgot that to
a human being who has wronged his fellow, forgiveness is an
infinitely more convincing proof of love than punishment can
ever be, and may, therefore, touch the heart as punishment will
seldom touch it.' Accepting this involves rethinking atonement
theology. 'The idea of vicarious suffering has nothing immoral
about it; under the conditions of human life love can hardly be
manifested in its highest degree without it. It is otherwise with the
idea of vicarious punishment.' It was this distinction on which
Rashdall insisted. The idea of vicarious punishment must be
rejected, along with retributive theory. 'On the other hand the
idea that the nature of God has received its fullest revelation in a
self sacrificing life and death is one against which the Moralist can
have nothing to say.'[41]

For Rashdall, notoriously, Abelard was the forerunner of any
worthwhile theology of atonement: the atonement is the very
central doctrine of Christianity in so far as it proclaims the
supreme Christian truth that God is love, and that love is the
most precious thing in human life. Christ's whole life was a
sacrifice which takes away sin in the only way in which sin can
really be taken away, and that is by making the sinner actually
better. David Nicholls has shown how the 'personality-centred'
theologies of Moberly and Rashdall went together with what was
effectively an advocacy of the welfare state.[42] As we shall see
below, this was part of a much larger movement.

It is instructive to look at the debate between Rashdall and
James Denney, a Scottish Free Churchman who continued to
advocate substitutionary atonement. In *The Death of Christ*, published in 1911, Denney argued that if the universal element, or
law, is eliminated from personal relations, then nothing intelli-
gible is left: no reason, no morality, no religion, no sin or
righteousness or forgiveness, nothing to appeal to mind or
conscience. In the widest sense of the word sin, as a disturbance
of the personal relations between God and man, is a violence
done to the constitution under which God and man form one
moral community and share one moral life. The New Testament

[41]   ibid., p. 312.
[42]   D. Nicholls, *Deity and Domination* (London, Routledge, 1989), pp. 54ff.

teaches that it is possible for God to forgive, but only through a supreme revelation of his love, made at infinite cost, and doing justice to the uttermost to those inviolable relations in which alone man can participate in eternal life. Denney offered a parable which was to become a commonplace of evangelical preaching. If I am sitting on the end of a pier and someone jumps into the water and drowns 'to prove their love for me', I should find it unintelligible, but if I am drowning and he jumps in, then I can say 'greater love has no man than this'. The more the meaning of Christ's death is realised as something there, in the world, outside us, the more completely does it take effect within us. If the atonement were not, to begin with, outside us – if it were not in that sense objective, a finished work in which God in Christ makes a final revelation of himself in relation to sinners and sin – in other words, if Christ could not be conceived in it as our substitute, given by God to do in our place what we could not do for ourselves, there would be no way of recognising it as a motive.

In his review of this book Rashdall maintained that Denney misrepresents the New Testament story. The parable ought to run: 'To show my love for you, I will allow myself to be thrown into the sea by those who have threatened to do so unless I abandon my work of preaching what I believe to be the kingdom of God, of preparing the way for his kingdom and for your admission thereto.' Death on this score awakens gratitude and love. The picture of Christ in the gospels appeals to the mind and religious consciousness of humankind. All human love is in some degree a revelation of God. In proportion as it is felt that human love reveals the love of God the answering love which the self-sacrifice awakens will be love to God as well as to man. In so far as the atonement shows us that God suffers, it remains the central doctrine of Christianity. For Greek theology, the incarnation was the atonement, and we should identify with that. Christ's whole life was a sacrifice which takes away sin in the only way in which sin can really be taken away, and that is by making the sinner actually better.

Both Rashdall and Denney appeal to results, to the actual effect of atonement doctrines. Those who believe in substitu-

tionary atonement have a familiar stock of conversion stories
which change little from generation to generation and which are,
it has to be said, belied by the history of nineteenth-century
prison ministry. At the end of the nineteenth century Frederick
Brocklehurst, a member of the Independent Labour Party
imprisoned for defying an order banning meetings, found in his
cell in Strangeways religious tracts for his edification, some of
which dated back to 1815. They contained warnings against
Hume's Deism, Paine's atheism, and against Owenism and
Chartism. 'Into this fare imagine a *soupçon* of warning against
eternal damnation, and a general exhortation to look upon
yourself as the blackest and vilest scum on earth, and you will
have a pretty fair idea of a medium sample of the moral and
elevating literature which is ladled out to brighten the lives and
cheer the hearts of the unfortunate dwellers in Her Majesty's
prisons.'[43] Stuart Wood, a petty criminal in and out of gaol at the
time Rashdall and Denney were debating, describes prison
sermons as informing prisoners 'how wicked we were and how
grateful we ought to be to society for giving us such an excellent
opportunity to mend our ways'.[44] Oscar Wilde agreed with
this account of prison sermons, and considered prison chaplains
'entirely useless'.

They are, as a class, well meaning but foolish, indeed silly, men. They
are of no help to any prisoner. Once every six weeks or so a key turns in
the lock of one's door, and the chaplain enters. One stands, of course, at
attention. He asks whether one has been reading the Bible. One
answers 'Yes' or 'No', as the case may be. He then quotes a few texts,
and goes out and locks the door. Sometimes he leaves a tract.[45]

Stuart Wood commented perceptively, 'the majority of them saw
nothing fundamentally wrong with the system because, after all, it
was only the logical application of the Mosaic Code in which
most of them had been nurtured'.[46] A narrow theology begot a
narrow practice.

[43] F. Brocklehurst, *I Was in Prison* (London, T. Fisher Unwin, 1898), p. 52.
[44] S. Wood, *Shades of the Prison House* (London, Williams and Norgate, 1932), p. 31.
[45] *Selected Letters of Oscar Wilde*, ed. R. Hart Davis (Oxford, Oxford University Press, 1979), p. 338.
[46] Wood, *Shades*, p. 39.

THE MEANING OF PUNISHMENT

As we saw in the previous chapter, the end of the eighteenth century witnessed the rise of the prison. The question of the nature of prison regimes dominated discussion in the century which followed. The rise of the prison has been the focus of a number of well-known studies, the most famous of which is Foucault's *Discipline and Punish.*[47] His book begins with the question why spectacular public executions gave way to imprisonment in the years between 1750 and 1820. His answer is in terms of a fundamental shift in the exercise of power, not as exercised by the state as such, but as it exists between different groups in society. The focus of punishment moves, he argues, from the body to the soul, and 'technicians' such as chaplains, psychiatrists and educationalists take over from the executioner, exercising the power they have through the knowledge they have of the subject. Foucault is sceptical of the good intentions of the prison reformers. Rather, what was being created was a 'disciplinary society', particularly adapted to the emergence of an industrial society. The prison creates delinquents as its deskilling of inmates leads to recidivism. The delinquent class is useful as a strategy of political domination, as it serves to divide the working class and reinforce respect for law and for property. As Garland puts it, 'the prison does not control the criminal so much as control the working class by creating the criminal'.[48]

As we have seen at a number of points, Foucault's hostility to giving a constructive role to ideologies was not shared by Michael Ignatieff's *A Just Measure of Pain.* Whilst Ignatieff allowed for the role religious motives played in the emergence of the penitentiary, he also argued that a new rhetoric largely took over from the old. In the place of a traditional view of crime as a form of human wickedness and sin social studies now pointed rather towards a 'society in crisis', and spoke rather of social envy, resentment, or desperation.[49] Reviewing

[47] M. Foucault, *Discipline and Punish*, tr. A. Sheridan (Harmondsworth, Penguin, 1977).
[48] David Garland, *Punishment and Modern Society* (Oxford, Clarendon Press, 1990), p. 150.
[49] Ignatieff, *JMP*, p. 210.

his argument five years later he felt that he had insufficiently emphasised the 'religious vernacular' of the reformers, and their commitment to a 'drama of guilt' for each offender, and this is consonant with what we have seen of the Victorian debate about atonement right up to the Gladstone Report of 1895.[50] Arthur Lyttleton's essay on atonement in *Lux Mundi*, published in 1889, remains, as we have seen, very firmly in the retributivist tradition. The climate of religious belief, therefore, was not only behind the early efforts of the prison reformers, but much more behind the retributivism of the Du Cane regime. This is nowhere clearer than in the classic statement of late Victorian atonement theology, R. W. Dale's Congregational Union lectures. In this period 'A sufficient measure of religious belief still persisted to allow earthly sanctions to appeal to a higher authority and hence to be explicit about its expiatory purposes.'[51]

David Garland's *Punishment and Welfare*, published in 1985, argues for changes in the penal agenda which we have seen to be mirrored in the theological. Garland distinguished between the penal practice of the bulk of the nineteenth century, which was based on the idea that crime was freely chosen, and that deterrence and retribution were the principal aims of imprisonment, and the rehabilitation agenda which followed the Gladstone Report. Where the earlier period, prior to Gladstone, appealed to the reason and responsibility of the criminal, welfare approaches relate to the individual 'not as an equal but as a benefactor, an assistential expert ... rescuing its subjects from vice and crime'.[52] Exactly these approaches are found to mark the theologies of the turn of the century. Moreover, as the measures proposed by the Gladstone Report went on the statute book in 1898, Tawney, William Temple and Beveridge were undergraduates at Balliol, all deeply influenced by Christian socialism and the new notions of welfare. The religious culture

---

[50] M. Ignatieff, 'State, Civil Society and Total Institutions: A Critique of Recent Social Histories of Punishment', in S. Cohen and A. Scull (eds.), *Social Control and the State* (Oxford, Martin Robertson, 1983), p. 92.
[51] D. Garland, *Punishment and Welfare* (Aldershot, Gower, 1985), p. 16.
[52] ibid., p. 31.

they represented influenced the formation of policy from the 1920s onwards, and served strongly to reinforce the belief in the necessity of rehabilitation. How this consensus collapsed, and gave place to the new retributivism will be the theme of the following chapter.

PART III

Contemporary directions in atonement and penal theory

CHAPTER 9

The gospel and retribution

> The prison authorities profess three objects: (a) Retribution (a euphemism for vengeance), (b) Deterrence (a euphemism for Terrorism) and (c) Reform ... They achieve the first atrociously. They fail in the second ... the third is irreconcilable with the first.
>
> G. B. Shaw

In Part II we have an overview, however partial and impressionistic, of developments in atonement theology and criminal justice during the eight centuries between Anselm and Moberly. Before sketching the present situation, and attempting a theological appraisal, I shall briefly review the argument.

Attitudes to crime and punishment in the West are, beyond argument, rooted deep in the Christian Scriptures. Here, alongside the ordinary punishments of criminal law, we find notions of expiation and atonement. In the texts of the Old Testament these run in and out of each other, and are not conceptually distinguished. In dealing with crime, which is also sin, a person must make *both* reparation and sacrifice. Murder is the great exception. For what would now be called 'first-degree murder' only capital punishment will do. The language which is used to theorise this is largely that of pollution.

The New Testament rests on these foundations. It exists as an attempt to interpret a judicial murder as a salvific event. Categories of sacrifice, possibly of scapegoating, are used to interpret it, but this attempt serves not to legitimate such practices but to critique them once and for all. 'No one understood Paul before Marcion', said Harnack, in a famous aphorism, 'and Marcion misunderstood him.'[1] Augustine, called the *Doctor gratiae* by the Schoolmen, was the interpreter of Paul for both Scholastics and Reformers, but, if Krister Stendahl is right, he too misunderstood him. The establishment of a new human order was soon understood in terms of pre-evangelical categories of sacrifice and the scapegoat. With the translation of the New Testament into Latin, the loss of Byzantium, and the hegemony of Latin as the language of both government and intellectuals, the New Testament was inevitably read through the interpretive lens of the Latin genius, which was law.

Enter Anselm. Legal categories obviously related in the first instance to church structure, and ecclesiology and canon law were always a major concern of the Western church. Anselm, however, not quite for the first time but in a quite new way, and with the force of genius, interpreted the atonement using a central legal category. Although the legal and societal framework of his day soon changed, what he bequeathed to posterity was the insight that atonement and a retributivist view of punishment belonged together. The brilliant city intellectual Abelard at once challenged this identification, but, although contemporaries felt the force of his arguments, they never became orthodoxy. The death of Christ dominated the 'structures of affect' of Europe for five hundred years, and in so doing they pumped retributivism into the legal bloodstream.

Rusche and Kirchheimer are able to show convincing correlations between the labour market and criminal justice during the late fifteenth and seventeenth centuries. When Europe was flooded with 'masterless men', at the beginning of the sixteenth century, repression was savage, and execution common. As the value of labour became more apparent, another way of dealing with excess labour was found: the workhouse, followed, from the mid seventeenth century on, by transportation. Mainstream theology continued to be solidly retributivist, though a mixture of Erasmian humanism and Anabaptism picked up the strain which came from Abelard. In the seventeenth century the mark of new political theories lay strongly on most forms of theology,

[1] A. Harnack, *History of Dogma* (7 vols., London, Williams & Norgate, 1905), vol. I, p. 89.

including theories of the atonement, as evidenced most distinctly by Grotius.

The industrial revolution, *laissez-faire* economics, the growth of the prison and the rise of utilitarianism came together. In the face of vindictive and savagely class-biased property laws most theologians sought to be useful to the magistrate. All forms of theology sought to mix the social cement. Archdeacon Paley offered theological support to Adam Smith, though his utilitarianism is less humane than that of Bentham. In England, only Law and Blake offered any theological resistance to this process.

The nineteenth century is the period of the penitentiary, of belief in the possibility of reforming prisoners. Chaplains and distinguished lay people such as Elizabeth Fry contributed to this effort, but theology remained stubbornly retributive. In debates on hanging, the bishops were amongst the most determinedly reactionary members. John Macleod Campbell's work, in mid century, reflects some of the debates going on about dealing with offences, but it is not until the very end of the century that theologians came out firmly in favour of rehabilitation. This move coincides with a critique of *laissez-faire* economics, and the growth of a more complex understanding of the human person. The prisoner was no longer the free moral agent, to be blamed for wrong choices, and able to choose whether or not to reform, but the damaged person, who needed the services of the educationalist and psychiatrist. In terms of the hegemony of assumptions the welfare age was already ushered in by 1914.

Is anything to be gained by looking at atonement and criminal law together over this long period? Is there any connection between the two, or are postulated connections purely arbitrary? Amongst the various analytical structures on offer I have argued that the cultural theory of punishment, advocated for understanding approaches to punishment by Spierenberg and Garland, offers a way of seeing a convincing connection. If a 'cause' is an intelligibility to be grasped between two sets of events, then I believe that there is such an intelligibility between satisfaction theory on the one hand and criminal justice on the other.[2] Even

---

[2]   For this concept of cause see my *God's Theatre: A Theology of Providence* (London, SCM, 1991), chap. 2.

today the rise of the 'moral majority' in the United States, committed to a fundamentalist form of Christianity, brings satisfaction theory and a retributive approach to punishment together. In the two concluding chapters I wish to consider the new retributivism, and to argue that, properly understood, the gospel leads to very different approaches to dealing with offenders.

THE RETURN TO RETRIBUTIVISM

In a famous, and often-quoted, speech in 1910 Winston Churchill, then Home Secretary, spelled out the considerations which needed to be borne in mind in penal practice:

The mood and temper of the public in regard to the treatment of crime and criminals is one of the most unfailing tests of the civilisation of any country. A calm and dispassionate recognition of the rights of the accused against the State, and even of convicted criminals against the State, a constant heart searching by all charged with the duty of punishment, a desire and eagerness to rehabilitate in the world of industry all those who have paid their dues in the hard coinage of punishment, tireless efforts towards the discovery of curative and regenerating processes, and an unfaltering faith that there is a treasure, if you can only find it, in the heart of every man – these are the symbols which in the treatment of crime and criminals mark and measure the stored-up strength of a nation, and are the sign and proof of the living virtue in it.[3]

The speech is an eloquent testament to that commitment to rehabilitation which became orthodoxy after the publication of the Gladstone Report in 1895. As Garland has argued, and as we saw with Rashdall, rehabilitation went together with an idea of the welfare state which needed to intervene on behalf of its weaker citizens. A good deal of confidence was placed in the possibilities of psychiatry and social work. From a Foucaultian perspective the initiatives of rehabilitation can be regarded as devious ways of getting people to conform, but J. A. Sharpe, reviewing punishment over a millennium, concludes that from the perspective of the late twentieth century the idealism and

---

[3] Supply (Report), Home Office, *Parliamentary Debates*, col. 1354, 20 July 1910.

energy represented in Churchill's speech 'look like the evidence of a lost Golden Age of penal policy'.[4]

Many factors contributed to the collapse of rehabilitationist ideas and the return of retributivism. Perhaps the most important was the failure of welfare programmes, slum clearance and full employment significantly to improve crime rates. Average crime rates in Britain remained fairly stable in the hungry thirties and the 'Never had it so good' sixties. Whilst rehabilitationists turned increasingly to the family as the source of delinquency, others concluded that 'nothing works'. This conclusion of Martinson's has been subject to severe criticism, which shows that it grossly oversimplifies the question of effectiveness. The upshot of the debate is that some treatments work on some offenders, but that there is no panacea for all offenders at all times.[5] Nevertheless, this conclusion represented a profound pessimism which shaped policy and moved it away from rehabilitation.

In addition there were intellectual criticisms from right, left and centre. As early as 1949 C. S. Lewis raised essentially Kantian objections to the welfare ideas of Barbara Wootton.[6] Reformative ideas, he contended, which think of all crime as essentially pathological, remove the concept of desert from punishment. The problem with this is that desert is the only connecting link between punishment and justice. Only as deserved or undeserved can a sentence be just or unjust. On this question every member of society can have an opinion, as moral beings who have a share in the Natural Light. Only experts, however, may come to a view about deterrence, or the chances of cure. Lewis foresaw a Huxleyan future in which good people, for the best reasons, sought to 'cure' those from whom they differed in 'Institutions for the Ideologically Unsound'. If crime is a disease which needs cure, rather than sin which needs pardoning, mercy is eliminated

---

[4] J. A. Sharpe, *Judicial Punishment in England* (London, Faber, 1990), p. 90. He notes that although the population of Britain has risen by only 17 per cent since 1945, the prison population has risen by 263 per cent. The Tory Government introduced the 'short, sharp shock' for young offenders in some institutions in 1979. A report on this in 1984 showed that it had no discernible effect on reconviction. It was, however, extended to all detention centres in 1985 to satisfy public clamour for revenge. Ibid., p. 128.

[5] B. Hudson, *Justice through Punishment* (London, Macmillan, 1987), pp. 29–30.

[6] 'The Humanitarian Theory of Punishment', *Twentieth Century* (March 1949). He had been unable to find a publisher in Britain, and was forced to publish in Australia.

from our society, for mercy is a 'mountain plant' which only grows on the rock of justice. These ideas were echoed twenty years later by liberals like Isaiah Berlin who maintained, correctly, that determinist accounts of human personality implied the end of morality.[7] Anthony Burgess explored this theme in his novel *A Clockwork Orange*, turned shortly into a film banned for its promotion of copy-cat violence. Burgess' scenario, of a violent gang leader being treated by lobotomy, was not so far from the truth as both drugs and surgery were used on some types of prisoner.

Far and away the most powerful of liberal critiques was that which emerged from American Quakers, some of whom had been gaoled for their opposition to the Vietnam War.[8] In 1971 they published an immensely influential manifesto, *Struggle for Justice*, which alleged that rehabilitationist practices represented an absolute disregard for the integrity of the individual. By insisting that guilty acts are intrinsically worthy of punishment we reaffirm social norms, recognise that the individual has a debt to society as a whole, and thus open the way to reformation.

On the left the work of Foucault summed up a variety of responses which included that of the psychiatrist R. D. Laing. Laing challenged definitions of normality, and the right to decide what counted as 'madness' in terms of them.[9] These thinkers denied the right of the state or moral majority to control what it regarded as 'deviancy' in the name of individual autonomy and freedom. Politically the tendency of this movement was towards anarchy. That they had a case was evidenced by the treatment of the 'Soledad Brother', George Jackson, who was politicised whilst in prison for a minor offence, and thereafter victimised until finally shot whilst trying to escape.

Finally, on the right were those who, all along, had been complaining about procedures which were 'soft on crime', and who had never abandoned retributive thinking. The fact that retributivism persisted right through the rehabilitationist era

---

[7] I. Berlin, *Four Essays on Liberty* (London, Oxford University Press, 1969).
[8] There is an entertaining account of this in L. Radzinowicz and R. Hood, 'The American Volte Face in Sentencing' in E. Tapper (ed.), *Crime, Proof and Punishment* (London, Butterworths, 1981).
[9] R. D. Laing, *The Divided Self* (Harmondsworth, Penguin, 1965); *The Politics of Experience* (Harmondsworth, Penguin, 1967).

derives from the fact that the justification for inflicting suffering at all is to be found in the assumption that the criminal owes retributive suffering to the community. Retributivism, in other words, always remained the backstop to penal policy. G. H. Mead explained its perennial power by observing that the legal process harnessed the aggressive instincts of society, and directed them at the criminal as a common enemy. 'The majesty of the law is that of the sword drawn against the common enemy ... Hostility towards the lawbreaker inevitably brings with it the attributes of retribution, repression and expulsion.'[10] It has also been argued that societies which cannot exact atonement for injuries run the risk of provoking the 'wild justice' of the vigilante.[11] The possibility of civilised life rests on the state channelling the energies of revenge.

Six years after the publication of *Struggle for Justice* the State of California abandoned its reforming practices and adopted a new, retributivist, penal code, in many cases returning once again to the death penalty. This return to retributivism was soon followed in Britain, where rehabilitation had worked through indeterminate sentences tailored to the offender rather than the offence, and through probation. The 'Justice Model' which replaced this sought determinate sentences, an end to disparity in sentencing and the relationship of punishment to desert. Its philosophy was spelled out in a report entitled *Doing Justice*, edited by A. von Hirsch. Punishment, the report argues, is about deterrence and desert. As Durkheim argued, the function of law is to reinforce moral boundaries and promote social cohesion.

RETRIBUTIVIST THEOLOGIES

Given Garland's premise that penal practice reacts back on ways of thinking, it is no surprise that atonement theologies which draw on retributivist ideas have followed this turn. I shall outline two of these before attempting an evaluation of the main arguments of retributive theory as they receive theological expression.

[10] G. H. Mead, 'The Psychology of Punitive Justice', *American Journal of Sociology*, 23 (1918), 577–602.
[11] S. Jacoby, *Wild Justice: The Evolution of Revenge* (New York, Harper & Row, 1983), p. 10.

In *The Actuality of the Atonement*, published in 1988, Colin Gunton insists that the Christian church stands or falls by whether it proclaims and lives by the gospel of the liberating grace of God, or whether its life degenerates into some form of self-salvation. For that reason, the doctrine of the atonement must continue to be at the heart of Christian theology, and the metaphor of the justice of God at the heart of the doctrine of atonement, if Christianity's orientation to the action of God in re-establishing free human life is to be maintained and articulated.[12]

He spells out the necessity for substitutionary atonement in the course of his critique of Moberly's theology. There are three points. The first is that penitence is insufficient. 'There must be a correspondingly objective demonstration of justice, or the world is a morally indifferent place.' Second, vicarious penitence does not require death on the cross. In exemplarist theologies the cross becomes simply an unfortunate completion to the human story. Third, Moberly's conception of sin is said to be too psychological. The unredeemed past is 'the objective disruption of the life and fabric of the universe', a breach of relationships so serious that only God can refashion them.[13]

Forgiveness alone will not do because this is to fail to take the offender and his or her acts seriously. Forgiveness without punishment is sentimentality. God cannot simply forgive because he wants to, for a mere declaration changes nothing. There can be no restoration of relationships unless the nature of the offence against universal justice is laid bare and attacked at its root.[14] To ignore the fact that Jesus is shown in Scripture as bearing the consequences, according to the will of God, of our breaches of universal justice – to forget that he was bruised for our iniquities – is to trivialise evil and deny the need for an atonement.

Richard Swinburne has also drawn on retributive theory in his account of the atonement, published in the same year.[15] If I do moral wrong, my situation is like that of a debtor who owes money: there is an obligation to do something like repaying.

[12] C. Gunton, *The Actuality of the Atonement* (Edinburgh, T. & T. Clark, 1988), p. 101.
[13] ibid., p. 163–4.
[14] ibid., pp. 159, 161.
[15] R. Swinburne, *Responsibility and Atonement* (Oxford, Oxford University Press, 1988).

Furthermore, the morally guilty person is unclean because guilt is 'a stain on the soul', which needs expunging. The way these two things are dealt with is by atonement, which involves repentance, apology, reparation and penance. Like Gunton, Swinburne argues that simple forgiveness will not do, as it fails to treat people seriously, and thus trivialises human relationships. Swinburne recognises that reparation is not always possible, at least in this life. 'Analogy and, I suspect, the intuitions of most of us educated in a semi Christian society, suggest that no wrong is so great that no atonement will suffice. However large your debt, some cheque would pay it off. So surely whatever evil a man has done in a few years of life on Earth would be remittable if he had the time and resources to make proper apology, due reparation and generous penance.'[16]

For Swinburne it is the fact that God exists as our origin and goal which turns wrongdoing into sin. All people owe atonement to God. Since we cannot make atonement, God comes to our aid, in the sacrifice of Christ. 'The sacrifice of Christ is ... Christ giving the most valuable thing he has – his life –; both a lived life of obedience to God, and a laid-down life on the Cross – as a present to God, whose benefits will flow to others, through the Resurrection.' This sacrifice is made available for us. 'Any man who is humble and serious enough about his sin to recognize what is the proper reparation and penance for it may use the costly gift which another has made available for him to offer as his sacrifice.' His death is not a strict equivalent of what men owe to God, but a reparation sufficient for a merciful God to let us off our due punishment.[17] Christ's self-offering makes reparation and penance for us. By appropriating it through the sacraments we share in the atonement.

Many of the main themes of retributive theory are present in these accounts. Implicitly or explicitly they appeal to the need for order, the sense of justice, the need to make sense of suffering and the need to deal with guilt. Both authors accuse non-retributivist theologies of 'trivialising evil'. Both insist that forgiveness alone will not do. For Swinburne reparation and penance are key

---

[16]   ibid., p. 89.
[17]   ibid., pp. 152–4.

aspects of atonement, corresponding to the two major concerns we have found in classical theory. Gunton adds the concern of eighteenth-century theologians, that unless Christ died a substitutionary death, God and the law are mocked. In addition, he attempts to impale the objector on the dilemma: either substitutionary atonement or self-salvation. I shall attempt to address these various elements of retributive theory and the issues they raise, before turning to an outline of alternatives.

RESTORING THE BALANCE

'Christ had to die for our sins. If he had not, evil would not be condemned, and the universe, or the universal moral order, would be fundamentally out of harmony.' There is overwhelming evidence that a sense of order is a key component in psychological wholeness. In the dis-ordered soul, 'chaos is come again'. To be the victim of crime is to find that wholeness threatened and called into question, and to need it restored. Personal wholeness is related to wholeness in society, for the one cannot exist without the other. It is but a short step from there to predicating metaphysical wholeness in the universe. This need for order seems to lie behind the powerful metaphor of justice as 'balance', the blindfold figure with the scales weighing evenly in her hand. Much of the persuasiveness of retributivist accounts of justice, and derivatively of the atonement, springs from this profound need. In the various versions of Anselm's theory Christ's death is seen to restore the wholeness which our transgression of the moral order ('sin') disturbs.

So deep is the sense of the human good addressed here that we have to recognise something which is inescapable in both penal theory and the theology of redemption. But how should it be framed? Contemporary accounts of balance theory suggest real limitations to the retributivist argument. Law, it is argued, is a way of seeing that the benefits and burdens within society are distributed fairly.[18] Those who play by the book help maintain this fairness, whereas crime consists in taking an unfair advantage

---

[18]   As, for example, by A. von Hirsch in *Doing Justice* (New York, Hill & Wang, 1976).

over others. The object of both retribution and restitution is to restore the distribution of rights which existed prior to the offence.[19]

A first problem with this account of 'balance' theory is that 'taking an unfair advantage' is a very odd way to talk about many of the worst crimes – rape, for example. Second, if the idea is pursued, it quickly breaks down into consequentialist arguments that punishment is a way of making sure that the law is obeyed.[20] But even if we allowed that this language was a possible way to talk about crime, it is quite unclear what would be meant by a 'fair balance' in an unjust society. The problem, as Duff puts it, is that to the extent that I do not receive a fair share of the benefits and burdens in question, I cannot owe this debt of obedience to my fellows. To the extent that my crime is motivated by a need which itself results from my unjustly disadvantaged position, or by a greed which is itself instilled and fostered in me by the very structures of my society, I cannot be accused of *wilfully* seizing an unfair advantage for myself in breaking the law. 'My punishment is then unjustified: it does not deprive me of a profit which I have *unfairly* gained, or restore a *fair* balance of benefits and burdens; and the state which treats me unfairly cannot claim the right to punish me in the name of fairness.'[21]

For Anselm the question of balance in this sense did not arise, because a 'just' society mirrored the order God had established, and that was hierarchical. But if 'balance' is conceived within a framework of radical equality between persons, then the metaphor is simply unworkable. The metaphor of balance takes no account of the problems which follow from an unequal society – the social disadvantage, personal need, and emotional inadequacy that is the real experience of human beings.[22] This argument for retributive theory, in other words, breaks down essentially on account of its *abstraction*. The world simply is not as it portrays it. This is as much a problem for Lewis as it is for Anselm, and is a

19 G. Davis, *Making Amends: Mediation and Reparation in Criminal Justice* (London, Routledge, 1992), p. 11.
20 R. A. Duff, *Trials and Punishments* (Cambridge, Cambridge University Press, 1986), pp. 212ff.
21 ibid., p. 209.
22 ibid., p. 66.

problem with many of the critiques of rehabilitation. In place of the person in an unjust society they place a theoretical construct who must be 'responsible'. Like the Victorian prison reformers they trade on the *type abstrait* of classical jurisprudence.[23] A theology of redemption has to respond to the world as it is – fundamentally marked by injustice. If 'harmony' is to be reintroduced, then it will be through the kind of 'balancing' of which the Magnificat speaks and not through the abstract balancing of retributive theory. The Hebrew image of justice, significantly, did not think of a blindfold goddess at all, but understood it as *essentially* vindicating the oppressed.

In a passionate introduction to Sidney and Beatrice Webb's *English Prisons Under Local Government* George Bernard Shaw insisted that to punish someone retributively was to injure them, whereas to reform someone was to improve them. 'And men are not improved by injuries.'

A punishment system means a pardon system: the two go together inseparably. Once admit that if I do something wicked to you we are quits when you do something equally wicked to me, and you are bound to admit also that the two blacks make a white. Our criminal system is an organized attempt to produce white by two blacks ... and thus we get the grotesque spectacle of a judge committing thousands of horrendous crimes in order that thousands of criminals may feel that they have balanced their moral accounts.[24]

Even if we allowed the validity of the balance metaphor, can Christ's death be centrally construed as restoring order and harmony? To the extent that the image of a fall from innocence, and the restoration of a previous state, is crucial to it, it is highly questionable. A messianic image of the work of Christ contributing to the *eventual establishment* of order might be more appropriate. It is not in the least clear, however, that Christ's *death* would do that. To explore reasons for the insistence on the suffering and death of Christ we need to turn to other aspects of retributive theory.

---

[23] See D. Garland, *Punishment and Welfare* (Aldershot, Gower, 1985), p. 25.

[24] Shaw in S. and B. Webb, *English Prisons under Local Government* (London, Longmans, 1922), p. liv.

DECONSTRUCTING THE LAW

Related to the idea of balance is the claim, in Gunton's words, that unless there is an objective demonstration of justice the world is a morally indifferent place. This puts in theological terms the demands of the right wing that we must not be soft on crime. We have seen and acknowledged, in a number of places, the need for the expression of moral outrage. When a judge lets off a rapist with the words that 'She was asking for it'; when a derisory sentence is passed on a youth who, through reckless driving, has killed two children and permanently and seriously disabled a third, people very properly express outrage. Such judgements call the worth of human life, and the seriousness of human responsibility, into question. However we understand the human moral sense, this seems to be deeply threatened by allowing offenders to go 'scot free'. Justice needs to be seen to be done to restore the sense of a moral universe in which we can be at home. This applies for the offender as well as other members of society, for the possibility of accepting guilt is part of what makes us human.

That responsibility is part of full humanness is accepted by both lawyers and theologians. For the theologian, however, it is not unproblematic. Colin Gunton offers us a choice between substitutionary atonement or self-salvation. Augustine rightly rejected the possibility of self-salvation because it rests on an absolutely inadequate account both of the strength of the human will and of the way in which humans are bound together in the evil that they do. Where the Pelagian thinks of a world of moral heroes, the Augustinian sees rather tragic protagonists, 'whose motivation is too unclear for them to be credibly heroic ... Moral or social improvement is clouded by the certainty of failure and regression; and guilt and virtue are elusive and ambivalent ideas ... There are seldom right answers.'[25]

The force of this picture is undeniable, but, translated into legal terms, the implication is that every offender could plead diminished responsibility, and that, retributivists correctly say, is to undersell human dignity.[26] Theologies of the atonement which

[25] R. Williams, *The Wound of Knowledge* (London, Darton, Longman & Todd, 1979), p. 87.
[26] See K. Menninger, *The Crime of Punishment* (New York, Viking Press, 1968).

presuppose retributive ideas and at the same time reject Pelagianism seem therefore to be involved in incoherence, as they are required both to affirm and to deny moral autonomy. In the shape of the 'predestined but guilty' debate this dilemma goes to the heart of Augustinian theology. It makes clear the way in which understandings of the human underlie both theological and legal debates. The attempt to reform raises, as the American Quakers saw, medical, psychological, social and moral issues. What they did not perceive, however, is that all of these issues need to be considered within the wider framework of what constitutes education, and what moral limits there are to that. This is a question to which we shall have to return.

Quite apart from this the connection made between the need for a public expression of 'justice' and the death of Christ is profoundly questionable. In Gunton's argument moral significance appears to be located exclusively in justice, rather than love, an odd view for a Christian theologian. We could say, in the light of the Sermon on the Mount and 1 Corinthians 13, that if there were no *love* the world would be morally indifferent, but could we say the same of justice? It is, of course, true that in an unjust world there is no love without justice, but the two are not identical. If the claim is that Christ bears our penalty on the cross, then Gunton's argument amounts to the acceptance of the idea that the law is only vindicated through the imposition of punishment. This was Aquinas' view: punishment is pure retribution. Its purpose is to humble the wills of those who oppose the law.[27] But to make this claim is to presuppose a morally objectionable picture of God, as Abelard had earlier pointed out. If it is punishment which gives us a moral world, on the lines of Kant's famous sentiment quoted earlier, then we need only remind ourselves of John Cottingham's remark, that such a view only makes sense if we presuppose a bloodthirsty deity. There is no punishment without a moment of pure violence. If there has to be punishment, it seems that this has to be as a *tragic* necessity, not as a positive good.

There is indeed a dialectical sense in which the cross is an

---

[27] Aquinas, *ST* 1a2ae 87 a.6. Cf. Duff, *Trials*, p. 196.

objective demonstration of justice – precisely in so far as it is an objective demonstration of *in*justice. By revealing the true nature of human religion, and of the political power it underwrites, it shows how hollow the claims to justice of the powers that be are. But it is not that without this the world is a morally indifferent place; rather, the cross shows that the world is a morally corrupted place which stands in need of redemption.

The doctrine of justification has, since the Reformation, been understood as the claim that there is indeed a righteous sentence against us, but that Jesus has taken all the blame on himself and absorbed it. If the cross records the in-justice of earthly systems of law, however, then it is more that all of our theories of crime and punishment are deconstructed, in exactly the same way that theories of sacrifice are deconstructed by the Letter to the Hebrews. That Christ is 'made a curse for us' is effectively *the overthrow of all retributivist theory*, its exposure and denial. When we realise the extent to which all punishment involves revenge, the maintenance of power, and scapegoating, we realise that only the mercy of God, as expressed in Christ's absolute self-giving, is supreme. Punishment involves our adopting a position of judgement which, in turn, denies the offender's real equality. This stance of judgement and punishment is *never* occupied by God, writes John Milbank, 'because he pronounces no sentences that we do not pronounce against ourselves, and permits us to judge him and condemn him to death here on earth, although he is beyond the reach of all condemnation. The trial and punishment of Jesus itself condemns, in some measure, all other trials and punishment, and all forms of alien discipline.'[28] The cross is not an endorsement of punishment but an announcement of its end.

MAKING REPARATION

Before turning to the crucial idea of expiation we need to distinguish it from something with which it is often confused, the idea of reparation. This notion has come to the fore in the past thirty years of penal debate through the realisation that criminal

[28]   J. Milbank, *Theology and Social Theory* (Oxford, Blackwell, 1990), p. 421.

justice has, hitherto, paid very little attention to the victim.[29] As we saw in chapter 4, reparation was a major feature of Anglo-Saxon law, only slowly dying out as the Crown assumed more and more responsibility for law and order. Reparation, it is suggested, can take the form of the payment of money to the victim, repair of damage, or other direct services. The guide to the level of awards drawn up by the Criminal Injuries Compensation Board in 1991 bears striking similarity to the Anglo-Saxon Commutations.[30]

The notion of reparation plays an important role in Richard Swinburne's theology of atonement. The extraordinary triviality of the examples of reparation he offers (giving a box of chocolates or a bunch of flowers, mending a bumper) and the statement that 'no matter how great the wrong, some cheque will pay it off' highlight the problem with it. Reparation in fact belongs to the sphere of offences against property, to the world of civil damages.[31] If I break your window, or damage your car bumper, then I can repair it. If, however, I murder your child, no cheque of any size can possibly make reparation. German 'reparations' to the State of Israel could not 'pay off' the guilt of the Holocaust. The death penalty was demanded for many offences against the person not to exact reparation, but in recognition of the fact that in these cases reparation was not possible. This was why, in Anglo-Saxon law, the most serious crimes were 'botless', unassuageable by monetary payment.

The insights of victim studies go deeper than the notion of reparation. Crime, it is pointed out, is traumatic because it undercuts autonomy, order and relatedness.[32] It is a profound expression of disrespect for the victim. More important than

---

[29] For theories of reparation cf. J. Dignan, *Repairing the Damage* (Sheffield, University of Sheffield, 1990) and J. Harding, *Victims and Offenders* (London, Bedford Square Press, 1982).

[30] Thus, an undisplaced nasal fracture qualifies for £650, loss of two front teeth £1,170, scar, young man, from ear to mouth £6,000, scar, young woman, from mouth to below jawbone £9,000, total loss of hearing in one ear £11,500, and total loss of vision in one eye £15,000. CICB Twenty-Seventh Report (London, HMSO, 1991).

[31] Swinburne's theory is an appropriate response to the highpoint of free-market capitalism in Britain, 1988.

[32] I am drawing on Howard Zehr, 'Respect in the Home', in *Respect in Prison*, transcript of a conference held in July 1991 at Bishop Grosseteste College, Lincoln.

restitution is action to let the victim know that he or she is not to blame, that something is being done to restore the situation. To do this, in a case of any seriousness, needs far more than the reparation Swinburne gives examples of. Mainstream Western theology of the atonement has, like criminal justice, centred on the offender, whose place Christ must take in order to avert damnation. Moltmann's theology of the cross, which emerged in the first instance as a response to the Holocaust, also marked a theological turn to the victim. This theology focussed not on Christ as making sacrifice or satisfaction, but on the fact that he suffered injustice, violence and betrayal alongside all the other victims of history. Of course, if Christ were just one more victim, then his suffering would have no particular significance. But, argues Moltmann, if God himself is *in* Christ (2 Cor. 5.19), then Christ brings eternal communion with God and God's life-giving righteousness through his passion into the passion story of this world and identifies God with the victims of violence. Conversely, we also have here the identification of the victims with God, so that they are put under divine protection and, though lacking human rights, have rights with God.[33]

This solidarity of God with the victim, adumbrated in the liturgy, is the theological foundation of victim support now urged by many concerned with criminal justice. As Moltmann himself has recognised, however, we cannot stay with but need to press the question of how, creatively, we deal with offenders. Classically this has been expounded through the notions of expiation or propitiation.

PUNISHMENT AS EDUCATION

The eighteenth-century jurist Blackstone, we remember, believed that punishment inflicted by the courts was in no way expiatory. This has not been the view of most of the Christian tradition, which has focussed especially on Isaiah 53.

In attacking the 'double mindedness' of bourgeois Christianity in the mid nineteenth century Kierkegaard effectively continues

---

the insight of the Deuteronomist, that God punishes those he loves. The one who wills the good in truth, he says, understands that punishment only exists for the sake of transgressors. It is a helping hand. The 'double-minded' person shuns punishment as a suffering, a misfortune, an evil, but it comes from 'the good'. 'It is the Good who, out of love for the pupil, has invented punishment.'[34]

Simone Weil applies this insight directly to the penal system. According to her, punishment is a method of procuring good for people who do not desire it. The art of punishing is the art of awakening in a criminal, by pain or even death, the desire for pure good. Those who are so estranged from the good must be reintegrated with it by having harm inflicted upon them. This must be done until the completely innocent part of the criminal's soul awakens with the surprised cry, 'Why am I being hurt?' This 'innocent part' of the soul must then be nurtured until it becomes able to judge and condemn past crimes and attain forgiveness.[35]

Perceptions such as these have formed the background of much Christian reflection about crime and punishment. Elizabeth Moberly wants to insist that punishment is an essential part of the response to crime.[36] Not to punish is not to take the wrongdoer seriously as a moral agent, for the victim of wrongdoing includes the agent. A sane offender has a right to be punished rather than manipulated or ignored, since his or her punishment expresses a proper response to his or her crime as the wrongdoing of a responsible moral agent. Punishment seeks to prevent continuation in hardness of heart, and to promote a return to goodness. Punishment does not spring from a pleasure in inflicting pain, as Nietzsche thought, but is a 'transforming agent'. As Walter Moberly argued, punishment is a symbol. It is an outward and visible sign of an inward and spiritual disgrace. It seeks both to forestall the consummation of wrongdoing and to promote its annulment.[37] All punishment as a secondary evil typifies primary

---

[34] S. Kierkegaard, *Purity of Heart*, tr. D. Steere (New York, Harper, 1956), p. 87.

[35] S. Weil, *Selected Essays 1934–1943*, tr. R. Rees (Oxford, Oxford University Press, 1962), p. 31.

[36] Elizabeth Moberly, *Suffering, Innocent and Guilty* (London, SPCK, 1978).

[37] W. Moberly, *The Ethics of Punishment* (London, Faber, 1968).

evil, which is moral and spiritual. Its aims are to deepen in us antipathy and counteraction to wrongdoing, to promulgate it to the world and stimulate it in the wrongdoer. Punishment is not opposed to forgiveness, as Rashdall argued, because forgiveness is not a desire to leave the wrongdoer subject to the entail of wrongdoing.

The problem with this argument is that, in the words of Iris Murdoch, 'The kind of suffering which brings wisdom cannot be named and cannot without blasphemy be prayed for.'[38] But the views just outlined not only name it, but seek to *prescribe* it for the criminal. Punishment as retribution seems to *coerce* criminals by inflicting suffering on them against their will. It alienates offenders. Nietzsche saw this absolutely clearly. Punishment, he notes, is the last thing to awaken 'the sting of conscience'. 'Generally speaking, punishment makes men hard and cold; it concentrates; it sharpens the feeling of alienation; it strengthens the power of resistance ... punishment *tames* men, but it does not make them "better".'[39] Against the enthusiasm for punishment, or suffering, we have to set Jeremy Bentham's well-known remark that 'all punishment is mischief, all punishment in itself is evil'.[40] Is this not an instance of the children of this world seeing more clearly than the children of light? Shaw, again, derided the notion that expiation could be made by suffering as 'superstition'. 'Human self-respect wants so desperately to have its sins washed away, however purgatorially, that we are willing to go through the most fantastic ceremonies, conjurations, and ordeals to have our scarlet souls made whiter than snow. We naturally prefer to lay our sins on scapegoats or on the Cross, if our neighbours will let us off so easily; but when they will not, then we will cleanse ourselves by suffering a penalty sooner than be worried by our consciences.'[41] Shaw's irony is heavy-handed, but he is right to draw attention to the dubiety of much thinking on expiation.

Many of Simone Weil's reflections in *Gravity and Grace* turn on

---

[38] I. Murdoch, *The Nice and the Good* (Harmondsworth, Penguin, 1969), p. 56.

[39] *The Genealogy of Morals*, tr. Walter Kaufmann (New York, Random House, 1969), 2.14, 15. Cf. Milbank, *Theology and Social Theory*, p. 421, in criticism of Walter Moberly.

[40] J. Bentham, *Principles of Morals and Legislation*, 13.2.

[41] Shaw, in Webb and Webb, *Prisons*, p. liii.

the issue of redemptive suffering. 'The extreme greatness of Christianity', she remarks, 'lies in the fact that it does not seek a supernatural remedy for suffering but a supernatural use for it.'[42] She seems to suggest that this supernatural use is a 'contagion' of goodness. Where our sin, for example bad temper, infects those around us, 'at the contact of a perfectly pure being there is a transmutation and the sin becomes suffering'. This was the function of the just servant of Isaiah, and of Christ. 'All the criminal violence of the Roman Empire ran up against Christ and in him it became pure suffering.' Expiatory suffering, she says, in a gnomic utterance, is the shock in return for the evil we have done. Redemptive suffering is the shadow of the pure good we desire.[43] Weil is raising issues of great importance which go beyond the idea that punishment can be educative, but which, in turn, raise further disturbing questions.

MASOCHISM AND EXPIATION

Dazzling as are many of Simone Weil's insights, it is difficult to read many of her most important texts without being repulsed by their implicit masochism. Masochistic attitudes have undeniably characterised a great deal of Christian art and spirituality. To what extent is expiation to be understood in terms of them?

In *Civilisation and its Discontents* Freud drew attention to the way repressed desire could be turned punitively either against the self or against others. From the conflict between our desires and our internalised controls arises the sense of guilt, which 'expresses itself as a need for punishment'.[44] 'An unconsciously punitive attitude towards one's own anti-social wishes may carry over into a projected punitive attitude towards those who have acted out such prohibited desires.'[45] Iris Murdoch illustrates this in her novel *Nuns and Soldiers*. Guy confesses that he wants to be judged:

Anne reflected. 'I wonder if it's a coherent idea? It seems to me a little like what you didn't care for about Christianity.'

---

[42]　S. Weil, *Gravity and Grace*, tr. E. Craufurd (London, Routledge, 1952), p. 73.
[43]　ibid., pp. 64–5.
[44]　*Civilization and its Discontents*, tr. J. Riviere (London, Hogarth Press, 1946), p. 105.
[45]　D. Garland, *Punishment and Modern Society* (Oxford, Clarendon Press, 1990), p. 240.

'I know exactly what you mean', said Guy ... 'It's romantic, sado masochistic, a story idea, not what it seems – indeed –'
'Do you mean judgement as estimation, a clear account, or as punishment?'
'Oh both. I think one *craves* for both.'[46]

E. P. Thompson noted how sacrificial, masochistic and erotic language all found a common nexus in the blood symbolism of early Methodist hymnology. Feelings of self-mortification were united with yearning for the oblivion of the womb and tormented sexual desire. 'It is difficult to conceive', he wrote, 'of a more essential disorganization of human life, a pollution of the sources of spontaneity bound to reflect itself in every aspect of personality.' Because joy was associated with sin and guilt, and pain (Christ's wounds) with goodness and love, so every impulse became twisted into the reverse, and grace was acquired only when performing painful, laborious or self-denying tasks. 'To labour and to sorrow was to find pleasure, and masochism was "Love".'[47]

Masochism is not simply a willing embrace of pain, but also represents perceptions about power. This is vividly illustrated in R. L. Stirrat's study of passion cults in contemporary Sri Lanka.[48] A number of shrines offering exorcism and healing have sprung up, attracting huge crowds. The priests who dominate the shrines act out the part of Christ, carrying a cross bare-foot in the central weekly rituals. The women who visit the shrines, meanwhile, understand their own sufferings as participating in the redeeming sacrifice of Christ, so that their suffering is not just a penance for their own sins, but a sacrifice for the sins of others. For the priests suffering is what gives them authority, and Stirrat notes that 'most of those who glorify suffering are those who in one way or

---

[46] *Nuns and Soldiers* (Harmondsworth, Penguin, 1981), p. 72.
[47] E. P. Thompson, *The Making of the English Working Classes* (Harmondsworth, Penguin, 1968), p. 409. The verses he has in mind run as follows:

> We thirst to drink Thy precious blood,
> We languish in Thy wounds to rest,
> And hunger for immortal food,
> And long on all Thy love to feast.

[48] R. L. Stirrat, *Power and Religiosity in a Post-Colonial Setting* (Cambridge, Cambridge University Press, 1992), pp. 99ff.

another are free of customary forms of subordination'. For lay women, however, suffering as sacrifice can be used as a means of exploring autonomy. Power relations, in other words, and the negotiation of authority within society, are crucial to the cult of suffering. Caroline Bynum has argued that this was true in the Middle Ages, and we may suppose that it lies behind many Enthusiast embracings of the passion.

<h2 style="text-align:center">DID CHRIST EXPIATE OUR SINS?</h2>

Abuse does not destroy use. That masochistic attitudes are found in many accounts of expiation does not prove that expiation is impossible.

We have seen that much of the power of the retributivist case stems from its ability to address guilt. When guilt is repressed, it destroys our self-respect. We may seek to restore this through undergoing suffering. When Henry II was whipped after the murder of Becket he was not making reparation, but the physical suffering he underwent expressed his remorse and 'cleansed' his soul. It was a 'sacrament', in Walter Moberly's sense. Expiation is made by penance, Duff suggests, by imposing on me, in painful and material form, a kind of suffering which symbolically represents the harm I have done to others and to myself. It aims to reconcile the penitent wrongdoer with others and himself or herself.[49]

If we take this as a fair account of expiation, a number of further questions arise. First, we can ask whether there are limits to it. If Henry could make expiation for the murder of Becket, could the Moors murders, or the murder of Suzanne Capper, for example, be expiated? Or are there some crimes which go beyond expiation? In Richard Swinburne's bizarre terms, what cheque could be written against them? Severe penance might convince those wronged, say the parents of the children tortured and killed, that the murderers were sorry. Would this wipe out their guilt? Is there not, in the background here, the fundamental principle of balance once more, the *lex talionis*, the aggressor's

---

[49]   Duff, *Trials*, p. 247.

suffering for the victim's? But it is entirely unclear whether suffering can be weighed in the balance like this. Helen Prejean's moving account of befriending prisoners on death row in the United States, and her encounters with victims' families, illustrates the problems. Some victims' families want nothing but revenge – an equal amount of pain for the murderer to that which the victim suffered, or more, and this does not assuage their pain. It becomes necessary for their own lives, so that they have to visit execution after execution. Others want not the death of a murderer, but just an apology.[50]

The question becomes even more pointed if we raise the problem of Auschwitz. Who or what could possibly atone for the Holocaust? Those who committed the crimes are unable to, being either dead or unrepentant. Can there, then, be vicarious expiation – identified by so many as the essence of the Christian claim?

We have noted throughout that vicariousness lies at the heart of the Christian vision of reality. The innocent can, and frequently do, bear the *punishment* of the guilty, and this can, in various situations, extend to dying for others. But what does it mean to bear another's *guilt*? The whole point of expiating guilt is that we own it, repent it, shun it in horror, and begin anew. This, said Rashdall, and many in the 'liberal' tradition before him, only the sinner himself or herself can do. Wrestling with this problem led Campbell and Moberly to the profound suggestion of vicarious penitence. For whilst an innocent person cannot become guilty, or be treated as guilty, he or she can certainly take the guilt of others to heart and seek to bear it. Such a perception lies behind the practice of the Carmelite nuns who keep a vigil of prayer at Auschwitz. But in what sense does this 'atone' for evil, or 'expiate' it?

It is because ideas of expiation were so obviously inappropriate in relation to the Holocaust that Christian reflection on the cross took a fundamentally different turn in the years after the Second World War, in the theology of the crucified God. From Anselm onwards attention was focussed on the *offender*, on the seriousness of sin. The death of millions in the camps, however, focussed

[50] Helen Prejean, *Dead Man Walking: An Eyewitness Account of the Death Penalty in the United States* (New York, Random House, 1993), *passim*.

attention squarely on the victims. In the theology which emerged in response to these events the significance of the cross is first of all God's solidarity with the *victims* of torture and murder. Beyond that lay the perception that only the victims can forgive. If there is to be forgiveness in God, it can only come from the God who is, as Godself, a victim. This turn reveals at the same time the extraordinary sensitivity of the theology of the cross to criminal theory, where likewise the victim was finally coming much more centre stage.

Moltmann, who provided the classic account of the crucified God, has more recently turned to the question of the torturer. What about him? Unexpiated guilt destroys us. Either justification of the self or destruction of the self follows. Most often, as Girard argues, the scapegoat mechanism is the means by which guilt is evaded. A 'guilty' person is sought on whom one can unload one's own failure and who then has to be 'guilty of everything'.[51] The expiation Christ makes on the cross is an alternative to such scapegoating. On the one hand there is no doubt that historically the preaching of the cross has enabled those with more guilt than they could bear to offload this on to Christ, and therefore to gain a sense of liberation. Christ, then, becomes the divine scapegoat. This process, however, leaves the scapegoat mechanism in place. Moltmann therefore speaks of Christ transforming human guilt into divine suffering by 'bearing' human sin, as the fourth Servant Song envisaged.[52] But when we speak of God 'bearing' our sin, here surely we are speaking of '*for*bearance', refusal to give up on us despite our failure. The suffering which Christ undergoes shows us the infinite cost, as well as the extent, of divine forgiveness. It does not, as such, 'wipe away' or 'cover over' our sin and guilt. In this context the observations of forensic psychiatrists, that perpetrators of the worst crimes never get rid of their guilt, may be instructive. Creative ways of dealing with guilt have to be found other than offloading on to others, even on to the Creator. I would therefore argue that notions of expiation seek to express the intuition rather that God will turn the flank of human wrongdoing, will use it

---

[51] Moltmann, *History and the Triune God*, p. 49.
[52] ibid., p. 50.

against itself, that what makes for life will be brought out of what makes for death.

Iris Murdoch, again, explores such an idea in her novel *The Unicorn*. In the passage which follows, two of the characters reflect on the position of Hannah, who has power because she has to exercise forgiveness:

Forgive is too weak a word. Recall the idea of Ate which was so real to the Greeks. Ate is the name of the almost automatic transfer of suffering from one being to another. Power is a form of Ate. The victims of power, and any power has its victims, are themselves infected. They have to pass it on, to use power on others. This is evil, and the crude image of the all powerful God is a sacrilege. Good is not exactly powerless. For to be powerless, to be a complete victim, may be another source of power. But Good is non powerful. And it is in the good that Ate is finally quenched, when it encounters a pure being who only suffers and does not attempt to pass the suffering on.[53]

On the cross Christ 'bears' our guilt, but this is not expiation. What happens there is the absorption of violence, the redefinition of power, and the establishment of the possibility of forgiveness. In the concluding chapter I turn, then, from understandings of Christ's death which have, one way or another, functioned to underwrite violence, legal and otherwise, to an alternative understanding, powerfully adumbrated by contemporary work on the rehabilitation of offenders.

[53] I. Murdoch, *The Unicorn* (St Albans, Granada, 1977), p. 9.

CHAPTER 10

Forgiveness, crime and community

> All Christian services and all Christian teaching in prison
> strike one with a sense of futility because the whole atmo-
> sphere of the prison life is a denial of Christianity. The
> forgiveness and love of God etc. are meaningless terms to a
> man who has never known forgiveness and love from men
> and is in prison because men refused to give them to him.
>
> Hobhouse and Brockway, *English Prisons Today*

Christian atonement theology is the attempt to spell out how
Christ is supposed to have helped us. It envisions the possibility
of recreating a broken world, of redeeming what would otherwise be lost. In Western society since at least the seventeenth
century the offender has been the paradigm case of such
potential loss, but the possibility of redemption in this life has for
much of that time hardly been in view. On the contrary, various
forms of punishment or retribution have been a surrogate for
eternal punishment. The motto guiding punishment has been
the motto Dante set over the gates of hell: 'Abandon hope.'
Over the past thousand years offenders have been hanged, put
in the pillory, transported, whipped, put in solitary confinement,
set on the treadwheel, and sent to Borstal. None of this has
reduced crime.[1] As we have seen, there are those who conclude
that, with regard to offenders, 'nothing works'. The introduction
to *Doing Justice* tells us that 'The quality of heady optimism and
confidence of reformers in the past, and their belief that they
could solve the problem of crime ... will not be found in this
document. Instead, we have here a crucial shift in perspective
from a commitment to do good to a commitment to do as little

[1] J. A. Sharpe, *Judicial Punishment in England* (London, Faber, 1990), p. 127.

mischief as possible.'[2] This could be taken as the expression, in the sphere of penality, of the 'Christian realism' advocated by Reinhold Niebuhr, a view which looks back to Augustine, and which understands the state principally as a bulwark against sin. The effect of this is to push the chance of redemption into another world. Hallowed as this is by popular caricature, such an approach is inconsistent with what we see in the New Testament. There we find that, in encounter after encounter, Jesus restores human beings to their communities here and now. For Paul and John the community itself, the 'body' of Christ, takes over this redemptive role, bringing enemies together and enabling forgiveness and reconciliation. Consistent pessimism is an odd option for those whose world view is determined by hope (Rom. 11.32), and we find a rejection of such pessimism amongst many contemporary criminologists and sociologists of punishment. Rehabilitation may not be very successful, it is argued, but at least it is inspired by humane considerations rather than vindictiveness, and seeks to reduce crime rather than just punish it. It has been shown repeatedly that imprisonment fails to reduce crime. At present in Britain nearly 70 per cent of male offenders reoffend within four years.[3] Other strategies, therefore, deserve urgent consideration. 'No one seriously believes we can "eliminate" crime or "remake" offenders', writes Roger Matthews, 'but there is nothing unrealistic about reducing crime or offering offenders a less damaging alternative to the traditional prison.'[4] In this final chapter I shall argue that such alternatives hinge crucially on our understanding of community. The difference between those who wish to return to rehabilitation, on the one hand, and 'radicals', on the other, consists, according to Barbara Hudson, in differing approaches to community. 'The former see the individual as the unit for action, whereas for radicals the target of change must be the society.'[5] Her distinction corresponds to the difference between so-called 'evangelical

---

[2] A. von Hirsch, *Doing Justice* (New York, Hill & Wang, 1976), p. xxxiv.

[3] Home Office Prison Statistics, England and Wales (London, HMSO, 1994). Cf. the conclusions of D. Farrington and P. Langan, 'Changes in Crime and Punishment in England and America in the 1980's', *Justice Quarterly*, 9 (1990), 5–46.

[4] R. Matthews , 'Decarceration and Social Control: Fantasies and Realities', in *Essays in the Sociology of Social Control*, ed. J. Lowman (London, Gower, 1987).

[5] B. Hudson, *Justice through Punishment* (London, Macmillan, 1987), p. 176.

Christians', who stake everything on individual conversion, and mainstream Christian teaching, both Catholic and Reformed, which has always begun with the community. Theologically the problem with the insistence on individual conversion is its extremely unbiblical individualism. To rephrase Anselm's famous remark, it has not weighed the *complexity* of sin, our mutual involvement in the sins of all, the very thing which the doctrine of original sin set out to emphasise. Retributivists are right that we must recognise responsibility, but this is always *mutual*. 'The critical human question is . . . *what are persons on the way to becoming?* How can we therefore work together to improve our *common* chances of becoming "better"?'[6] Conventional forms of punishment regularly 'fail' because '*it is only the mainstream processes of socialization* (internalized morality and the sense of duty, the informal inducements and rewards of conformity, the practical and cultural networks of mutual expectation and interdependence etc.) which are able to promote proper conduct on a consistent and regular basis'.[7]

Since the early nineteenth century it has been shown again and again that imprisonment creates criminality. As the North American Judge Dennis Challeen puts it:

> We want (prisoners) to have self worth . . .
> So we destroy their self worth.
> We want them to be responsible . . .
> So we take away all responsibilities.
> We want them to be positive and constructive . . .
> So we degrade them and make them useless.
> We want them to be non-violent . . .
> So we put them where there is violence all around.[8]

At the conclusion of their study of English prisons under local government, Sidney and Beatrice Webb felt that, 'It is probably quite impossible to make a good job of the deliberate incarceration of a human being even in the most enlightened of dungeons.' Prisons, they said, cannot be expected to have a beneficial result

---

[6]   D. Jenkins in *The Meaning of Imprisonment*, Proceedings of a Conference at Lincoln, July 1989.

[7]   David Garland, *Punishment and Modern Society* (Oxford, Clarendon Press, 1990), p. 289 (my italics).

[8]   D. Challeen, *Making it Right: A Common Sense Approach to Criminal Justice* (Aberdeen, S. Dak., Melius & Peterson, 1986).

on the intellect, emotions, or character of any prisoner, and in this they echoed countless studies of the Victorian penitentiary.[9] A prison chaplain from the early years of the century noted gloomily that 'Preaching a religion of brotherly love to convicts while you are treating them upon a basis of hatred is a discouraging performance.'[10] Back in 1922 Hobhouse and Brockway were of the opinion that the only useful reform for most English prisons was dynamite.[11] Why, then, are our prisons now fuller than ever, and retributive attitudes stronger? Is it because of a lack of alternatives? In this final chapter I shall argue that there are compelling alternatives to retributivism both in theology and penal practice. I shall begin by outlining some of the alternative strategies to punitive justice currently envisaged.

STRATEGIES OF RECONCILIATION

In seeking a response to crime we have to begin with the observation that criminal justice and social justice are correlative. That poverty and crime are important correlates has been observed in countless studies from Quetelet onwards. Whilst improving living standards do not necessarily *lower* crime rates there are indisputable connections between, for example, poverty, unemployment, poor education and crime.[12] Moreover, it cannot be an accident that most of those who end up in prison are young men from the bottom two social classes. This on the one hand expresses ruling-class blindfolds about the seriousness of white-collar crime and on the other shows that social deprivation is one of the most fundamental causes of criminal behaviour. It is perfectly clear that, whilst crime will never be eliminated by social engineering, the construction of a more just society can go a very

9 S. and B. Webb, *English Prisons under Local Government* (London, Longmans, 1922), p. 247; for Edwardian assessments of the harmful effect of prisons see D. Garland, *Punishment and Welfare* (Aldershot, Gower, 1985), p. 60.

10 T. M. Osborne, *Within Prison Walls* (New York, Appleton, 1913), p. 324.

11 S. Hobhouse and A. Fenner Brockway, *English Prisons Today* (London, Longmans, 1922), p. 91.

12 Hudson, *Justice through Punishment*, p. 96; D. West and D. Farrington, *Delinquency, its Roots and Careers* (Cambridge, 1977); V. Gattrell and T. Hadden, 'Criminal Statistics and their Interpretation', in E. Wrigley (ed.), *Nineteenth-Century Society* (Cambridge, Cambridge University Press, 1972).

long way to removing the more obvious causes of crime. As Rusche and Kirchheimer put it, 'the crime rate can really be influenced only if society is in a position to offer its members a certain measure of security and to guarantee a reasonable standard of living. The shift from a repressive penal policy to a progressive programme can then be raised out of the sphere of humanitarianism to constructive social activity.'[13] If we are seeking to improve our common chances of becoming 'better', therefore, social justice is where we begin.

Social justice also includes a sense of fairness within society as a whole. Anthony Bottoms suggests that in social conditions where social justice seems non-existent, the legitimacy of the criminal justice system ebbs away.[14] The situation in England in the 1720s, where ancient common rights were removed, is a case in point, as are contemporary societies where gross disparities of reward are encouraged. The Poll Tax did great damage to the local tax system because it was, to most people outside the governing class, unfair and therefore illegitimate. Legitimacy, Bottoms suggests, is the crucial issue which links criminal justice with social justice. One of the reasons rehabilitationist policies failed, it may be suggested, is that prisoners were well aware of the injustices which trapped them into a particular way of life. This awareness of injustice, and of the way religion sanctified it, illustrated by the role of chapel in the prison regime, explains the sullen resentment encountered by so many of the Victorian prison chaplains. The chaplain was not just an ineffectual do-gooder – he was a class enemy. Once again, only a real dismantling of class antagonism can begin to deal with this problem.

Behind the debate about social justice lie contrasting attitudes to society and the human project. David Faulkner has shown how retributive views on punishment go with social philosophies which emphasise personal freedom and individual responsibility, the discipline of competition and market forces, and regard criminal justice as the central instrument of social control. The counter view lays more emphasis on public duty and social responsibility,

---

[13]   G. Rusche and O. Kirchheimer, *Punishment and Social Structure* (Columbia, 1938), p. 207.

[14]   A. Bottoms, 'Avoiding Injustice, Promoting Legitimacy and Relationships', in *Relational Justice*, ed. J. Burnside and N. Baker (Winchester, Waterside, 1994), p. 62.

seeks participation within industry, and does not expect criminal justice to solve social problems. With regard to offenders, the first view emphasises correction and punishment, the second education and welfare. The issues of criminal justice, in other words, are bound up with the whole orientation of society as regards relationships, authority and education.[15]

Let the objections to welfare programmes be granted, however, and let us agree that they will never produce a society without crime, violence and cruelty. Nevertheless, the claim that offences can be answered other than in kind is at the heart of the gospel. The most constructive attempts at alternatives explored over the past thirty years are in terms of conflict resolution, and have as their theoretical underpinning the perception that all crime represents a breach of relationships. Conflict resolution seeks to bring aggrieved parties together, often in the presence of a mediator, to sort out their differences by argument. Jimmy Boyle's autobiography, *A Sense of Freedom*, illustrates the possibilities here with particular force. Boyle had been dubbed 'the most violent man in Britain', and had had many convictions for wounding and assault before being finally gaoled for murder. Moved from one top-security unit to another, he caused mayhem, attacking prison Governors and destroying padded cells. The move to the Special Unit at Barlinnie changed his life. Here, instead of being treated as a dangerous animal, stigmatised and frequently attacked, he was part of a small group on Christian-name terms where differences were resolved by putting anyone committing an anti-social act in the 'hot seat', where they had to explain the reason for their actions. 'The key to the whole thing', wrote Boyle, 'lies in the relationship of the people with the group, and the understanding that no one person is bigger than the Community, that the commitment is to the Community, and not the individual ... I've experienced all sorts of punishments in my life and all have been very easy in comparison with the Community hot seat.'[16] Boyle's concluding remark here is

---

[15]   D. Faulkner, 'Law, Citizenship and Responsibility: Teaching Children Right from Wrong'. Unpublished paper presented at the Howard League Annual Conference, November 1994.

[16]   J. Boyle, *A Sense of Freedom* (Edinburgh, Canongate, 1977), p. 252.

important in view of Susan Jacoby's argument, already noted, that a society which fails adequately to signal its rejection of wrongdoing risks triggering vigilante violence. What is proposed in the 'hot seat' strategy is a non-alienating form of *punishment*, which is clearly marked off from revenge.

Conflict resolution can also be a means of helping victims and offenders to meet and express their views and feelings.[17] Boyle gives a vivid account of the way in which offenders in prison quickly come to perceive themselves as victims. Where face-to-face meeting with victims is possible, however, this does not happen. 'On hearing for the first time the victim's side of the story, the offender's defensive strategy of "neutralising" his or her actions by denying responsibility, or the level of seriousness of the offence, is undermined.' Moreover, and this takes us back to the discussion of forgiveness, offenders who have difficulty in relating to adults because of poor parenting can have new possibilities of trust opened up by receiving their victim's forgiveness. As far as can be measured, these schemes seem to be remarkably successful.[18] At the same time they address the lack of respect which is the heart of the victim's experience of crime, a lack of respect reinforced by the treatment the prisoner receives in gaol. For that reason respect, justice and fairness in prison lie at the centre of the recommendations of the Woolf Report.[19]

Neighbourhood Dispute Centres, which seek to resolve disputes before they develop into crimes, are quite independent of the criminal justice process. Mediation and reconciliation initiatives have been formalised in the New Zealand legal system to the extent that they represent a real alternative to the adversarial model. In cases involving young people (excluding murder, manslaughter and rape) Family Group Conferences bring together victims, offenders and their families to bring about reconciliation. Fred McElrea has suggested that this could be extended to adult conflicts as well, by constituting Community

---

[17]　G. Davis, *Making Amends: Mediation and Reparation in Criminal Justice* (London, Routledge, 1992).

[18]　N. Baker, 'Mediation, Reparation and Justice', in *Relational Justice*, pp. 74–5.

[19]　Rt Hon. Lord Justice Woolf, Prison Disturbances April 1990: Report of an Inquiry (London, HMSO, 1991).

Group Conferences.[20] The importance of mediation initiatives is that they do not operate by scapegoating, thrusting offenders *outside* the community, into gaol, but recognise that offenders have to be dealt with *within* the community. The most exciting suggestion in this field is that the procedures of conflict resolution ought to become a standard part of primary education so that children are socialised from the very first to understand both that there are other ways to solve problems than through violence, and to respect and understand the feelings of others. These procedures are being followed today between Muslim and Catholic children in Croatia, and are advocated by David Faulkner.[21] Such education might go some way to fill the gap caused by the breakdown of traditional moral structures. Christians ought to recognise in these suggestions the teaching on 'church discipline' in Matthew's gospel (18.21–35) and its outworking in the two letters to Corinth. Mary Grey has, following the lead of the Victorian women novelists, used feminist insights to insist that atonement must be reimaged as the restoration of right relationships, and her work is consonant with these initiatives for dealing with crime.

Reparation has also been reconceived, through Community Service Orders, with a view to reintegrating offenders into the community. Reparation may involve apology, money, repair or construction work of general benefit to the community. A number of important things are going on here. We noted, in the discussion of 'balance theory', that the intuitive force of justice as fairness is very great. Reparation addresses feelings of injustice which address risible sentences, or the feeling that the victim simply gets ignored in the criminal process. Ashworth notes that 'the element of reparation involved in community service is symbolic'.[22] In fact what happens is that a rhetoric and symbolics of mediation and apology replaces the adversarial rhetoric of the courtroom, where, as Boyle again illustrates, it is easy for the offender to feel

---

[20]   F. McElrea, 'Justice in the Community: The New Zealand Experience', in *Relational Justice*, pp. 93ff.

[21]   I owe this information to Sarah Woodhouse. See also Penelope Leach, *Children First*, (Harmondsworth, Penguin, 1994); Faulkner, 'Law, Citizenship and Responsibility'.

[22]   A. Ashworth, *Sentencing and Criminal Justice* (London, Weidenfeld & Nicolson, 1992), p. 268.

in turn victimised. It is the moral values of the community which are symbolised, not by punishment, as Durkheim envisaged, but by recognising the needs and rights of victims. At the same time, by looking at the problems of communities and taking victims and offenders together a break is made with the individual pathology approach to crime and delinquency. Mediation and reparation put the community, rather than the offender, at the centre of the process.[23] David Faulkner has spelled out the difficulties which attend attempts at reparation, for example where a person denies an offence, or where a person is pressured to admit to an offence he or she has not committed, and the dangers of similar cases having different outcomes.[24] He nevertheless urges government action in furthering such initiatives.

These initiatives, and the project of making the administration of justice more locally based, might be understood as a reversal of the trend to abandon community law and replace it with state law, which began in the tenth century. The old community law was reconciliatory and compensation-based, like the initiatives just mentioned. Just as state law emerged together with the nation state, so a movement back to community law may accompany its demise and increasing replacement by federal systems.

A third creative initiative turns on our understanding of punishment. Durkheim argued that punishment was essentially an extension of moral blame, and Antony Duff has recently taken this suggestion up. Moral blame seeks to persuade the offender, by rational moral argument, of the wrongness of his or her conduct. It seeks to arouse the repentant recognition of guilt which is, in fact, a form of pain. 'Such pain must be mediated and aroused by his own understanding of and judgement on his conduct ... Blame ... seeks the participation of the person blamed: for its aim is not a kind of suffering which I can impose on him, but one which he must impose on himself.'[25] Punishment might operate, Duff suggests, on the lines of the church discipline of penance. Penance is a self-imposed punishment through which the offender expresses his or her repentance and thus restores

23 Hudson, *Justice through Punishment*, p. 179.
24 D. Faulkner, 'Relational Justice: A Dynamic for Reform', in *Relational Justice*, p. 171.
25 ibid., p. 59.

himself or herself to the communion from which sin separated him or her. The 'hot seat' at Barlinnie was a concrete example of this form of punishment.

The work of John Braithwaite, on reintegrative shaming, approaches this form of punishment from another angle.[26] Braithwaite considers the role of shame within the 'mainstream processes of socialization'. It is, in his view, largely what educates our conscience. John Locke had already recognised this in the seventeenth century. He advocated sparing use of corporal punishment in education because 'The smart of the rod if shame accompanies it not, soon ceases, and is forgotten, and will quickly, by use, lose its terror.' In fact, 'Shame of doing Amiss and deserving Punishment is the only true Restraint belonging to Vertue.'[27] The prison reformer William Eden, we recall, believed that 'the finger of shame' should follow offences, rather than harsh sentences. Guilt is failure to live up to the standards of our conscience, and shame is reaction to criticism by other people. Shame, however, can be either reintegrative or disintegrative. The latter simply leads to stigmatisation and the formation of sub-cultures which are impervious to shaming except from fellow members of the group. Reintegrative shaming is a form of moral control which draws offenders back into the mainstream. Whilst it is more intolerant than liberal permissiveness, it maintains bonds of respect and love and terminates disapproval with forgiveness. On the micro level it is family life which shows that shaming and punishment are possible within the bounds of respect. In terms of cultures Japan is the main example of a society which has a low crime rate, which is not needing to send ever more people to gaol, and which secures compliance through shaming mechanisms. McElrea argues that in the New Zealand experience it is family shame, experienced at the Family Group Conference, which goes home in a way that courtroom condemnation does not.[28] This experience echoes, of course, the central parable in

---

[26]   J. Braithwaite, *Crime, Shame and Reintegration* (Cambridge, Cambridge University Press, 1989).

[27]   Locke, *Thoughts on Education*, cited in M. Ignatieff, *A Just Measure of Pain: The Penitentiary in the Industrial Revolution 1750–1850* (Harmondsworth, Penguin, 1989), p. 72.

[28]   McElrea, 'Justice in the Community', p. 97.

Moberly's theology of atonement. Two things are needed for shaming mechanisms to work: first, an emphasis on the community, rather than the individual; second, as for Duff, a recognition of the possibility of repentance. Cultures which hold up models of adopting the repentant role, Braithwaite argues, will be cultures which succeed in shaming that is reintegrative. Such role models do exist in Christian cultures of the West, even though the Prodigal Son is not one of our leading folk heroes.[29]

As a theologian John Milbank echoes these views in saying that the only finally tolerable and non-sinful punishment for Christians must be the self-punishment inherent in sin. The offender calls down social anger on himself or herself, but the aim has to be 'to reduce this anger to a calm fury against the sin, and to offer the sinner nothing but goodwill ... This instance of real punishment is also the instance of its immediate cancellation.'[30]

COMMUNITY AND REDEMPTION

All these practices of reconciliation presuppose a wider community within which such practices occur: they cannot take place only in Special Units, Rehabilitation Centres or prisons. The question of community lies at the heart of responses to crime, as the essays in *Relational Justice* see clearly, just as it does for some versions of the atonement. Christie Davies argues that the networks of local communities in late Victorian England, such as churches and Sunday schools, must be understood as having a bearing on declining crime rates at the end of the century.[31] Conversely, the disintegration of local community as facilitated by some aspects of modern technology, such as cars and telephones, the growth in size of institutions, and the centralisation of government has played a real part in the present burgeoning crime rates.

Two questions must be put to any attempt to focus redemptive hope on the community. The first relates to the sheer injustice of

[29] Braithwaite, *Crime, Shame and Reintegration*, p. 162.
[30] J. Milbank, *Theology and Social Theory* (Oxford, Blackwell, 1990), p. 421.
[31] Christie Davies, 'Crime and the Rise and Decline of a Relational Society', in *Relational Justice*, pp. 31ff.

present human forms of community. Reviewing his proposals for reconceiving punishment, Duff is finally pessimistic. Given that the burden of punishment falls undeniably on the poor of any community, given, in other words, the structural sin of which criminality is in some ways but a symptom, it can be argued that punishment is not justifiable until we have brought about deep social, political, legal and moral changes in ourselves and our society – by which time there might be no need for punishment.[32] To those who maintain that we can, without injustice, preserve enough of our existing system of law to avert disaster Duff replies that this shows unwarranted optimism either about the extent to which our existing legal institutions and practices can be adequately justified or about the likely consequences of abandoning them.[33] He sees little alternative but to continue in an unhappy compromise. Barbara Hudson's 'radicals' are more hopeful. They address these problems by demanding programmes for tackling unemployment, community regeneration schemes, and improving the environment of dangerous areas (for example by better street lighting or late-night bus services). These proposals are far from utopian. Some are sketched out as possibilities for future political action in the Report of the Social Justice Commission.

A related but more far-reaching challenge to putting community at the centre of redemptive initiatives arises from analyses of postmodernity.[34] Zygmund Bauman characterises the postmodern condition in terms of 'widespread aversion to grand social designs, the loss of interest in absolute truths, privatization of redemptive urges, reconciliation with the relative ... value of all life techniques, acceptance of irredeemable plurality of the world'.[35] If this is an accurate description of where Western society to a large extent now finds itself, the rejection of rehabilitation in recent penal practice can be understood as part and parcel of the reaction against social engineering. There is very good reason for this aversion, for postmodernism is in part

[32] Duff, *Trials*, p. 294. Cf. J. Murphy, *Retribution, Justice and Therapy* (Dordrecht, Reidel, 1979).

[33] Duff, *Trials*, p. 297.

[34] I have been much helped, in the following paragraphs, by conversations with Graham Ward.

[35] Z. Bauman, *Modernity and Ambivalence* (Cambridge, Polity Press, 1991), p. 97.

generated by the perception that the social-engineering characteristic of modernity could lead to the Holocaust. Modern genocide
is not the product of passion but the attempt to bring about, by
'rational' means, that 'ambivalence-free homogeneity that messy
and opaque social reality failed to produce'.[36] A profound
suspicion of 'normalizing' procedures is included in it, and
Bauman finds this to be one of its most creative features.
Modernity ruled by assimilation, by denying the right to difference. It was characterised by internalised discipline, 'a strategy of
cost-efficient domination that homogenises, simplifies, regiments
and scientises an otherwise messy practical world of hungry,
passionate and creative human beings'.[37] Stanley Milgram's
famous experiment, in which ordinary middle-class citizens were
apparently invited to administer potentially lethal electric shocks
to their victims, showed how far this compliance could go.[38]

One of the key problems, then, is the rejection of 'normalising'
values. Another is the loss of community. The postmodern world
has replaced the failed 'liberty, fraternity, equality' of modernism
with 'liberty, diversity and tolerance', and it is these values which
constitute today's Western 'mentality'. As Bauman recognises,
however, this new creed is also a failure, for these values are
defined by the market. 'Liberty' means consumer choice, and
only that diversity is tolerated which benefits the market. For all
its positive affirmation of pluralism, difference and diversity,
postmodernism is, in Frederic Jameson's phrase, part of the
cultural logic of late capitalism. A crucial aspect of this logic is the
way in which the demands of a mobile labour force and the
priority of consumption have dissolved the rooted communities in
which human beings have lived for most of their history. Post-
industrial, consumerist human beings live rather in ever-shifting
groupings of the like-minded in which people never stay long
enough to put down roots, and in which they need the 'heritage'
industry, selling them 'tradition', to convince them that they are

[36]   ibid., p. 38.
[37]   Colin Sumner, 'Foucault, Gender and the Censure of Deviance', in L. Gelsthorpe
       and A. Morris (eds.), *Feminist Perspectives in Criminology* (Milton Keynes, Open Uni-
       versity Press, 1990), pp. 27–8.
[38]   S. Milgram, *Obedience to Authority: An Experimental View* (London, Tavistock, 1974).

at home. In the postmodern condition 'contingency is destiny', which involves 'the acceptance that there are other places and other times that may be with equal justification ... preferred by members of other societies, and that however different they are, the choices cannot be disputed by reference to anything more solid and binding than preference'.[39] At the centre of this picture stands the lonely individual constantly confronted with the need for decision and desperate for community. Alas, the old communities have disappeared, and what has taken their place is a neo-tribal world, where the tribes are formed by a multitude of individual acts of self-identification.

Such agencies as might from time to time emerge to hold the faithful together have limited executive power and little control over co-optation or banishment ... 'Membership' is relatively easily revocable, and is divorced from long term obligations ... Tribes 'exist' solely by individual decisions to sport the symbolic traits of tribal allegiance. They vanish once the decisions are revoked or their determination fades out. They persevere thanks only to their continuing seductive capacity. They cannot outlive their power of attraction.[40]

It is because ours is an age that lacks community, Bauman argues, that it is the age of lust for community, search for community and invention of community.

The possibility of a community which was more than 'neo-tribalism', and of going beyond a false normalisation, is of critical importance if we accept the axiom, articulated by many sociologists of punishment as well as by some theological traditions, 'no community, no redemption'. I shall begin with some remarks on the problems of consensus and norming. Postmodernism celebrates the crucial significance of difference rather than consensus. In his experiments Milgram found that when his subjects were presented with equally prestigious but conflicting authorities, their action was paralysed. Bauman comments, 'In the face of the *pluralism* of authority, the moral drives of the subjects reasserted themselves and regained control over their conduct. Ethics returned, so to speak, from the enforced exile.'[41] It is the

[39] Bauman, *Modernity*, p. 235.
[40] ibid., p. 249, summarising the account of 'neo-tribalism' of Michel Maffesoli.
[41] ibid., p. 51.

recognition of a plurality of values which is the source of ethics. Barbara Hudson's 'radicals' in penal theory are socialists, but for postmodernism socialism is merely 'modernity's last stand', and the social engineering of the welfare state has no future. With whose values, we are asked, are we supposed to be reintegrating the offender? Are they those 'normal' values which would practise cruelty if told to do so by men in white coats? As we saw in the first chapter, however, the very legitimacy of law, and in parti- cular the institution of trial by jury, presupposes widely shared values. Hart argues that law rests on very obvious generalisations, indeed truisms, concerning human nature the force of which is that there are certain rules of conduct which any society must recognise to be viable.[42] Postmodernism gives us an ethic of critique, but it is not clear that the society it reflects realises the extent to which consensus is necessary for there to be a human project at all. Prioritising critiques of normality and deviance, for example, calls into question all forms of education, all of which involve schooling in community mores, or 'norming'. Pedagogic theory, Hudson notes, is based on notions of similarity, and this implies limits to deviance both in school and in prison when this is conceived of as an arena for reform.[43] Accepted limits to deviance are one of the things which create a law-governed community. A law which is consensual, rather than repressive, is, like education, one of the things constitutive of that *community* without which human beings cannot survive.

The challenge we face, then, is to structure a genuine *community* – where values as well as material goods such as energy resources or means of transport are held in common – which does not at the same time repress and marginalise those who are different and which does not rule by a false normal- isation. I wish to make the, at first sight implausible, suggestion that there may be resources for this project within the Christian tradition.

In his discussion of the rise of nationalism, Benedict Anderson coins the phrase 'imagined community'. All communities are 'imagined', he argues, in that the image of their communion lives

---

[42] H. L. A. Hart, *The Concept of Law* (Oxford, Clarendon Press, 1961), p. 188.
[43] Hudson, *Justice through Punishment*, p. 34.

in the mind of each member.[44] The nations of the modern world are held together not primarily by ethnic ties, but by constructed stories. Whilst these stories are usually the products of ruling elites his analysis calls into question the primacy of the contingent individual in Bauman's account of neo-tribalism. The vigour of contemporary nationalism evidences the extent to which most people live within *traditions*, even if these are traditions of recent invention. Alasdair MacIntyre's landmark study *After Virtue*, published in 1982, effectively engaged with the problem of the collapse of normality, taking it as a threat rather than a promise. There his solution to the collapse of consensus was the formation of new Benedictine-style communities, but when he returned to the discussion six years later the postmodern problematic we have outlined was discussed in terms of a *conflict of traditions*.[45] If there is a criticism to be made of Bauman's analyses, it might be that they fail to recognise the extent to which the condition of postmodernity is framed within post-Enlightenment traditions. Anderson rightly sees that all the great religious communions are imagined communities, imagined in and through the continuities of their traditions, and notes the problems this posed for the nineteenth-century European colonisers. The Christian church was from the very beginning, I would like to argue, an 'imagined community', not just in Anderson's sense but also in the sense of a utopian community, not rooted in kinship (Mark 3.31f.), whose purpose was to provide a messianic 'home', or rooting, for human beings. In a society characterised by very stable, religiously undergirded family ties Jesus calls into being a community of *voluntary* commitment, willing to take on the hostility of this society.[46] It was as a utopian, imagined, community that it both structured and sought further to envisage the possibilities of redemption, seeking to break down the fundamental barriers of the ancient world (Gal. 3.25). One thinks, for example, of the famous descriptions of Christian community in the *Apologies* of Justin and Tertullian.[47] These descriptions are not so much idealised as visionary. It could

[44] B. Anderson, *Imagined Communities*, 2nd edn (London, Verso, 1991), p. 6.
[45] A. MacIntyre, *Whose Justice? Which Rationality?* (London, Duckworth, 1988).
[46] J. Howard Yoder, *The Politics of Jesus* (Grand Rapids, Mich., 1972), p. 45.
[47] Justin Martyr, *First Apology* 66–7; Tertullian, *Apology* 39.

be argued, then, that the situation analysed by postmodern theory is precisely the situation envisaged by the church from the beginning, namely one in which rooted communities are often barriers to redemption, and in which redemption, the restoration of relationships, is brought about only by the creation of an 'imagined' community athwart all existing communities. The community called 'church' contributes to that struggle and negotiation for forms of social life properly called human by faithfulness to and proclamation of this tradition and, in every period and culture, by the creation of such communities. In so doing it enters into the debate between traditions, and it is by respecting the *debate* that the problems of normality are approached. The problem of respecting the stranger, of allowing difference, hangs together with an approach which recognises that another tradition may be rationally superior 'in respect precisely of that in the alien tradition which it cannot as yet comprehend'.[48]

To such a claim it can properly be objected that if we want examples of a false normalisation which needs to be critiqued, we need go no further than the church which has upheld 'just' wars, exploitative economics and retributive justice. The examples I have given of strategies of reconciliation all come from the secular community, specifically from those who have not abandoned the idea of redemptive education (rehabilitation). Do we need to talk about the church at all? I believe that it continues to make sense to do so because the creation of a different kind of social space, in which people can find creative ways of coping with difference, disagreement and sheer downright evil, presupposes the immense work of education which we call the reappropriation of tradition. If there is anything in claims that the gospel is redemptive, this must be in virtue of the fact that the founts of the tradition themselves, 'Scripture', constantly deconstruct positions of power and privilege, and therefore positions which legitimate oppressive normality. The church 'semper reformanda' is the church constantly reconscientised. With Pieter Spierenberg Christians believe that human sensibilities can change for the better, and

48 MacIntyre, *Whose Justice?*, p. 388.

that the gospel plays a crucial part in this. Thus the abolition of slavery can be read not only as a cynical response to changes in the mode of production, which is doubtless part of the truth, but also as the result of changes in attitude which made it henceforth intolerable to treat other human beings in this way, at least publicly and officially, because the ideological legitimacy of slavery collapsed. Garland illustrates the way in which changes in economic thinking went with changes in the understanding of penality, in the emergence of interventionist economics and the welfare state. In the same way the church, on the ground of its founding texts, needs to attack the related ideologies of neo-liberal economics and retributivism, to contribute to their deconstruction. At the heart of this attack lies a conception of human life grounded not on violence, and the logic of an eye for an eye, but on forgiveness.

THE LOGIC OF FORGIVENESS

In holding before us the claims of an imagined community the New Testament, far from providing legitimation for retributivist practice, in fact advanced the claims of an alternative, non-violent, way of life. Forgiveness, I shall argue, lies at the heart of that – not as a benign doctrine, but as a remorselessly difficult *praxis*.

A repeated retributivist claim, as we have seen, is that to forgive without punishing is to condone evil, to reduce grace to sentimentality. Behind such claims seems to lurk the idea that to forgive is to let someone off, but this is absolutely not what happens in forgiveness. When Jesus forgives the woman taken in adultery (John 8.1–11), he neither insists on her punishment nor condones her sin. Forgiveness is a creative act, *sui generis*, which heals by restoring people to community, by recognising the mutuality of guilt ('Let him without sin cast the first stone').

The story of the healing of the paralysed man in Mark's gospel is a parable of the power of forgiveness (Mark 2.1–12). The sinner is paralysed by sin and guilt, a burden to all (he is carried by four friends). It is forgiveness which 'looses' him, enables him to stand on his feet, rejoin society and begin a new life. Only retribution, it is claimed, recognises guilt and therefore responsibility, but this is false, for a recognition of guilt and responsibility is *implicit* in any real act of forgiveness. Forgiveness, in fact, changes both the past and the future. 'If you forgive', writes Brian Frost, 'often you can free a trapped yesterday and make possible a different tomorrow. In other words a paradigm shift occurs and a new ingredient has become available whose impact can be not only the changing of perceptions ... but roles and regulations too.'[49]

'The whole trouble is', wrote Tolstoy, reflecting on the criminal justice system, 'that people think there are circumstances when one may deal with human beings without love, but no such circumstances ever exist ... human beings cannot be handled without love ... it cannot be otherwise, because mutual love is the fundamental law of human life.'[50] In *Crime and Punishment* there is much discussion of Raskolnikov's need to 'accept suffering' to expiate the guilt of the murder he has committed. It is true that he has an inner need to undergo punishment, but it is not suffering which redeems him in the end but Sonia's *love*: 'It was love that brought them back to life: the heart of one held inexhaustible sources of life for the heart of the other ... Life had taken the place of dialectics.' What I suggest is that the tradition which begins with Abelard may be offering us not a reductive rationalism, but an insistence of precisely this creativity.

In *Atonement and Personality* Moberly argued that forgiveness could only morally follow repentance. The way this happens is beautifully illustrated in the last scene of *The Two Gentlemen of Verona* (Act 5, sc. 4). Proteus has systematically betrayed his friend, and is at last found out. 'Proteus', says Valentine, 'I am sorry I must never trust thee more, But count the world a stranger for thy sake.' The dialogue goes on as follows:

> *Proteus*: My shame and guilt confounds me.
> Forgive me, Valentine; if hearty sorrow
> Be a sufficient ransom for offence,
> I tender't here; I do as truly suffer
> as e'er I did commit.

[49]　Brian Frost in *Respect in Prison*, transcript of a conference held at Bishop Grosseteste College, Lincoln, July 1991, p. 93.

[50]　*Resurrection*, tr. R. Edmonds (Harmondsworth, Penguin, 1966), p. 450.

Valentine: Then I am paid;
And once again I do receive thee honest.
Who by repentance is not satisfied
Is nor of heaven nor earth,
for these are pleas'd;
By penitence th'Eternal wrath's appeas'd.

Shakespeare here embraces the main tenet of Socinianism, which might have brought him to the stake had he worked it out in a theological tract. Forgiveness does not require all the conditions which Swinburne sets out, the acts of reparation which *prove* that I am in earnest. On the contrary, forgiveness is prevenient – it *enables* reparation, expiation, 'atonement'. To attach conditions to forgiveness is to attach conditions to love – but there are no such conditions, for love is free, for nothing. This is the true meaning of the *sola* in the various Reformation watchwords: *sola fide, sola gratia* – love without conditions, for a love with 'ifs' and 'buts' is not love. The charter of love's creativity is set out in 1 Corinthians 13. Earlier I posed the question whether there were crimes which could not be expiated, mentioning the Moors murders as a particularly horrific crime. Myra Hindley has, as far as can be ascertained, 'repented', is full of remorse for her actions. If she could not expiate them, could she be forgiven? 'Once again I do receive thee honest.' This is not to say that she can ever *forget* – live without guilt, though this must be an eschatological possibility. It does mean, however, that a new life is enabled. The problem is to know who could declare forgiveness in such a case, for just as there are forms of suffering which cannot be preached without blasphemy, so forgiveness cannot be blandly urged by those not directly affected. Once again, Helen Prejean's narrative is illuminating. Some of the victims' families she knew could forgive, whilst others condemned her for her work with murderers. Forgiveness, she remarks, has to be prayed for, struggled and won each day.[51] It is not sentimentality but part of the way of the cross.

Iris Murdoch, as we have seen, draws attention to the way in which forgiveness itself can be an exercise of power, but that such power is refused is what is redemptive in the crucifixion. As she

---

[51]   H. Prejean, *Dead Man Walking: An Eyewitness Account of the Death Penalty in the United States* (New York, Random House, 1993), p. 245.

puts it in another novel: 'To love and to reconcile and to forgive, only this matters. All power is sin and all law is frailty. Love is the only justice. Forgiveness, reconciliation, not law.'[52] Despite the difficult questions about who could possibly be authorised to forgive, apart from the victims, we have to recognise that it is forgiveness alone which breaks the vicious circle by which disrespect breeds disrespect, and alienation causes alienation.

FORGIVENESS AND SACRAMENTAL PRAXIS

I have argued that the church was from the beginning an 'imagined community', and that at the heart of its gospel is a praxis of costly forgiveness. How does this relate to the current retributive penal climate, and to the strategies of reconciliation I have outlined? We have seen that the conclusion of two centuries of penal experimentation seems to indicate that, although crime will never be eliminated, the only way of tackling it effectively is through 'mainstream processes of socialisation' and not through retribution. The imagined community called church is not this community of redemption *in toto*, but it is so *sacramentally*. The General Synod working group finely note that Christian experience shows that God's response to human misdeeds does not require suffering or pain as a condition for acceptance, or demand retaliation or condemn or exclude the offender. It does not primarily aim to express divine wrath. Instead 'God accepts the offender without condoning the offence; requires the offender to face up to the reality of that offence; invites the offender into a community of reconciliation; encourages the offender to lead life with a new attitude; declares the offender to be free from the offence; invites the person to follow in service as a "disciple".'[53] The community of reconciliation (not the church, but the church sacramentally) is the means through which atonement is effected, which is the reason, presumably, Christ bequeathed us not a set of doctrines or truths but a community founded on betrayal and the survival of betrayal.

[52]   *The Nice and the Good* (Harmondsworth, Penguin, 1969), p. 315. On this theme Portia's great speech in *The Merchant of Venice*, Act 4, sc. 1 also has much illumination to offer.
[53]   See C. Wood, *The End of Punishment* (Edinburgh, St Andrew Press, 1991).

Pierre Allard, Director of Chaplaincy Correctional Service in Canada, has a moving story to illustrate this. He has taken it as an axiom that prisoners cannot be ministered to by 'chaplains', but only by a community of faith. In his experience it takes five to ten years to educate a faith community about prisoners. In one congregation, after a number of years addressed by prison chaplains and other prison workers an ex-offender was finally invited to speak:

As he shared his story with much effort, the people's hearts were touched. This church of 800 people gave him a standing ovation. Two weeks after, he was still shedding tears over it. The ovation did more for him than many of our more sophisticated programmes, to help him believe that he had a place again in our community.[54]

This story shows very clearly how the work of conscientisation, of the creation of new sensibilities, goes on. In reflecting on what it is God has done for us in Christ we need to shift the centre of our reflection from satisfaction to the biblical roots of redemption and reconciliation. Christ 'redeems' us from the principalities and powers, from the social structures which warp human behaviour and produce violence and crime, partly by laying bare the way in which they scapegoat and exclude, but also, correlatively, by inaugurating a continuing practice of reconciliation.

The faith community, then, if it is true to its founding insights, is constituted as a sign or parable of how 'offenders' should be treated, just as seventeenth- and eighteenth-century Protestants maintained, though to very different effect. For earlier Protestantism, the offender was the sign of the sinner in all of us, and his or her punishment a dreadful warning. According to satisfaction theory it was judgement which made reconciliation possible. By analogy, the offender had to make satisfaction before reconciliation could take place. The great Victorian prisons all proclaim the need to make satisfaction. Their high walls are at least as much about the exclusion of the scapegoat as they are about protecting 'the public'. Liberal theologians like Schleiermacher and Hastings Rashdall complained that the imagery of satisfaction theory went back to

---

[54] *Respect in Prison*, transcript of a conference held in Lincoln, July 1991, p. 24.

'the crudest human conditions'. In this they were not wrong. Their mistake was, first, to suppose that we might have outgrown such conditions and, second, to fail to see the immense power implicit in the rhetoric of satisfaction. For all its power, however, we have seen that the sub-text of the doctrine is a subtle rhetoric of violence, a violence which has underwritten both state sadism and individual masochism. Nothing is gained by simply inveighing against this rhetoric. Its engagement with the springs of human action has to be recognised. The point, however, as Marx says, is not just to understand it but to change it. This can only be done through an alternative praxis.

A different construal of redemption, a recognition that it is about enabling those excluded to be included, enabling the acceptance of blame and penance by those who share the blame and must also do penance, calls for a different regime for offenders. In such a regime the faith community is, or ought to be, the sign of what human community, at large, is on the way to becoming – the community of forgiven sinners, the community always in need of reformation. The church, argues John Milbank, has to recognise the tragic necessity of alien punishment – the need, for example, for society to be defended against serial killers. However, it must also seek to be an asylum, a social space where a different, forgiving and restitutionary practice is pursued.[55] The good of order, the need both to express and work through moral outrage, the need for guilt to be shriven, all have to find expression in the creation of such alternative space, as also does the acceptance of difference. In such a praxis, as Moberly argued, the work of atonement is continued by the church. Satisfaction theory has expressed some of the deepest human needs, but it has at the same time distorted them. The redeeming power of the cross needs to find deeper, and more effective, expression, in which the realities of human wickedness and guilt, on the side of both the offender *and* the judiciary, are creatively addressed. Over the past two centuries it has been shown beyond peradventure that the idea that punishment functions to deter offenders is an illusion: it has no statistical basis. The need to show that justice is

---

[55] Milbank, *Theology and Social Theory*, p. 422.

done, to satisy the moral *sensus communis*, is real, but this is not equivalent to saying that we are compelled to continue in present policies of imprisonment. The upshot of two centuries of penal experimentation is that nothing but 'mainstream processes of socialisation' is of any use in rehabilitating offenders. The demand that the church should offer an alternative social space, therefore, and that it might be this which is the redemptive alternative to retribution, is neither nostalgia for a vanished past nor facile Pickwickian optimism. It is, rather, a sober account of the only realistic and creative way of dealing with human fecklessness and evil which we have discovered.

Select bibliography

THEOLOGY

AUTHORS WRITING BEFORE 1900

Abelard, Peter *The Letters of Heloise and Abelard*, tr. B. Radice, Harmondsworth, Penguin, 1974

Petri Abelardi Opera, ed. V. Cousin, Paris, 1859

Anselmi Opera Omnia, ed. F. S. Schmitt, 6 vols., Edinburgh, Nelson, 1946

Aquinas, T. *Summa Theologiae*, New Blackfriars edition, 60 vols., London, Eyre & Spottiswoode, 1964–81

Butler, J. *Works*, 2 vols., Oxford, 1820

Calvin, J. *Institutes of the Christian Religion*, tr. H. Beveridge, Grand Rapids, Eerdmans, 1975

Campbell, J. Mcleod *The Nature of the Atonement*, London, James Clarke, 1959

Fairweather, E. R. (ed.) *A Scholastic Miscellany*, London, SCM, 1956

Harnack, A. *History of Dogma*, tr. J. Millar, 7 vols., London, Williams & Norgate, 1897

Howard, J. *The State of the Prisons*, London, 1777

Keynes, G. (ed.) *The Writings of William Blake*, 2 vols., London, 1925

Kierkegaard, S. *Purity of Heart*, tr. D. Steere, New York, Harper, 1956

Law, W. *Works*, 9 vols., Hampshire, 1892

Munzer, Thomas *The Collected Letters and Writings of Thomas Munzer*, ed. P. Matheson, Edinburgh, T. & T. Clark, 1988

Owen, J. *The Death of Death*, in *Works*, ed. Goold, 23 vols., London and Edinburgh, Johnstone and Hunter, 1852, vol. x

Paley, W. *The Principles of Moral and Political Philosophy*, 2 vols., London, 1785

Priestley, J. *Works*, 25 vols., Hackney, 1871–1931

Socinus, F. *Opera Omnia*, Irenopolis (Amsterdam), 1656

Stillingfleet, E. *Collected Works*, London, 1710

WORKS WRITTEN THIS CENTURY

Bottrall, M. *The Divine Image: A Study of Blake's Interpretation of Christianity*, Rome, 1950

Bronowski, J. *William Blake and the Age of Revolution*, London, Routledge, 1972

Brown, R. *The Epistles of John*, London, G. Chapman, 1983

Bultmann, R. *Theology of the New Testament*, tr. K. Grobel, 2 vols., London, SCM, 1952, vol. 1

Bynum, C. *Jesus as Mother: Studies in the Spirituality of the High Middle Ages*, Berkeley, University of California Press, 1982

Childs, B. *Exodus*, London, SCM, 1974

Chilton, B. *The Temple of Jesus: His Sacrificial Program within a Cultural History of Sacrifice*, University Park, Pennsylvania State University Press, 1992

Davies, J. G. *The Theology of William Blake*, Oxford, Oxford University Press, 1948

Davies, W. D. *Paul and Rabbinic Judaism*, London, SPCK, 1965

Denney, J. *The Death of Christ*, London, James Clarke, 1950

Eichrodt, W. *Theology of the Old Testament*, vol. II, tr. J. A. Baker, London, SCM, 1967

Erdman, D. *William Blake: Prophet Against Empire*, Princeton, Princeton University Press, 1954

Gunton, C. *The Actuality of the Atonement*, Edinburgh, T. & T. Clark, 1988

Hinkelammert, F. *Sacrificios humanos y sociedad occidental: Lucifer y la Bestia*, Costa Rica, DEI, 1991

Hooker, M. *Jesus and the Servant*, London, SPCK, 1959

Jeremias, J. *The Eucharistic Words of Jesus*, London, SCM, 1955
New Testament Theology, London, SCM, 1971

McIntyre, J. *St Anselm and his Critics*, London, Oliver & Boyd, 1954

Milbank, J. *Theology and Social Theory*, Oxford, Blackwell, 1990

Miranda, J. *Marx and the Bible*, London, SCM, 1977

Moberly, E. *Suffering, Innocent and Guilty*, London, SPCK, 1978

Moberly, R. C. *Atonement and Personality*, London, J. Murray, 1909

Moberly, W. *The Ethics of Punishment*, London, Faber, 1968

Moltmann, J. *History and the Triune God*, tr. J. Bowden, London, SCM, 1991

Myers, C. *Binding the Strong Man*, New York, Orbis, 1990

Nicholls, D. *Deity and Domination*, London, Routledge, 1989

Rad, G. von, *Old Testament Theology*, tr. D. Stalker, London and Edinburgh, Oliver & Boyd, 1962

Rashdall, H. *The Idea of the Atonement in Christian Theology*, London, Macmillan, 1925
The Theory of Good and Evil, Oxford, Oxford University Press, 1907

Sanders, E. P. *Paul and Palestinian Judaism*, London, SCM, 1976

Schussler Fiorenza, E. *The Book of Revelation*, Philadelphia, Fortress, 1985

Segundo, J. L. *Evolution and Guilt*, tr. J. Drury, London, Gill and Macmillan, 1980

Stendahl, K. *Paul among Jews and Gentiles*, London, SCM, 1977

Swinburne, R. *Responsibility and Atonement*, Oxford, Oxford University Press, 1988

Taylor, V. *The Atonement in New Testament Teaching*, London, Epworth, 1940

Weil, S. *Selected Essays 1934–1943*, tr. Rees, Oxford, Oxford University Press, 1962

Weingart, R. E. *The Logic of Divine Love: A Critical Analysis of the Soteriology of Peter Abelard*, Oxford, Clarendon Press, 1970

Westermann, C. *Creation*, tr. J. Scullion, London, SPCK, 1974
  Isaiah 40–66, tr. D. M. G. Stalker, London, SCM, 1969

Yoder, J. Howard *The Politics of Jesus*, Grand Rapids, Mich., Eerdmans, 1972

SOCIOLOGY, LAW AND CRIMINOLOGY

Anderson, B. *Imagined Communities*, 2nd edn, London, Verso, 1991

Bauman, Z. *Modernity and Ambivalence*, Cambridge, Polity Press, 1991

Bentham, J. *A Comment on the Commentaries*, ed. C. W. Everett, Oxford, Oxford University Press, 1928

Braithwaite, J. *Crime, Shame and Reintegration*, Cambridge, Cambridge University Press, 1989

Burnside, J. and N. Baker (eds.) *Relational Justice*, Winchester, Waterside, 1994

Carrithers, M., S. Collins and S. Lukes (eds.), *The Category of the Person*, Cambridge, Cambridge University Press, 1985

Cottingham, J. 'Varieties of Retribution', in *Punishment*, ed. R. A. Duff, Aldershot, Dartmouth, 1993

Davis, G. *Making Amends:Mediation and Reparation in Criminal Justice*, London, Routledge, 1992

Denning, T. *The Changing Law*, London, Stevens, 1953

Doob, A. and E. Greenspan (eds.), *Perspectives in Criminal Law*, Aurora, Ont., 1985

Douglas, M. *Purity and Danger*, London, Routledge, 1966

Duff, R. A. *Trials and Punishments*, Cambridge, Cambridge University Press, 1986

Durkheim, E. *The Division of Labour in Society*, tr. W. D. Halls, London, Macmillan, 1984

Dworkin, R. *Law's Empire*, Cambridge, Mass., 1986

Eden, W. *Principles of Penal Law*, 2nd edn, London, 1771

Elias, N. *The Civilizing Process*, Oxford, Blackwell, 1994

Finnis, J. *Natural Law and Natural Rights*, Oxford, Clarendon Press, 1980

Foucault, M. *Discipline and Punish*, tr. A. Sheridan, Harmondsworth, Penguin, 1977

Garland, David *Punishment and Modern Society*, Oxford, Clarendon Press, 1990
   Punishment and Welfare, Aldershot, Gower, 1985

Garland, D. and P. Young (eds.) *The Power to Punish*, Aldershot, Ashgate, 1992

Girard, R. *Things Hidden Since the Foundation of the World*, tr. S. Bann and M. Metteer, London, Athlone Press, 1987

Hart, H. L. A. *The Concept of Law*, Oxford, Clarendon Press, 1961
   Punishment and Responsibility, Oxford, Clarendon Press, 1968

Hirsch, A. von *Doing Justice*, New York, Hill & Wang, 1976

Hobhouse, S. and A. Fenner Brockway, *English Prisons Today*, London, Longmans, 1922

Howe, Adrian *Punish and Critique*, London, Routledge, 1994

Hudson, B. *Justice through Punishment*, London, Macmillan, 1987

Ignatieff, M. *A Just Measure of Pain: The Penitentiary in the Industrial Revolution 1750–1850*, Harmondsworth, Penguin, 1989

Lowman, J. (ed.) *Essays in the Sociology of Social Control*, London, Gower, 1987

Maine, H. S. *Ancient Law*, London, John Murray, 1906

Malinowski, B. *Myth, Science and Religion and Other Essays*, Westport, Conn., Negro Universities Press, 1971

Marx, K. and F. Engels, *Collected Works*, Moscow, 1975ff.

Nietzsche, F. *The Genealogy of Morals*, tr. Walter Kaufmann, New York, Random House, 1969

Pollock, F. and F. W. Maitland, *The History of English Law before the Time of Edward I*, Cambridge, Cambridge University Press, 1895

Potter, H. *Hanging in Judgement*, London, SCM, 1993

Prejean, H. *Dead Man Walking: An Eyewitness Account of the Death Penalty in the United States*, New York, Random House, 1993

Radzinowicz, L. *A History of English Criminal Law and its Administration from 1750*, vol. 1, London, Stevens, 1948

Radzinowicz, L. and R. Hood, *The Emergence of Penal Policy*, Oxford, 1990

Roebuck, D. *The Background of the Common Law*, Oxford, Oxford University Press, 1988

Rusche, G. and O. Kirchheimer, *Punishment and Social Structure*, New York, Columbia University Press, 1938

Spierenburg, P. *The Spectacle of Suffering: Executions and the Evolution of Repression*, Cambridge, Cambridge University Press, 1984

Vinogradoff, P. *The Jurisprudence of the Greek City*, London, Oxford University Press, 1922

Webb, S. and B. *History of English Prisons under Local Government*, London, Longmans, 1922

Wood, C. *The End of Punishment*, Edinburgh, St Andrew Press, 1991

Wrigley, E. (ed.) *Nineteenth-Century Society*, Cambridge, Cambridge University Press, 1972

SOCIAL AND CHURCH HISTORY

Ashton, T. S. *The Industrial Revolution*, London, Oxford University Press, 1948

Bates, D. *William the Conqueror*, London, G. Philip, 1989

Beattie, J. M. *Crime and the Courts in England 1660–1800*, Oxford, 1986

Beier, A. L. *Masterless Men: The Vagrancy Problem in Britain, 1560–1640*, London, Methuen, 1985

Briggs, Asa *The Age of Improvement 1783–1867*, London, Longman, 1979

Clark, J. C. D. *English Society 1688–1832*, Cambridge, Cambridge University Press, 1985

Clay, W. *The English Convict System*, London, 1862

Dickens, A. G. *Reformation and Society in Sixteenth Century Europe*, London, Thames & Hudson, 1966

Dronke, P. *Poetic Individuality in the Middle Ages*, Oxford, Oxford University Press, 1970

Duffy, E. *The Stripping of the Altars*, New Haven, Yale University Press, 1992

Durant, W. and A. *The Lessons of History*, New York, Simon & Schuster, 1968

Faller, L. B. *Turned to Account*, Cambridge, Cambridge University Press, 1987

Fisher, H. A. L. *A History of Europe*, 2 vols., London, Longmans, 1935

Gatrell, V. A. C., B. Lenman and G. Parker, *Crime and the Law: The Social History of Crime in Western Europe Since 1500*, London, Europa, 1980

Glasscoe, M. *English Medieval Mystics: Games of Faith*, London & New York, Longman, 1993

Grimm, H. *The Reformation Era*, New York, Macmillan, 1954

Hanning, R. W. *The Individual in Twelfth Century Romance*, New Haven, Yale University Press, 1977

Hay, D. et al. (eds) *Albion's Fatal Tree*, Harmondsworth, Penguin, 1975

Hill, C. *Reformation to Industrial Revolution*, Harmondsworth, Penguin, 1969

  A Tinker and a Poor Man: John Bunyan and his Church, New York, W. W. Norton, 1990

Hilton, Boyd *The Age of Atonement, The Influence of Evangelicalism on Social and Economic Thought 1785–1865*, Oxford, Oxford University Press, 1988

Hobsbawm, E. J. *The Age of Revolution*, London, Sphere, 1977

Huizinga, J. *The Waning of the Middle Ages*, tr. Hopman, Harmondsworth, Penguin, 1965

Langford, P. *A Polite and Commercial People*, Oxford, Oxford University Press, 1989

Lecky, W. E. *The History of the Rise and Influence of Rationalism in Europe*, 2 vols., New York, Appleton, 1914

Le Goff, J. *Medieval Civilization*, tr. Barrow, Oxford, Blackwell, 1988

Linebaugh, P. *The London Hanged: Crime and Civil Society in the Eighteenth Century*, Harmondsworth , Penguin, 1991

Moeller, B. *Imperial Cities and the Reformation*, tr. H. Midelfort and M. Edwards, Philadelphia, Fortress, 1972

Morris, Colin *The Discovery of the Individual 1050–1200*, London, SPCK, 1972

Ozment, S. *The Age of Reform, 1250–1550*, New Haven & London, Yale University Press, 1980

Powers, Edwin *Crime and Punishment in Early Massachusetts 1620–1692*, Boston, Mass., Beacon, 1966

Priestley, P. *Victorian Prison Lives*, London, Methuen, 1985

Sharpe, J. A. *Judicial Punishment in England*, London, Faber, 1990

Southern, R. *Anselm, A Portrait in a Landscape*, Cambridge, Cambridge University Press, 1990

   The Making of the Middle Ages, London, Pimlico, 1993

   Western Society and the Church in the Middle Ages, Harmondsworth, Penguin, 1970

Stenton, D. M. *English Society in the Early Middle Ages*, Harmondsworth, Penguin, 1965

Thomas, K. *Religion and the Decline of Magic*, Harmondsworth, Penguin, 1973

Thompson, E. P. *The Making of the English Working Classes*, Harmondsworth, Penguin, 1968

   Whigs and Hunters, Harmondsworth, Penguin, 1975

   Witness against the Beast: William Blake and the Moral Law, Cambridge, Cambridge University Press, 1993

Thomson, J. A. F. *The Transformation of Medieval England*, London, Longman, 1983

Ullmann, W. *The Individual and Society in the Middle Ages*, Baltimore, Johns Hopkins University Press, 1966

Willey, B. *The Eighteenth Century Background*, Harmondsworth, Penguin, 1940

Index

CAMBRIDGE STUDIES IN IDEOLOGY AND RELIGION